# THE AMERICAN GARDENER'S

# BOOK OF BULBS

# THE AMERICAN GARDENER'S BOOK OF BULBS

BY **T. H. EVERETT**

*Horticulturist of The New York Botanical Garden*

*with the assistance of* Howard Swift *on special aspects and containing a chapter on flower arrangements by* Ann Hagan

*Foreword by* Walter Roozen *of the Associated Bulb Growers of Holland*

**RANDOM HOUSE**
**NEW YORK**

TO Allan Falconer

*Associate of Honour of the Royal Horticultural Society, an outstanding professional gardener and an amiable tyrant under whom the author served in his youth as a journeyman gardener and from whom he learned the importance of attention to detail and of timeliness in all gardening work.*

FIRST PRINTING · COPYRIGHT, 1954, BY RANDOM HOUSE, INC.

*All rights reserved under International and Pan-American Copyright Conventions. Published in New York by Random House, Inc., and simultaneously in Toronto, Canada, by Random House of Canada, Limited.*

Grateful acknowledgment is made to the Associated Bulb Growers of Holland for their generous help in gathering for this book the work of the following photographers: Paul E. Genereux, Max Tatch, Josef Muench, Gottscho-Schleisner, Jack Roche, Malak of Ottawa, Cottlieb A. Hampfler, Ray Atkeson, L. O. Huggins. Pictures for the How-To-Do-It section were taken by the author with the exception of picture number 6 on page 234 and picture number 4 on page 235, which are used with the kind permission, respectively, of Germain's, Los Angeles, and M. Van Waveren & Sons, New York.

LIBRARY OF CONGRESS CATALOG CARD NUMBER: 54–7801

MANUFACTURED IN THE UNITED STATES OF AMERICA

DESIGNED BY PETER OLDENBURG

# CONTENTS

# FOREWORD

BY Walter Roozen

My interest in bulbs began when I was just five years old, when, at my pleadings, my parents gave me my own tiny plot of sandy soil. In it I clustered tulips, daffodils, hyacinths, and crocuses. The following year I was able to present to my mother a beautiful bouquet on the occasion of her birthday. I still remember how delighted she was that I had grown her gift myself. I loved my little garden, but I knew even then that it was crudely planned. I dreamed of some day having a big garden and a plan for planting my bulbs.

Over the years other interests have come into my life. Many of them are long since forgotten, but my love for bulbs has never changed. Sometimes when all else seems transient only a flower remains beautiful, sturdy . . . and forever the same. Wars, devastation, floods, pestilence, changes of governments—none of these things affects the eternal beauty of the tulip. And as life has pressured me I have increasingly turned to my bulb garden for peace and relaxation. Every fall finds me planning and planting . . . and in the spring, from the time of the earliest crocus, my heart becomes gay with the flowers.

So I know you will understand what a pleasure it is for me to see a great publishing house undertake a book for which I have long felt a need. Here—in *The American Gardener's Book of Bulbs*—is a work designed for the average gardener. Not just another guide to different flowers, but a book that, with several hundred beautiful color pictures, shows in a practical way just how and where to plant most effectively. It will help even the most uncertain gardener to achieve excellent results.

I like to think of bulbs as a symbol of hope for the future. When a man plants his spring garden he does so in the fall—a full seven or eight months earlier. He is looking forward and planning ahead. As he stands in his garden in September, with a handful of bulbs, he knows that he is holding all the beauty that will surely blossom forth next spring.

To my tiny nation—Holland—bulbs have brought world-wide fame. Holland traditionally has a kind of picture-postcard, storybook charm for most people:

the windmills and canals . . . wooden shoes . . . Hans Brinker and his silver skates . . . apple-cheeked Dutch girls with lace bonnets . . . and the boy who held his finger in the dike.

But most of all you remember that Holland is the land of tulips. In fact, tulips just about spell out the word "Holland" whenever this pretty flower brings color to gardens and back yards all around the world.

Over the years the growing and exporting of flower bulbs has become much more than just a popular pastime. It has become one of the main industries of Holland. In an area about fifteen miles long and four miles wide some two to three billion bulbs are grown every year and then shipped to almost every corner of the world to provide beauty for twenty-five million gardens.

As the Director of Information for the Associated Bulb Growers of Holland, I am in touch with the gardening enthusiasts of twenty countries. I can say truly that there is an international fraternity of bulb gardeners. It started in Holland but is now world-wide in scope. There is a strong, intangible bond among the members of this group. They are eager to share their gardening secrets and to discuss new varieties. The common bond: they have learned what beauty comes from just a handful of bulbs in a plot of soil!

It is doubtful that one could find many men anywhere who are better equipped to write a book on bulbs than the author of this volume. Thomas H. Everett, the horticulturist of The New York Botanical Garden, is a recognized authority who has written and lectured on his subject in many countries. Constantly in demand as a judge at foremost exhibits and shows in America and Europe, he brings not only encyclopedic knowledge to his task but a practical awareness of the amateur's needs gleaned from his background as a respected advisor and popular teacher.

He is to be congratulated for having tackled a formidable task and succeeded so well. But I know he would join with me in more important congratulations: to the American gardener—because it is his interest in bulb gardening that has shown the way for such a book to come into being. Thank you for making a five-year-old's dream come true!

# PREFACE

## What Are Bulbs?

Botanically speaking, bulbs are buds, commonly subterranean, producing roots from their undersides, and consisting of layers of fleshy rudimentary leaves, called scales, attached to abbreviated stems. They are organs in which food is stored so that the plant may persist through such unfavorable periods as summer droughts and winter cold.

If we accept this botanical definition the determination of whether or not a particular plant is a bulb is relatively simple: it depends upon the morphology of the storage organ. But if we do so, many plants that the gardener considers bulbs—such as crocuses, dahlias, cannas, and calla-lilies—are ruled out. These, and many other plants not technically bulbs, have bulblike organs that function in the same way as bulbs but structurally are not scaly buds. They include solid, thickened stem bases called corms (crocuses, gladioluses), thickened terminal portions of stems called tubers (caladiums, begonias), elongated thickened stems called rhizomes (cannas and calla-lilies), and swollen tuberlike roots (dahlias).

Ordinarily the gardener uses the word "bulb" to include all organs obviously bulblike as well as true bulbs. In this book the gardener's terminology is followed. But this necessitates some arbitrary decision as to what to include and what to exclude for we are no longer leaning on the neat and easily applied technical definition of the botanist. Individual gardeners differ as to which plants should be classified as bulbs. These differences of opinion apply to borderline cases only, for all include such obvious plants as tulips, gladioluses, and dahlias in their bulb categories. Some go so far as to consider day-lilies, peonies, plantain-lilies, astilbes, and butterfly weed as bulbs. We do not do this. In general the criterion we accept is whether the bulb may be kept out of the ground in a dry condition without roots during its resting season. Note the word "may"; there is no implication that keeping the bulb out of the ground and divesting it of roots is beneficial—indeed in the cases of lilies, amaryllises, and some others it is decidedly detrimental—but it does permit them to be handled with ease for commercial sale. But we are not inflexibly consistent. You will find included in this book lily-of-the-valleys, lily-of-the-Niles, and clivias, none of which are acceptable if we apply the yardstick stated. The first named are discussed because cold storage "pips" are handled for indoor cultivation in much the same way as certain bulbs, the last two because they are such mighty good terrace plants and are at least semi-bulbous. This is not, from one viewpoint, very logical. Perhaps there are other deviations and inconsistencies. The reader's indulgence is asked.

## The Pattern of This Book

In this book detailed information is offered on the *selection* and *uses* of bulbs in gardens, as well as instruction on *how to grow* them. Because people are often faced with particular problems presented by specific locations, and want to know how to landscape and decorate them and what is best to plant, it seemed to the author that it is important to consider bulbs from that point of view. Accordingly, in the first part of this work you will find chapters dealing with such defined problems as those concerned with the rock garden, the perennial flower border, temporary bulb beds, the production of cut flowers, the growing of bulbs indoors, and so on, as well as a chapter by Miss Ann Hagan on flower arrangement. In this section, too, you will find chapters on the propagation of bulbs and on disease and pest control.

But problems of a different kind may confront you. You may want information on a particular type of bulb . . . details of its cultural needs, some knowledge of its kinds, its approximate height and time of bloom. Perhaps you are interested in getting a general idea of the geographical areas from which a certain bulb and its relatives originally came. Such information you will find in the alphabetical encyclopedic section of this book . . . which in a way is a series of recipes telling simply and concisely how to grow many hundreds of kinds of bulbs, with a little other information added for good measure.

In an age that appreciates "visual education" as a popular means of instruction, we are just awakening to the truth of the Chinese proverb that one picture is worth ten thousand words. It is hoped that the photographs of actual operations connected with growing bulbs that form the "How To Do It" section of this book will clarify and amplify the text, and that the splendid color pictures will convey some suggestions regarding the uses of bulbs—and also something of the magnificence and beauty of their blooms and of their infinite variety.

## Acknowledgments

The author is indebted to Miss Ann Hagan for contributing the chapter "Flower Arrangement" and to Howard Swift for many helpful ideas on the uses of bulbs that are incorporated chiefly in chapters 3, 4, 9 and 10, and for aid in selecting the colored illustrations. He acknowledges, too, the valued assistance of Miss Nancy Callaghan and of his wife, Ellen Brunt Everett, in posing for many of the "How To Do It" pictures. To Miss Elizabeth C. Hall he expresses thanks for expert assistance in involved library research. He is grateful to Ellen Brunt Everett for so carefully typing his almost illegible handwritten manuscript. In matters of nomenclature, this book follows, with very few exceptions, the excellent *Hortus Second* by L. H. Bailey and Ethel Zoe Bailey, published by the Macmillan Company.

### If You Want Help

No book can adequately cover *all* phases of bulb gardening nor can any author anticipate *every* question his readers may wish to ask. As Horticulturist of The New York Botanical Garden, the author of this volume is privileged to serve the public by answering its horticultural questions. If you wish to avail yourself of this free service of the Garden write to T. H. Everett, The New York Botanical Garden, Bronx Park, New York 58, New York, enclosing a stamped, self-addressed envelope for reply.

On behalf of The New York Botanical Garden, the author extends to all a cordial invitation to visit its plantings, library, and herbarium and to make use of its facilities and services. The New York Botanical Garden is a public, non-profit institution supported largely by contributions and membership fees. If you would like to know more about the privileges of membership, write to the New York Botanical Garden, New York 58, New York.

T. H. EVERETT

# HOW TO USE
# AND ENJOY BULBS

*In Holland tulip bulbs are grown to perfection to supply the markets of the world. Here workers are removing the flowers so that all the plant energy will go into developing first-class bulbs.*

# BULBS

# FOR EVERY

# GARDENER

Plant bulbs if you crave lavish color in your garden . . . if you wish floral profusion with minimum trouble . . . if you want sure-fire results from your horticultural adventures . . . if you seek quick returns from your gardening efforts. Plant bulbs, too, if you would like to test your skill in cultivating a selection of the choicest, rarest, and most tantalizingly capricious plants that can be grown.

There are bulbs for every gardener. A few kinds respond only to the persuasions of those whose thumbs are so green that they can almost cause a table leg to sprout roots, but many, many more will flourish for the veriest beginner provided just a little care is taken in selecting and planting them. So whether you belong to that small group of skilled horticulturists who can discuss learnedly the ways and needs of *Nomocharis* and rare Fritillary (or to that even smaller group who can grow them); whether you are an absolute beginner who can't recognize a crocus from a snowdrop; or, which is much more likely, if you belong to that great middle-of-the-horticultural-road group that has done a little gardening, and gets fun out of growing things and satisfaction from having attractive, colorful gardens and lots of flowers for cutting, bulbs are for you.

As a matter of fact you don't even need a garden to know the delights of bulb growing. Hyacinths, narcissuses, tulips, and many other popular kinds can be brought into glorious bloom in the home with little effort, in a few short weeks, and without even using soil if you prefer to use fiber, pebbles, or water instead. Lily-of-the-valleys can be had in bloom in three weeks from the time they are planted, colchicums even more quickly. What other group of plants offers so much . . . for so little?

Undoubtedly the ease with which most bulbs can be grown appeals. That is one reason why millions of tulips, narcissuses, hyacinths, crocuses, snowdrops, squills, grape-hyacinths, etc., are planted each fall, why gladioluses, dahlias,

3

cannas, tuberous begonias, gloxinias, and other summer-bloomers are popular for spring planting. Give these favorites but half a chance and they will reward you handsomely and unfailingly.

Excitement and adventure lie ahead if you really pursue the idea of acquiring a collection of the rarest bulbs. You may find yourself in correspondence with nurseries and individuals in Europe, South America, India, Kashmir, South Africa, and other distant lands, as well as with dealers, amateur gardeners, botanists, and others in our own country, for it is a fact that many fine native American bulbs are not commonly available. But such explorations are not for you until you have acquired a little of the know-how of handling the more easily obtainable kinds.

So begin bulb growing by planting generous quantities of those that are commonly available . . . kinds that are listed in most seedsmen's catalogs . . . types suitable for beginners. You can scarcely fail if you pay attention to their few simple needs. A modest monetary investment will provide amazing dividends in beauty and pleasure.

There you have *one* of the secrets of the popularity of bulbs . . . they give so much for so little. But bulbs offer many other attractions for the average amateur as well as for the horticulturally elite. Consider these.

(1) Bulbs make it possible to have a continuous succession of beautiful, spectacular, and interesting flowers outdoors or indoors throughout the year.

(2) No matter what kind of soil you have, if it will grow anything at all, it is suitable for some kinds of bulbs.

(3) There are bulbs that need shade, bulbs that need sun, bulbs that need moisture, bulbs that need drier conditions. There are bulbs that may be chosen, with every confidence of their success, for almost every conceivable garden condition and situation.

(4) Bulbs offer infinite variety in color, form, and texture. When in bloom they vary from an inch or two in height to several feet; their foliage characters are as diverse as their flowers. They are useful in practically every kind of landscape plan.

(5) The flowers of most bulbs last well when cut and are exquisite for use in flower arrangements.

(6) Bulb gardening requires a minimum of work—and most of that is done in the most pleasant seasons of the year.

(7) Bulbs give a high percentage of successful results even for the newest amateur.

(8) Bulbs, in great variety, are easily procured.

(9) Bulb gardening can be undertaken by the beginning amateur and, as his competence increases, he can find in bulbs a constant challenge to his skill, even though he become a most expert gardener.

## Historical Notes

Bulbs have a long and favorable record as garden plants. The history of bulb gardening spans the history of gardening itself; I can attempt no more here than a brief outline.

Because great civilizations originated in lands where bulbs were natively plentiful we must believe that these showy flowers were found in the earliest gardens, and such records that we have support this view. An Egyptian papyrus dating eighteen centuries before the birth of Christ, written by a priest, mentions colchicums and squills as being used in medicine. They were probably cultivated in sacred groves, prototypes of monastic herb gardens of the Middle Ages. There are records that the Pharaohs grew anemones in their gardens and that narcissuses and lilies were employed by the ancient Egyptians in funeral wreaths. Solomon, of the Old Testament, had an herb garden containing lilies and crocuses. As early as 380 B.C. the Greeks were using crocuses, lilies, and hyacinths in ceremonial crowns. These flowers were grown in gardens about their homes and presumably on a commercial scale also, for in Athens a regular flower market was in operation.

Theophrastus, who died about 287 B.C., writes of alliums, anemones, crocuses, cyclamens, gladioluses, grape-hyacinths, lilies, narcissuses, ranunculuses, scillas, and urgineas. Dioscorides, who lived in the first century A.D., lists, in addition to some of those mentioned by Theophrastus, colchicums, pancratiums, hyacinths, and ornithogalums. The Roman author Pliny the Elder, who lived about the time of Dioscorides, mentions four varieties of lilies and three of narcissuses, as well as alliums, scillas, anemones, gladioluses, ornithogalums, and crocuses.

During the Dark Ages that followed the fall of the Roman Empire interest in gardening in Europe fell to a low ebb. The spark was kept alive in the monasteries, and it was a monk of the Abbey of St. Gall near Lake Constance who authored the earliest known medieval book on gardening, a poem called "The Little Garden." Walafrid Strabo wrote this book in the ninth century and in it recorded his love for lilies as well as roses in these words:

> Better and sweeter are they than all the other plants and rightly called the flower of flowers. Yes, roses and lilies, the one for virginity with no sordid toil, no warmth of love, but the glow of their own sweet scent, which spreads further than the rival roses, but once bruised or crushed turns all to rankness. Therefore roses and lilies for our church, one for the Martyr's blood, the other for the symbol in His hand. Pluck them, O maiden, roses for war and lilies for peace, and think of that Flower of the stem of Jesse. Lilies His words were and the hallowed acts of His pleasant life, but His death re-dyed the roses.

The designations "lily" and "white lily" as used in those times referred to *Lilium candidum*, the Madonna lily. In 812 A.D. a list was published of the herbs grown in the imperial gardens of the Emperor Charlemagne; it includes the candidum lily. The earliest known original work on gardening in English, of which a manuscript copy written in 1441 still exists, lists ninety-seven plants actually growing in an English garden; among these are daffodils, candidum lilies, *Hepatica triloba,* and *Crocus sativus.*

The Crusades, and the Renaissance that followed, revived interest in plants and gardens. People were traveling, seeing strange lands, becoming acquainted with foreign customs and unusual plants. Interest first centered in the Mediterranean region and in lands to the east of it, but before long the New World was discovered and floral treasures as well as other wealth were introduced from the Americas to Spain and Portugal and to other European countries.

All over Europe increasing attention was given to gardens. The Italians, French, Spanish, Germans, Austrians, Dutch, and English played parts in the movement and many exotic plants were introduced to their home countries. Because bulbs withstood long delays incident to the transportation of the day better than most plants, they were undoubtedly prominent among the successful introductions. Records indicate that during the last half of the sixteenth century and the first half of the seventeenth the following bulbs were brought for the first time into England: Martagon lilies, crown imperials, Persian fritillaries, Persian ranunculuses, double-flowered hepaticas, yellow crocuses, and tulips.

The tulip, now one of the most popular of garden bulbs, was not known in Europe before 1554, when the Ambassador of the Emperor Ferdinand to the Sultan of Turkey told in a letter of seeing flowers "which the Turks call tulipam" between Adrianople and Constantinople. The first record of tulips blooming in Europe is 1559. But long before this they were popular in Eastern gardens. The Turks grew many kinds and that fierce warrior and great gardener Mohammed Babar (Emperor Zehireddin Mohammed) gave attention to them and recorded, when marching through the mountains of Afghanistan:

> The ground is richly diversified by various kinds of tulips. I once directed them to be counted, and they brought in thirty-two or thirty-three different sorts of tulips. There is one species which has a scent in some degree like a rose, and which I termed *laleh-gul-bui* (the rose-scented tulip). This species is found only on the Sheikh's Plain, in a small spot of ground, and nowhere else.

Mohammed Babar died in 1530, but before he died this Great Mughal had traveled widely and built many gardens. He visited Samarkand and made a long list of the gardens surrounding the city. It was there that the Lala-Zar, or tulip fields, were located. In the magnificent garden he made at Agra, his Indian capital, he planted fragrant narcissuses—and undoubtedly tulips.

In the New World, too, great civilizations had given attention to gardening . . . . and to bulbs. In 1520 the Conquistador, Cortez, in a letter to Charles V told of the wonders of Montezuma's pleasure gardens. In the finest of these, at Hauxtepec, there grew along with many other decorative plants amaryllises and dahlias. In Peru the Incas were especially fond of nosegays, and in that bulb-rich land it is certain that bulbous plants must have been appreciated

*This field of double tulips growing in the rich bulb soil of Holland calls for expert attention and much hand work to give of its best.*

. . . and cultivated. The earliest known American book dealing with plants is the Badianus Manuscript, an Aztec Herbal of 1552. In it, clearly shown in color, is a picture of a dahlia. Like other adventurers of the day the Conquistadors sent to their home lands strange plants they found. The canna found its way from America to Spain and Portugal in this way.

Holland, which now supplies the world with most of its tulips, did not receive its first bulbs until 1571. Sixty-three years later a tulip mania broke out in that country and lasted for three years. Speculation in the bulbs rose to fantastic heights and many were bankrupted when the inevitable crash came. A similar extravagance occurred in Turkey early in the eighteenth century.

Increase in the number of different kinds of bulbs grown in gardens continued steadily. Tradescant, listing the plants he grew in his garden at Lambeth in London in 1656, mentions (among others) more than ten kinds of crocuses, five kinds of cyclamen, six kinds of fritillaries, four kinds of gladioluses, twenty-five kinds of hyacinths (he includes grape-hyacinths), several kinds of colchicums, bulbous irises from Persia and Africa, cannas (which he calls "redflowered Indian Cane and yellow Indian Cane"), many tulips and many narcissuses, leucojums, anemones, alliums (including a "Virginia Garlick from America"), *Ornithogalum arabicum* and *Ornithogalum neapolitanum*, crown imperials, ranunculuses, anemones, and, of course, lilies.

The establishment of the Dutch in South Africa in 1652 resulted in the first "Cape plants" being sent to Europe, a foretaste of the vast wealth of magnificent plants, particularly bulbs, that South Africa was to give to the world. Among the first sent home were two kinds of oxalis. Not too long afterward followed nerines, freesias, gladioluses, and clivias.

But colonists not only collected bulbs of the new lands and sent them home; they brought with them familiar kinds from the old countries and planted them in their new homes.

From 1640 on the Dutch settlers in New Amsterdam (New York) each had "a patch of cabbages, a bit of tulips," and Adrian Van der Donck who came to New Amsterdam in 1642 later reported upon "the flowers in general which the Netherlands have introduced." He included "different varieties of fine tulips, crown imperials, white lilies, the lily frutularia [sic] and anemones."

From the beginning of the seventeenth century geographical exploration and exploitation proceeded rapidly. Wealth accumulated in many of the old countries and some of the new. Interest in plants and gardens continued to expand. New plants of all types, including bulbs, were collected more or less systematically and became available to gardeners. The stream of new introductions that began at that time has flowed continuously, although at various rates at different times, to the present day.

John Bartram, first great American botanist, sent to Europe bulbs of native erythroniums as well as those of *Lilium philadelphicum* and *Lilium superbum*. The latter bloomed in England for the first time in 1738, the former a year later. Contemporaries of Bartram were also actively collecting plants.

In 1772 the first of a long line of professional plant hunters, Francis Masson, was sent from Kew Gardens in England to South Africa, charged with the particular purpose of collecting and sending home live plants and seeds. To Masson and his successors through the next eighteen decades we are indebted for many fine bulbous plants we now grow. Among Masson's own introductions was the unbelievable green *Ixia viridiflora* and red-flowered *Boophone distachya*. The first tiger lilies (*Lilium tigrinum*) were sent by William Kerr from China in 1804. Although new to Western gardens this lily had been cultivated in the Orient for more than a thousand years. It is a species that alert American hybridists have successfully used to produce some of the fine hybrid lilies that are such a noteworthy development of the mid-twentieth century.

The exploration of western North America brought to notice a grand lot of new bulbs including *Camassia esculenta* which David Douglas was the first white man to see when he was collecting in the early years of the nineteenth century.

Dr. F. P. von Siebold, a Dutch surgeon, made horticultural history when he returned to Europe in 1829 with bulbs of *Lilium speciosum* and *Lilium maculatum* from Japan, a country then practically closed to Westerners. The magnificent *Lilium auratum* was obtained from Japan by Veitch in the early 1860s, and Augustine Henry sent home from China *Lilium Henryi* soon afterward. Last of the really great lilies to arrive was the regal lily obtained by "Chinese"

Wilson in the Min valley of China when he was collecting for the Arnold Arboretum of Jamaica Plain, Massachusetts, and sent home by him in quantity in 1911. During the twentieth century other new bulbs have been introduced from the wild to our gardens. The names of such collectors as Wilson, Forrest, Ward, Elliot, Farrer, Rock, Balls, and others rightly belong with those of the great plant introducers of the ages.

The history of plant collecting is a long and glorious one. Justice cannot be done to it here. I shall be content if I can awake in a few of those who plant bulbs today an appreciation of the work of the princes and emperors, the monks and missionaries, the soldiers and sailors, the professional plant collectors and the amateurs, the gardeners and nurserymen, the naturalists and botanists, whose devotion and labors through the centuries have made it possible for us to decorate our gardens and homes with gorgeous bulbous plants from all parts of the world.

But our indebtedness does not cease there. We owe much, too, to the keen-eyed selectors and propagators of those plants that varied from their fellows in a sufficiently favorable manner to make their continuance desirable, and to the hybridizers who by crossing wild species have produced new kinds; for modern bulb gardening relies fully as much on varieties that are developed and fostered by man as it does upon nature's wild types.

*The glowing flowers of tulip Katherine Truxton show to advantage against a groundcover planting of Ajuga.*

# THE CARE

# $2$ AND FEEDING

# OF BULBS

In nature all plants except those that inhabit tropical rain-forests and a few other favored locales face one or more difficult periods each year during which growth is impossible. This may be because of low winter temperatures or because of lack of moisture during the dry season. Whatever the cause, the survival of the species depends upon its persistence in some form or other through these unfavorable times. Such continuance is provided for by various procedures and devices.

Annuals simply die at the end of the season favorable to growth, leaving seeds capable of surviving and giving rise to new individuals at the commencement of the next growing season. Deciduous trees and shrubs shed their foliage and present to the drying influences above ground their bark-protected stems and branches only. Evergreens, such as yuccas and pines, resist desiccation because their leaves have a tough cuticle and so do not lose water rapidly when exposed to wind and sun. Some plants lose all or many of their leaves and exist through the times of stress entirely or mainly by virtue of the tenacity of life of their underground parts. In many cases these parts are fat and swollen and serve as storage organs for elaborated food materials and for water. Such organs the gardener calls "bulbs."

The chief regions in which bulbs occur naturally are those that have a "mediterranean" climate—where an extended dry warm period alternates with a moist warm period, areas such as the steppes of Russia, where a cold winter is succeeded by a short growing season and that in turn by a hot dry period, and the woodlands of temperate regions, where winters are cold and summers reasonably moist. This last-named locale permits a short spring growing season before the overhead canopy becomes too dense to admit sufficient light and before the roots of the trees become so active that they absorb most available moisture and keep the soil about the bulbs much drier than might be sup-

*For a kaleidoscope of bright color in early spring plant a formal flower bed thickly with mixed double early tulips.*

posed. California, Mexico, South Africa, and the Mediterranean region and its eastward extensions are all regions where bulbous plants abound naturally; most are sun-lovers. In eastern North America, central and northern Europe, and parts of eastern Asia a considerable selection of chiefly woodland bulbs have their homes; the majority of these are shade-lovers.

Most soils in which bulbs grow naturally are dry or definitely dryish during those periods when the top and root growth of the bulbs is inactive, that is, when the bulbs are at rest. There are just enough exceptions to validate this rule—a few swamp lilies, the lesser celandine, and certain camassias, for example, grow in soils that are always moist. In the long evolutionary development of plant life these may represent dry-region species that have invaded humid soils and have not yet lost the organs that served them well in droughty areas.

An appreciation of the conditions under which bulbs grow in nature is of considerable help in understanding their needs in cultivation, but is by no means all-sufficient. When plants are grown away from their native homes— and perhaps are accommodated in pots indoors—they may respond to quite different soils, temperatures, moisture conditions, etc., than those to which they are subjected in the wild. Cultural practices for any specific bulb should be based on a triad of informational sources: one is a knowledge of its native environment, another an acquaintance with the practices and recommendations of those who have successfully cultivated it, and the third personal experience based on trials and experiments with its cultivation. When growing any kind of bulb for the first time judgment as to its treatment must of necessity be based upon evidence provided by the first two of these sources. The wise gardener quickly adds to his learning by carefully observing the responses and behavior of the newcomer to the treatment it is accorded.

*Beautiful overall flower patterns may be had by bedding tulips closely together.*

### Care in Handling Bulbs

There are some important general principles to be observed in the cultivation of bulbs. Because they are fleshy they must be handled carefully to avoid physical injury. When lifting bulbs and when digging and cultivating among mixed plantings of which they form a part they are easily mashed, punctured, and scraped unless particular care is taken to prevent this. Any wound provides easy access for disease and encourages decay, which may spread rapidly to kill the entire plant. A spading fork is the safest tool to employ for lifting bulbs; if a spade is used too many are apt to be sliced. By marking with stakes or in other appropriate fashion the locations of bulbs planted in areas where soil operations are likely to be carried out during times when the bulbs have no top growth, the risk of damaging the bulbs is greatly reduced. If bulbs are injured unavoidably, prompt treatment consisting of smoothing the edges of the wounds and dusting them with sulphur of Fermate is advisable.

### Proper Soil

Most bulbs prosper in what we speak of as good garden soil—an earth midway between sand and clay and containing a generous measure of organic matter. Because their roots extend well down it should be made agreeable to a depth of at least eight inches and more for kinds that are planted deeply.

### Manner of Planting

Although there are exceptions, bulbs are generally set with their tops about three times the diameter of the bulb below ground; small bulbs deeper proportionately. In most cases it is the pointed end of the bulb which should be uppermost—but some tubers are planted horizontally. Some few, such as anemones, give no clear indication as to which end is "up" but close examination will usually disclose some sign of previous stem or root sources, and of course the stem scar should face upward.

## Moisture and Drainage

It is essential that all bulbs have plenty of moisture when growing actively. Efficient drainage to prevent water from standing around them is very necessary for nearly all. An overabundance of water during the dormant period is particularly harmful.

## Storage of Nourishment

Bulbs are warehouses in which the plant stores food to provide nourishment for next year's crop of foliage and flowers. In many spring-flowering kinds

*A border a few inches wide provides a home for these spring crocuses. Sweet Alyssum or California poppies sown over them when the crocus flowers have faded will give a long season of summer bloom.*

embryonic leaves and flowers are completely formed within the bulb before winter comes, and these remain quiescent until spring warmth stimulates growth; in others no foliage or flower parts are present, but the foodstuffs needed for their development are stored. Most summer-flowering bulbs have enough food within themselves to provide a vigorous spring start, but that needed for the production of later foliage and flowers is manufactured by the leaves from elements taken from the soil and air as growth proceeds. The nourishment that the plant stores for the next season is prepared by the green leaves of the current year; therefore it is imperative not only that enough green leaves to carry out this process be developed and retained but also that they be kept in good condition until their work of food manufacture is complete, which is indicated by natural yellowing and eventual browning. When cutting flowers from bulbs, it is always important not to remove too many leaves if the bulb is expected to produce flowers the following year. When bulbs must be dug before the ripening process is completed, it is just as important that the leaves be given as good a chance as possible to complete their work and to ripen normally. Success with bulbs demands that everything possible be done to encourage and retain healthy leaf growth.

## Fertilizers

Like all plants, bulbs respond to fertile soil, but manures and fertilizers must not be used carelessly or more harm than good may result. The value of well-rotted manure to improve soil structure and to provide nutrients is recognized. It may be used to great advantage as long as there is a good protective layer of soil between the bulbs and the manure. Fresh manure coming in contact with the underground parts of any plants in this group is likely to be disastrous and should not be permitted; neither should manure mulches be used except with great caution.

Slow-acting fertilizers other than manure are particularly recommended for feeding bulbs. Bone meal is one of the best, and five or six pounds to a hundred square feet is not too heavy an annual application. Other good fertilizers are cottonseed meal, dried blood, tankage, and wood ashes, as well as complete commercial fertilizers in which the nutrient elements are neither too rapidly available nor too concentrated; a regular 5-10-5 fertilizer such as is used in vegetable gardens is suitable.

## Mulches

Mulches can be employed with excellent effect. Those used in summer can be very helpful in aiding to retain moisture in the soil, in keeping the ground cool, and in discouraging weeds. Peatmoss, buckwheat hulls, clippings from lawns, and even decayed sawdust can be used successfully. Mulches intended for protective winter cover should be applied after the top surface of the ground has frozen and be removed after bulb growth is well started in the spring. For this purpose, branches of evergreens, buckwheat hulls, pine needles, salt hay, and leaves of deciduous trees that do not pack down (because of their tendency to do this maple leaves are not very suitable) are recommended. The purpose of winter covering is not to keep the bulbs warm but to lessen the hazards of alternate freezing and thawing which may lift and expose bulbs that are not far below the surface and may tear and break the roots of others. Winter protection should not be applied until the top couple of inches of soil are frozen.

## Housekeeping

Good housekeeping—seeing that cultivated and adjacent areas are kept free of debris and that injured and infected foliage is diligently removed—is essential. Incurably diseased plants should be promptly removed and burned. When seeds are not desired, the early removal of faded flowers channels plant energy which would normally be used for seed production into building stronger bulbs. It also aids in keeping the garden neat.

*May-flowering tulips are unsurpassed for spring bedding arrangements. These lawn beds will be filled with summer flowers when the tulip blooms have passed.*

## Insects and Diseases

In dealing with insects and diseases, proper diagnosis of the trouble is of primary importance; it is not reasonable to resort to medication, surgery, or more drastic measures without being sure what is wrong. Such practices may be both expensive and wasteful of time. Particularly when rare or expensive varieties are concerned is it desirable to know what the chances are of a diseased plant being saved by removing the affected parts and nursing what is left back to a healthy condition. Frequently when disease appears among a planting, lifting the healthy bulbs, disinfecting them, and moving them to an area not previously used for growing bulbs of the same kind will save them from infection.

## Storage

Many bulbs are dug, transported for great distances, stored in stock bins of bulb merchants, and displayed at retail outlets for extended periods before they are delivered to the customer. After delivery there may be further delay before the bulbs can be set in the garden. Some bulbs—like narcissuses and tulips—withstand this treatment amazingly well. They are often dug in July and are not put back in the ground until late November or December. It is agreed, however, that most bulbs should not be out of the ground longer than necessary. New bulbs should be procured from retailers as soon as they are available and, except in a very few cases, be planted as soon as is practicable. A few, such as amaryllises and lilies, have fleshy perennial roots attached to their bases when dug. These are usually removed or are very seriously battered before they reach the purchaser. Because these roots are so essential and must be replaced before the plant can fully resume its normal activities, it may take a year or more for such bulbs to re-establish themselves after planting. Lily bulbs which have soft fleshy scales and a maximum amount of exposed surface ( as well as other kinds known to be very susceptible to serious drying) should be kept in sawdust, peatmoss, buckwheat hulls, vermiculite, or similar material while out of the ground. A storage atmosphere that is either too dry or too damp can be disastrous to all kinds of bulbs. Dahlias, cannas, and some others often benefit from the protection of being packed in dry soil, peatmoss, or other material which may even have to be sprinkled occasionally to lessen the water loss which causes them to wither. The know-how of handling bulbs in storage is in most cases a matter of realizing the effect of atmospheric conditions on their physical make-up and using common sense.

## Buying Bulbs

When purchasing bulbs avoid "cheap jack" offers of extraordinary "bargains." Deal with suppliers of known integrity, place your order as early as possible,

LEFT:   *A flowering crabapple and tulips decorate this easy-to-maintain courtyard garden. White tulips are used generously; they repeat the coolness of the white boundary wall and with it serve to prevent discords between other tulips, the brick pavement, and the crabapple flowers.*

RIGHT:   *Narrow borders filled with groups of flowering bulbs and perennials here skirt plantings of flowering trees and shrubs.* Ajuga *and* Alyssum saxatile *are the perennials in bloom in the front of the border. A little more variation in the sizes of the flower groups would be advantageous.*

and expect to pay fair prices. Good bulbs should be heavy for their size, firm of flesh, and plump. They should be free of bruises and scars, their coats intact (except that tulips sometimes tend to lose their skins and this does no harm provided the flesh beneath is not damaged).

Bulb sizes often puzzle the amateur. They are expressed in different ways for different kinds and, unfortunately, dealers are not always consistent in their application. "Top size," "jumbo size," "exhibition size," "extra size," "number one size," and similar terms are freely used—and sometimes misused. When sizes in inches or centimeters are given they usually refer to the circumference of the bulb, but in some cases—freesias and tuberous begonias, for example—to the diameter. Such sizes are a good guide when comparing bulbs of the same variety and sometimes when making comparison between different varieties of the same kind. This latter does not always hold, however; some varieties of narcissuses, for example, have consistently larger bulbs than others, the very biggest bulb of a poeticus being of a size that would be small for a "King Alfred." It pays to buy large bulbs, but not always the largest. "Bedding size" hyacinths, for instance, are more suitable for outdoor planting than exhibition size; freesias not over three quarters of an inch in diameter are generally preferred to bigger ones.

No matter how fine the bulbs you purchase are, if you mistreat them afterward they will deteriorate. Open the packages immediately upon arrival. Examine the bulbs carefully for defects and, if you find any, request a replacement at once. If planting has to be delayed, store the bulbs in the bags they come in with their tops opened in a cool, well-ventilated place where mice, squirrels, and other rodents cannot get at them, or spread them out in flats or shallow trays and store them under the same conditions. Keep them away from furnaces and other sources of dry heat. Too high temperatures and excessive dryness will cause shriveling and may work other serious harm. The best temperature for storing is between 60 and 65 degrees.

*This border, set against a background of shrubs and planted almost solidly with tulips arranged in informal groups, provides a rich picture that is much more pleasing than if the bulbs had been planted in geometrical patterns.*

# 3
## SPRING BULBS
## IN BEDS
## AND BORDERS

Our earliest American flower gardens were extremely simple and were made close to the house. Here there was protection for cherished plants and less risk of destruction by romping children, by saddled horses left to nibble grass while their owners made calls, or by cows and chickens escaped through inadequate fences. Having the garden near at hand, the housewife could at odd moments keep back encroaching weeds and supply the needs of a few sturdy ornamentals.

As the pioneers became sufficiently settled and could stretch their resources to improve the surrounding land aesthetically, they kept selected areas grass- and weed-free for the growing of decorative plants. These were the first American flower beds and borders, the prototypes of those that adorn our gardens today.

It is of such beds and borders that the beginning gardener first thinks when he considers planting bulbs to provide lavish spring color. Such features afford the more experienced ample opportunity to exercise taste and skill in creating breath-taking effects with daffodils, hyacinths, tulips, and other bulbs. With the planning and planting of such areas this chapter is concerned.

Spring-flowering bulbs are used in two principal ways in beds and borders. They are massed alone or in combination with other spring-blooming plants in "bedding arrangements" and they are planted in groups with perennials and perhaps biennials and annuals in informal mixed borders. Bedding arrangements are distinctly formal and are temporary. They are disassembled at the completion of the spring blooming season and the beds are then replanted with decorative summer-bloomers. Bulbs planted in mixed borders form part of more permanent plant collections which are selected to provide long successions of bloom without the necessity for completely clearing and replanting

The collector of bulbs will usually plant his treasures in small groups as these narcissuses are planted. Such groups are easily accommodated in the perennial borders and at the front of shrubberies. Here we have groups of Narcissus Duke of Windsor (top), Cheerfulness (center), and Fortune (bottom).

*Narcissuses planted in irregular groups add color to borders beneath this avenue of birches. They are planted among ferns and other shade-tolerant plants that cover the ground during summer.*

the beds oftener than once every few years. Such plantings are much more informal than stylized bedding and because of this they often fit better into contemporary gardens.

## Formal Beds

Formal bedding can be used to fine advantage in enclosed gardens laid out in geometric patterns and in association with architectural features. It is suitable for bordering walks, for setting against retaining walls, for planting near formal pools, and for installing in appropriately placed lawn beds, but it is out of place in free landscapes and in naturalistic parts of the garden.

*Hedges of boxwood, stretches of greensward, and a backdrop of fresh young tree foliage and of dogwoods and wistaria in bloom, provide a perfect foil for this well-planned bedding arrangement of May-flowering tulips.*

Hyacinths and tulips are the most important bedding bulbs. Planted in blocks of single colors or in patterned designs in various hues they are spectacular. Good effects may also be had with narcissuses, Spanish and Dutch irises, and, in mild climates, with ranunculuses and poppy-anemones. Such other bulbs as scillas, grape-hyacinths, crocuses, and glory-of-the-snows are of minor importance as bedding subjects but they may sometimes be employed with other spring-bloomers to produce unusual and interesting displays.

When bulbs alone are planted in a formal bed they may be of one variety, as for instance a solid bed of hyacinth "Queen of the Pinks" or of tulip "City of Haarlem." Two or more varieties of the same kind in contrasting or harmonizing colors may be used together; for example, violet-flowered tulip "The Bishop" could be planted with the soft yellow tulip "Niphetos" . . . or deep pink, blue, and white hyacinths might be used in lively mixture or in a more formal design. Lastly, more than one *kind* of bulb may be used in a single bed as, for example, when Spanish bluebells are used—as they can be so charmingly —with May-flowering tulips. As the mixtures become more complex, so the need for careful thought and the exercise of good taste becomes more important. No one can go wrong with a single variety in a bed, but it is easy to blunder when different *kinds* of bulbs are used together. Since the single variety bed provides little opportunity for creativeness and individual expression, the mixed bed often makes more appeal. When selecting bulbs for such plantings it is important to choose kinds intended to give desired color combinations that will surely bloom together.

But bulbs in formal beds need not be used alone. Lovely spring effects may be had by employing them in combination with such plants as English daisies, pansies, violas, arabises, aubrietas, *Alyssum saxatile* (both the golden-yellow- and the lemon-flowered kinds), blue *Phlox canadensis*, forget-me-nots, polyanthus primroses, and wallflowers. These non-bulbous plants, set out as ground-covers beneath hyacinths, narcissuses, and tulips, can be extremely effective.

Many pleasing arrangements can be worked out, including some that involve exciting and daring color associations as well as others that are more subtle. A bed of blue forget-me-nots interplanted with rose-pink tulip "Princess Elizabeth" is in excellent taste; so is a planting of a pale yellow tulip such as "Mrs. John T. Scheepers" with a carpeting of forget-me-nots or of blue *Phlox canadensis*. The rich brown tulip "Don Almo" is a fine companion for viola "Apricot." A more daring result is achieved by using glowing orange Siberian wallflowers with an almost black tulip such as "Black Eagle" or "La Tulipe Noire" . . . or by planting the brilliant red tulip "Charles Needham" among blue forget-me-nots.

Hyacinths growing among pansies of contrasting or harmonizing hues are pleasing and they can also be associated very effectively with English daisies. Deep pink hyacinths with pink daisies beneath are lovely. Pink daisies are also beautiful with pale blue hyacinths, but no more so than are white daisies with rich purple hyacinths.

Narcissuses, a little less suitable than tulips and hyacinths for formal beds, need carefully chosen companion plants to be seen at their best; polyanthus primroses are appropriate and so are pansies.

*Such lavish massing of color as is seen in this tulip border is better adapted to public plantings than to the home garden. In private gardens the groups of the individual varieties that form the border should be much smaller.*

A very gay result is secured by planting mixed tulips among a variety of spring-blooming carpeting plants to form a real medley of bloom. Such a very mixed planting should occupy a fairly large bed; in small areas one or two varieties are better. It is also possible to achieve a very satisfactory result by using a single groundcover—arabis, pansies, or violas, for example—and to interplant it with hyacinths, tulips, Spanish bluebells, and Spanish irises to ensure having a succession of bulbs blooming over a long period with the same underplanting constant for all. This, again, is most appropriate for sizeable beds; many different kinds of plants in a tiny bed rarely look well.

Anemone blanda *blooms with early tulips. Here, it is planted in bold groups in a partially shaded place, with other spring-flowering bulbs.*

*A bed of tulips underplanted with pansies and forget-me-nots borders one side of a stone-paved path, azaleas in bloom and rhododendrons the other. The tulips are rather widely spaced to accommodate the interplanting.*

### Informal Borders

Symmetrical beds filled with spring-flowering bulbs are gay and decorative but are not suitable for all locations, and they do present the necessity for summer plantings to follow. Most frequently in today's gardens spring-flowering bulbs are used informally with perennials, biennials, annuals, and summer- and fall-blooming bulbs. This makes possible a spring-to-fall succession of flowers in one border, which is completely replanted every four or five years with minor replanting in intermediate years. Such borders may be established close to the house, may extend in long sweeping curves along the edge of woodland or stream, may be planted against a background of trees or shrubs or against a hedge or wall.

When selecting bulbs for grouping in mixed borders, remember that the number needed for each patch may be relatively small if their flowers are of good size—a great deal larger if the flowers are small—that the larger the border, the bigger the groups should be. In borders of modest size, narcissuses and tulips are most impressive when planted fifteen to thirty together, small subjects such as glory-of-the-snows and crocuses in lots of fifty or more. Easy-to-grow bulbs of various flowering heights are readily available, so kinds may be chosen for the front of the border and for all points to the very back. Bulbs should never be "stuck" in without particular thought just because there happen to be vacant spaces in the border. The groups should have irregular, pleasingly curved outlines rather than be square, circular, or elliptical. The bulbs should be spaced at approximately even distances within the groups but should not be in straight rows, and the groups should be spaced at irregular intervals.

Locate kinds that have long, coarse foliage such as narcissuses, Spanish blue-bells, and the more leafy alliums behind perennials which will grow up and hide the unsightly yellowing bulb leaves after the flowers have passed. If annuals are to be used for color to follow the bulbs, allow enough space between or adjacent to the bulbs to permit filling in with annual seedlings.

Many bulbs break ground surprisingly early. Even in New York City, February, and sometimes late January, finds us poking around the garden looking for the first comers. There is excitement in finding firm bundles of bulb leaves pushing through brown earth before winter has finally departed, for we know that in a month or less we shall have colorful winter aconites, snowdrops, grape-hyacinths, glory-of-the-snows, scillas, and crocuses. Snowdrops and some of the crocus species, notably *Crocus Korolkowii,* are among the first to pop, and how grateful we are for those first blooms!

April comes and soon the trees are misty green with tiny foliage. Early shrubs burst into flower even before they leaf. A few colorful taller perennials such as yellow doronicums and Virginia bluebells are of special value as companions for early bulbs.

Now is the time to start keeping records of flowering dates, plants that combine well, and other pertinent data that will help you plan a better border and perhaps other borders and other gardens. Continue this practice throughout the year. Wherever you live you will find tables of flowering dates invaluable —and making such lists is something that can be done in anticipation of having a garden even before actual garden work is started. Planning combinations of plants is one of the most enjoyable pleasures of gardening and is without backaches! It is of special importance in arranging mixed borders, for to do this well you must be acquainted with the flowering sequence of the plants you wish to use.

The first perennial flowers other than bulbs to appear are those of low-growing plants that are choice as groundcovers with bulbs. These include arabises, aubrietas, moss pinks, and evergreen candytuft. Although more conspicuously in bloom a month later these can be depended on to provide welcome foliage and some flower color to accompany such early flowers as the brilliant Fosteriana tulip "Red Emperor" and the single and double early tulips. These first tulips have great value for early color and, even though their stems are so short that underplanting is not requisite, low perennials planted to cover the ground do help to prevent their flowers from being splashed with mud in spring showers . . . and also make effective edgings. Drifts of perennials which hug the earth closely add interest and richness to the fronts of mixed borders when associated with early tulips, narcissuses, hyacinths, scillas, grape-hyacinths, snowdrops, crocuses, *Iris reticulata,* and other spring bulbs.

In choosing varieties of early tulips to use in the foreground of borders, the most intense colors often prove irresistible. After the dullness of winter we hunger for a crescendo of brightness—so why not satisfy that hunger? To prevent too-vibrant associations of very strong colors such as bright red and vivid yellow, use patches of white flowers or masses of green foliage as separators. Brilliant color used in studied sequence and perhaps repeated along the border can be exciting. On the other hand, soft pastels, which blend with the delicate colors of opening leaves and with early shrub flowers such as those of pale yellow Cornelian dogwood, lavender-pink *Daphne Mezereum*, blush *Viburnum Carlesii*, and creamy white Japanese tandromeda can be charming.

Hyacinths can be used in the border very much in the same manner as early tulips. They are stiffer and more formal in appearance and ordinarily should not be employed as freely as tulips. They offer tones of blue and purple not provided by tulips in addition to a delightful selection of pinks, reds, lavenders, soft yellows, and whites. Their stalwart spikes add interest and a variety of flower form.

*Nine bulbs each of white hyacinths and Red Emperor tulips are sufficient to plant attractive small contrasting groups at the front of this border.*

Narcissuses are more permanent in borders than are hyacinths and tulips. Under favorable conditions they persist and increase. Because of this they should be placed where they need not be disturbed. Narcissuses vary greatly in form and size of flowers and in their flowering times. They do not possess the wide color range of tulips and hyacinths. Yellows and whites predominate, with orange and subdued pinks offering occasional variation. Despite their limited range of color, the diversity of hues displayed within this range by the hundreds of available varieties is amazing—and what an astounding number of combinations there are! Their flower forms include those with large trumpets (the true daffodils) and those with trumpets so shallow that they suggest nothing so much as crinkled caps of pop bottles. The flowers are borne one to a stem or in clusters. Some are double, and some have fragrance as an added attraction.

Narcissuses are valuable not alone for their flowers but also for their clean, luxuriant foliage. This becomes something of a problem, however, for after the flowers have faded the foliage continues to grow and then needs a long period of ripening before it can be safely cut away. For this reason, place your narcissuses where their leaves will be somewhat hidden by perennial plants during late May and June.

Catalogs usually group tulip varieties to give some indication of their flowering periods, but they do not often do this with narcissuses. There is no more satisfactory way of selecting narcissuses (and other spring-flowering bulbs too, for that matter) than to visit gardens where they are grown—those of friends and acquaintances—and public gardens that accommodate collections. Here you will find practical help as well as opportunity to note varieties best suited for your garden and combinations which have a particular appeal. Do not fail to take sufficient time out to visit other gardens.

*Pleasing results are obtained by combining different kinds of bulbs. Here deep blue grape-hyacinths are interplanted with single early yellow tulips.*

*A narrow border of ranunculuses atop a terrace wall provides a brilliant spectacle in this California garden. Note that yellow pansies in the lower border have been cleverly used to repeat the yellow of the ranunculuses. The absence of other color emphasizes the beauty and richness of this planting.*

May, in New York and places with approximately similar climates, is one of the most thrilling months of the garden year. Trees and shrubs expand their leaves with unbelievable rapidity, and flowers develop no less slowly. Throughout most of North America spring brings rapid climatic changes that speed the growth of plants. In consequence we enjoy a procession of flowers accelerated in their development to an extent that is not fully appreciated unless compared with the more leisurely growth characteristic of climates such as that of England. But, alas, our flowers do not last. The same factors that speed their coming hasten their passing. Flowering seasons may span an entire month in England and but a short two weeks here. This makes careful planning for constant garden color a much more exacting task. Hit-or-miss planting is more likely to be unsatisfactory where the plants remain in bloom for a short season than where longer displays from individual kinds can be expected.

In mixed borders, a great number of delightful May combinations are possible, but it is best to restrict oneself to those kinds which are truly worth-while and to avoid too wide a selection. Very pleasing effects are obtained by repetition of forms and colors throughout the length of a border. Trying to include too many varieties may easily cause an objectionable spottiness. This is particularly important to remember when choosing tulips and narcissuses, which are available in such diversity that there is danger of adding more and more instead of repeating groups of a few favored varieties and combinations. Of course if you are primarily a collector of plants, with garden design as a secondary interest, this need not apply.

Consideration of color is of great importance in planning mixed borders. Good taste in its use is best developed by keen observation and by studying pleasing combinations. The problem of how to place spring colors in a border may be approached by locating the patches of tulips first. This is a very satisfactory procedure for working out May color schemes. For instance, one might start at the center of a border with white and follow through progressive shades of color such as pastel pink, deeper pink, rose, lavender, mauve, lilac, red to purple or deep maroon—using the same sequence in either direction from the center. Many other color progressions can be worked out. They lend rhythm and balance to border design. Perennials, and bulbs other than tulips, which flower at the same time may then be fitted in to harmonize with the basic color line—starting with the low perennials that are so effective for foreground and underplanting and continuing with taller kinds.

*Tulips, narcissuses, and grape-hyacinths combine here well with creeping phlox and other plants. The yellow flowers in the foreground are annuals grown in a greenhouse and transferred outside when in bloom.*

Varying levels give an opportunity to create distinctive garden pictures. This stone retaining wall makes a lovely background for an informal border of tulips and daffodils with perennials for later bloom. An unpretentious path, an inviting seat, and a pale-pink-flowering cherry in bloom complete the picture.

Clumps of tulips are used here effectively among the evergreens that form the foundation planting of a modest home.

This border, well stocked with non-bulbous irises and other perennials, is brightened in spring by groups of tulips and other bulbs planted between the perennials.

*Tulips and apricot-colored pansies have been selected to complement the yellow-brown stone of this terrace wall. A clump of evergreen candytuft repeats, in the front corner, the white of the dogwood in the distance.*

Ajuga, alyssum, snow-in-summer, candytuft, sweet woodruff, *Phlox canadensis* and *Aethionema* are low perennials valuable for association with the May-flowering bulbs. Among biennials (plants which flower from seed sown the previous year) are violas, pansies, forget-me-nots, English daisies, and Siberian wallflowers. Several of the most popular tulips have petal bases of contrasting color which can be pleasantly matched with the color of low perennials. Scarlet "Marshal Haig" with pale yellow *Alyssum saxatile citrinum* and cardinal red "City of Haarlem" with blue forget-me-not are examples.

Of taller-growing perennials colorful in May, bleeding heart (*Dicentra spectabilis*) is one of the best loved. Its graceful branches hang thickly with delicately formed pink flowers—a beautiful background for groups of carefully chosen tulips or Spanish bluebells. The early bearded irises come in May too—and what a wealth of colors are offered by firms which specialize in these aristocrats! The old-fashioned globeflower (*Trollius*) is not to be overlooked. Columbine and blue flax are musts for any spring border, and the earliest day-lilies can be counted on to flower before the first of June.

Tulips of Darwin, Breeder, and Cottage varieties are sometimes grouped together in catalogs, with other tulips that bloom in May listed separately because of their more distinct characters. Parrot tulips are the most fantastic of these. They have fancy petals that are slashed, fringed, crinkled, and marked

*Hyacinths are among the loveliest bulbs for spring bedding. Here they are used with daffodils to create a charming effect near an entrance.*

so that they resemble colored feathers. Their value in a mixed border is limited to providing additional interest and variety—and, as the stems of nearly all parrot varieties have a tendency to weakness, inconspicuous staking is generally necessary. The lily-flowering tulips have reflexed, pointed petals and add a note of gaiety and casualness to border plantings. Double, peony-flowered varieties are suitable for patches of color in the border foreground. Species or botanical tulips may be used advantageously at the fronts of mixed borders. Among the best for this purpose are *Tulipa Clusiana, T. Kaufmanniana, T. Greigii,* and *T. Fosteriana.*

Bulbous irises of the Spanish, Dutch, and (less frequently offered) English types are very different from ordinary garden (rhizomatous) kinds. They grow from deeply planted bulbs exactly as do tulips, and they are just as easy to care for. They do not produce great masses of foliage like the bearded, Japanese, and Siberian irises. Their stems are wiry and stand up well. Each supports a solitary, fragrant flower three to four inches in diameter. The flowers range in color from white through cream to deep yellow and from pale blue to deep purple. They bloom slightly later than the tulips and may be grouped in exactly the same fashion in the border. These irises are somewhat more tender than tulips. In the north they need a sheltered location and heavy winter protection.

Stately foxtail-lilies (*Eremurus*) come into bloom before roses herald the

*Red Emperor tulips are used here with other early-flowering varieties and masses of soft-yellow perennial* Alyssum saxatile luteum *to bring color to the garden before the border of May-flowering tulips in the rear comes into bloom.*

arrival of June. These are magnificent accent plants for planting in twos or threes at the rear of the border. Set them where they will not be disturbed. Their multiflowered spires of white-, of pink-, and of yellow-toned blooms may attain heights up to eight or nine feet. They are really conversation pieces.

The bulbs discussed in this chapter are the chief border bulbs of spring. There are a few others such as *Allium zebdanense* for the front and *Allium Rosenbachianum* for spaces toward the rear of the border. Clumps of summer

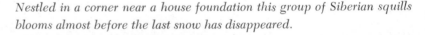

*Nestled in a corner near a house foundation this group of Siberian squills blooms almost before the last snow has disappeared.*

snowflakes as well as masses of smaller grape-hyacinths, crocuses, snowdrops, and other small bulbs may be included in the foreground.

If the area is shaded, use quantities of Spanish bluebells in blue and white. Camassias, and all the more robust bulbs recommended in Chapter 6 for the woodland garden, are other possibilities.

*An underplanting of pansies in complementary colors adds greatly to the decorative value of this bed of Darwin tulips.*

## Planting and Culture in Beds and Borders

When making mass plantings, prepare the ground thoroughly to a depth of at least a foot and preferably eighteen inches. Fork quantities of rich organic matter—compost, leafmold, humus, peatmoss, or old well-rotted manure—into the undersoil. If you use manure, make sure it is far enough below the bulbs to be out of contact with them. Enrich the upper earth by mixing with it organic matter (but not manure) as well as bone meal and a complete fertilizer.

You may plant in one of two ways. One method is to excavate the entire bed to the depth at which the bulbs are to be set, prepare the undersoil, level it, tread it moderately firmly, set the bulbs evenly and at appropriate distances apart, and cover to grade with enriched topsoil. The other method is simply to plant each bulb with a trowel in soil that has been well prepared without excavating. In either case, when planting is completed make the soil moderately firm by treading it (when it is fairly dry, not when it is wet enough to stick to your shoes) and rake the surface level. The excavation method gives assurance that the soil is prepared uniformly, that organic matter is well beneath the bulbs, and that the bulbs are at an even depth—all important factors to ensure uniform height at flowering time. The other method involves less labor and is entirely satisfactory provided particular care is taken to set all bulbs of the same kind at uniform depth. When planting bulbs in mixed borders, prepare the soil as thoroughly as for massed plantings in beds. There is no need to follow the excavation plan of planting; careful trowel work will do the trick and will give results uniform enough for borders, where slight variations in height normally add to rather than detract from the charm of the resulting picture.

In cold climates, bulbs planted in beds and borders are "put to bed" at the beginning of winter by covering them with salt hay, leaves, branches of evergreens, or some similar protection that admits air fairly freely. This protection should not be applied until the top inch or two of soil has frozen; otherwise mice may be attracted to the bulbs. Then begins the long wait for spring. The gardener relaxes in full knowledge that below ground busy roots are threading through unfrozen soil and are becoming well established to nurture future

*Lavender-pink aubretias and yellow* Alyssum saxatile *spill over the front of this wall. Behind, in small groups, is planted a diversified collection of hyacinths and early tulips.*

*Tulips in pastel pinks and creamy whites, informally grouped near broad sweeps of perennial, lavender-blue* Phlox canadensis, *create a simple satisfying picture.*

bloom. When severest winter weather has passed, the covering is gradually removed. This must be done before the new shoots become long and weak.

At the end of their flowering season, bulbs in formal beds are usually replaced with temporary plantings that provide a long season of summer bloom. Lantanas, heliotropes, fuchsias, dwarf dahlias, petunias, verbenas, and marigolds are popular for this purpose. Before these summer flowers are planted, the bulbs are ordinarily lifted and stored. That is the preferred practice. You may, however, leave the bulbs undisturbed and sow over them such shallow-rooted annuals as portulaca, sweet alyssum, and California poppies for summer display.

Spring bulbs in formal beds are usually lifted after flowering, but in mixed borders it is practicable to leave them in the ground year after year—lifting them only when they become so crowded that division is necessary or when the entire border is being remade. Some specialists recommend taking tulips up each year—even when they are part of a mixed planting—to store them until it is time for fall planting, but this is not necessary. If the bulbs are to be lifted, they may be segregated in the border by planting them in easily made baskets of half-inch wire mesh which facilitates lifting and, incidently, offers protection against rodents.

Before the bulbs are stored, they must be completely ripened. Their foliage and stems must have died naturally. If this stage has not been reached when it is time to set the summer plants, carefully dig the bulbs with a spading fork —taking care to preserve both tops and roots (leaving as much soil attached as possible)—and plant them closely together in shallow trenches with their stems and leaves above ground. Select an out-of-the-way spot in light shade for this purpose. There keep them watered and leave them until the tops are entirely brown and withered. Once ripening is complete, clean the soil, old roots, broken skin, and other debris from the bulbs and dust them with sulphur. Place them in a cool, dry, shaded place, either suspending them in well-ventilated paper bags or old nylon stockings, or spreading them in shallow layers on wire mesh. Let them remain there until fall planting time. These old bulbs, whether left in the ground or stored through the summer, will not bloom as evenly as new ones. Their flowers will vary in size and length of stem. In formal beds it is better to use new bulbs each year. Bulbs previously used may be planted with good effect in less formal areas and in the cutting garden.

# 4
# SUMMER AND FALL
# BULBS IN BEDS
# AND BORDERS

Somewhat arbitrarily we divide the bulbs used in our flower gardens into two groups—the spring-flowering and the summer- and autumn-flowering. No rigid calendar date defines the division, yet every gardener is aware of its existence. Perhaps the passing of late tulips, most surely the fading of Dutch and Spanish irises, marks the end of the season of spring bulbs.

The summer- and autumn-blooming kinds are a varied group. They include some so hardy that they flourish outdoors from year to year even in northern climates, others so susceptible to cold that they may not be set outside until well after it is safe to plant tomatoes.

Certain summer bulbs, notably cannas, begonias, caladiums, and dahlias, provide gay displays for many weeks and remain attractive until the coming of frost. Others such as alliums, gladioluses, montbretias, acidantheras, lilies, colchicums, and lycoruses bloom more briefly, the flowers of individuals lasting for a relatively short period. The flowering season of some—gladioluses and

*An evergreen hedge provides a dignified background for this narrow border of mixed tuberous begonias. The hedge provides shelter from winds which is very necessary for these bulbs.*

montbretias, for example—can be lengthened by planting bulbs every ten days or so throughout late spring and early summer. The seasons of lilies, alliums, and a few others can be extended by using several species that bloom in natural succession.

In perennial borders and mixed borders bulbs that bloom briefly can be used with delightful results. So too can kinds of longer duration, but for massing solidly in beds that are to be attractive all summer the only ones that are useful are those that give colorful displays over a long season. We shall consider these first.

## Bulbs for Summer Bedding

Easiest of summer-bedding bulbs to grow over most of North America are cannas, dahlias, and elephants-ears. Begonias and fancy-leaved caladiums are somewhat more exacting but are highly satisfactory where conditions suit them. Because cannas in brilliant yellows and fiery reds so often have been used inappropriately in public plantings—frequently arranged in concentric circles with edgings of scarlet salvia—prejudice has resulted that causes them to be regarded with disfavor by many home gardeners. As a result, they are not grown as frequently as their fine qualities deserve. Yet by using modern varieties, bold of foliage and gorgeous in bloom, beds can be created that rival in magnificence anything offered; and, with imagination and good taste, these can be used in just the proper places to produce stunning results. The modern gardener also has available cannas in more subtle colors that may be used with greater freedom. Of these the ones named for familiar operas—"La Bohème," "Mme. Butterfly," "Rigoletto," and so on—are especially pleasing.

Cannas are bold in appearance and beds of them belong most appropriately in fairly large landscapes where they may be viewed from some distance; this is particularly true of the strong-colored varieties. They are not recommended for beds six or eight feet in diameter set in front lawns that measure fifty by thirty!

Even bolder in foliage than the canna is the elephants-ear, correctly known botanically as *Colocasia antiquorum* but often cataloged as *Caladium esculentum*. This noble aroid is grown for its magnificent leaves; its flowers are of no garden significance. The leaves have blades that measure three feet or more long and two thirds as wide and are held aloft on stalks six to eight feet high. Elephants-ears, rich green and tropical looking, are especially attractive for planting by the waterside.

Dahlias suitable for bedding are mostly of the mignon and dwarf types, which grow to a height of about eighteen inches and include the well-known "Coltness" and "Unwin" hybrids. Although these dahlias have tuberous roots like the taller kinds and can be stored in the same way over the winter, they are usually discarded after flowering and new plants are raised each year from seeds sown indoors in February. There is no reason, however, why tubers of

*The Goldband Lily,* Lilium auratum, *is not always easy to grow but it is one of the choicest and most magnificent lilies for the late-summer flower border.*

*Madonna lilies planted in association with foxgloves, as they are here, or with delphiniums, are happy combinations in early summer flower borders.*

particular favorites from among a bed of seedlings should not be saved and propagated by division or by cuttings.

Seedling dahlias vary in color but because most have at least one open flower at planting time, it is easy to make selections for particular effects and to arrange them pleasingly. A mixed bed provides a wealth of variety and interest and the colors can generally be depended upon not to be discordant. Low-growing dahlias are splendid plants to fill beds from which tulips have been lifted.

Choicest of all summer-bedding bulbs are tuberous begonias but, alas, these are at their best only where nights are moderately cool—a restricting requirement throughout much of the United States and Canada. The cool, damp climate that favors many places on the Pacific Coast is superb for tuberous begonias, and flowers of magnificent size and quality are common there. Although decidedly tricky in the vicinity of New York City, there are places not far away—such as the Massachusetts Berkshires—where they can be grown luxuriantly, and places nearer where they can be grown very creditably. In the hot, dry plains and prairie states where cannas and elephants-ears thrive so well, tuberous begonias are almost impossible. Wherever they can be grown with reasonable success plant them freely, making sure that they are sheltered from whipping winds, that they have some shade during the heat of the day, and that they are kept moist.

Tuberous begonias come in many flower forms including crested, camellia-flowered, carnation-flowered, and large single-flowered varieties, all of which have blooms six inches or more in diameter. Their colors range through pinks, reds, yellows, and apricots, and there are fascinating two-toned kinds as well as some with pure white blooms. The smaller-bloomed multiflora types bear a great profusion of flowers in an equally delightful color range. All have beautiful foliage which adds great richness to their appearance.

Fancy-leaved caladiums are admirable for summer beds in sheltered locations. They revel in high temperatures and do well in full sun or in partial shade provided the air is not too dry. The bulbs may be bought in a mixture of varieties or separately according to color and name. They produce an excellent growth of magnificent heart-shaped leaves, which in different kinds exhibit a great variety of color patterns with shades of green, red, and pink as well as of white predominating; contrasting color usually follows the veins or mottles the surface. In some the leaves are sheer even to transparency. These plants have flowers—white or colored and shaped somewhat like those of a jack-in-the-pulpit—but they are usually hidden beneath the ample foliage. The flowers are fleeting but the foliage is so richly colored that the absence of floral display is of no particular importance.

Beds for summer bulbs should be spaded and enriched with compost, leaf-mold, or humus; bone meal mixed in at the rate of a quarter to half a pound to a square yard helps too. Wait until the weather is definitely warm and settled before planting. Make sure that the plants are hardened off by having been kept outdoors in their pots for about a week before the planting date, and soak them thoroughly with water a few hours before they are set out. Take

*Here, carefully staked gladioluses afford a stately display of blooms in a carefully cultivated border. Geraniums line the front of the border.*

care not to break their root balls. Plant so that the tops of the balls are covered with half an inch of soil. Pack the soil firmly around the roots and soak with a fine spray as soon as planting is completed.

Because formal beds are normally expected to be in bloom over as long a period as possible it is usual to start summer bulbs to be used in them indoors early. By this means sizeable plants in four- or five-inch pots are available at setting-out time. Cannas, elephants-ears, caladiums, and begonias *can* be grown from bulbs planted directly outdoors, but this is rarely done for bedding purposes because too long a period must then elapse before they come into bloom.

## Hardy Bulbs for Summer Borders

In perennial and mixed borders the flush of early bulbs that concludes with tulips and Dutch and Spanish irises is followed by a brief period when few bulbs flower. During this lull the parade of alliums (flowering onions) that began at tulip time continues. In early June astonishing *Allium albopilosum* opens its myriads of silvery lilac, star-shaped flowers. These are massed in

LEFT: *Tigridias or Mexican shell-flowers need a really sunny position and a light well-drained soil. They come in a great variety of flower colors.*

RIGHT: *Tritonias are among the many fine bulbous plants that flower in spring in the greenhouse that come to us from South Africa.*

*Ismenes or basket-flowers are most excellent summer bulbs. Their blooms are deliciously fragrant; they are seen to good advantage when set toward the front of the border.*

globular heads that measure eight to twelve inches across and top stalks one to two feet tall. A group of three, five, or seven spaced twelve inches apart toward the front of the border never fails to command attention and interest. At about the same time *Allium Moly* opens much smaller heads of clear buttercup-yellow flowers that show to fine advantage against its broad, bluish green foliage. Mass this onion where it gets part-day shade; in full sun its flowers are likely to bleach. *Allium Moly* starts into growth late; take care not to destroy its young shoots when digging and cultivating. The Naples onion, *A. neapolitanum*, blooms at the very beginning of June. Its pure white flowers sport rosy stamens and are in loose heads on slender foot-tall stems. This graceful Mediterranean species is hardy in New York City in sheltered locations but is not reliable under winter conditions much more severe. Like the others so far mentioned, it loses its foliage when in bloom or immediately afterward and so, like them, should be set behind plants that cover the ground when it retires from view.

There are numerous other alliums, but make selections with care because a few, such as *A. cyaneum*, are too frail for general border planting and many others although vigorous enough are in other ways unsuitable, a common fault being the undistinguished purplish flowers that characterize so many of the clan. One excellent species that flowers later than most and that retains its foliage from spring to fall is *A. tuberosum* (sometimes offered as *A. odorum*). This white-flowered kind grows thirty inches or so tall, blooms in June and July, and—believe it or not—is as fragrant as heliotrope. Enjoy its scent from a little distance; if you break or bruise it, an unmistakable alliaceous odor is released. This plant increases rapidly by offsets and from self-sown seeds. It is one of the finest border alliums.

After bleeding hearts, columbines, and bearded irises have faded, richly colored peonies, tall spires of delphiniums, day-lilies, and early phloxes make a conspicuous showing on the perennial border. At this time bulbs come again into prominence; it is in this elegant company that the first true lilies make their debut. Surely lilies are among the handsomest of all plants grown from bulbs. Species and varieties may be selected to flower one after another from June through July, August, and September. Not all are easy to grow in all localities and some test the skill of the gardener anywhere. For border planting it is wise to restrict one's choice to kinds that grow without undue difficulty, and these are likely to be found among the ones mentioned here. A special word of warning must be sounded. Do try to secure disease-free bulbs because lilies are subject to several serious bulb-borne diseases and infected stock will not only be unsatisfactory itself but will serve to infect any healthy lilies you may have in your garden.

The candlestick lily (*Lilium dauricum*) is one of the first lilies to bloom and is one of the easiest to grow. It attains a height of two feet or so and its up-turned flowers, which in its typical form are bright orange-red spotted with purplish black, make bold splashes of color in the June border. *Lilium dauricum* comes in several color variations. *Lilium hollandicum,* a name which covers a hybrid swarm rather than a natural species, is often sold as *L. umbellatum* although this name rightly belongs to a western American species. The *hollandicum* lilies range from one and a half to two feet tall, are available in many fine color varieties ranging from deep crimson to apricot and yellow, and bloom in June. At about the same time, a related hybrid lily, *Lilium maculatum* (*elegans*), opens its upright goblets for their fill of sunshine. The many varieties of this lily run through about the same color range as those of *L. hollandicum.*

Beyond all doubt the Madonna lily (*L. candidum*) is outstanding among earlier-blooming kinds. It is a magnificent addition to any border and shows to fine advantage when it is among peonies, near climbing roses, or when grouped to provide that popular combination—Madonna lilies and delphiniums. Madonna lilies may be set well back in the border. Sturdy stems lift their fragrant white horizontal trumpets to an impressive height of three or four feet. Success with this lily is dependent upon planting it shallowly and early (in late summer). Its leaves remain in evidence all winter.

Scarcely later than the Madonna is the regal lily (*L. regale*). This is one of the best loved and easiest to grow of all lilies. Its funnel-shaped, fragrant flowers, mostly white, are washed with rose-purple on their outsides and are light yellow deep in their throats. Combined with stately foxgloves or planted near deep purple buddleias or *Clematis Jackmanii,* it forms a picture not likely

*If you live where summer nights are not too dreadfully hot, plant tuberous begonias in partially shaded places beneath trees.*

Modern cannas are greatly superior to old-fashioned varieties. They may be used to bring glowing color as well as soft pastel shades to the summer flower border.

to be forgotten soon. With the cool dark hues of early monkshoods, the leopard or panther lily (*L. pardalinum*) offers sparkling contrast. As many as thirty flowers grace each stem. They have recurved petals and in the typical form are bright orange spotted with reddish brown for about half their length, but many variations occur. All are lovely. About the time that such summer shrubs as vitex and caryopteris begin to flower, *L. tigrinum*, the tiger lily, comes into bloom with red-orange flowers thickly spotted with black, its petals stiffly recurved.

In late July and in August *Lilium Henryi* also displays its pendant flowers, five to twenty on each five- to eight-foot stem. The flowers are light orange with darker spots and are distinguished by a green stripe which runs the length of each petal. In sun their color fades; it is better to plant this fine lily where it gets a little shade. Because of its unfailing dependability and prolific increase in almost any soil, it is not one to be omitted.

Even later, when September anemones are in flower, *L. formosanum* blooms, each stem carrying a few very large trumpet-shaped flowers of great beauty. It is white inside and colored with purple on the outside; the petal tips are recurved. At this time when most of the border perennials have finished blooming and early chrysanthemums and asters are beginning to show color, bold masses of the Formosan lily are especially desirable.

There are many other lilies including numerous new hybrids and selected forms of kinds listed above. The "Mid-Century" hybrids between *L. umbellatum* and *L. tigrinum* (which bloom in June and July) and the "Aurelian" hybrids of *L. Henryi* (which flower in July and August) are outstanding examples of fine new lilies. Check catalogs of bulb dealers for others and be bold in trying those that have originated from parents that are dependable in the garden.

For colder sections of the country queenly lilies and their more plebeian relatives the flowering onions afford the greatest number of different kinds of summer-flowering border bulbs that are surely hardy, but there are some others that should not be overlooked—colchicums, for example, which come into flower in late summer and fall and have huge crocus-like flowers of purest white, lavender-pink, pink, and rosy violet. They are quite naked of foliage at flowering time and indeed for many weeks before they bloom; because of this they must be set among a low, permanent front-of-the-border plant such as *Sedum album* or creeping thyme if they are in full sun, or among ajuga or sweet woodruff if they are in partial shade. In spring their broad bold leaves come up and are attractive while they are green but become rather messy looking when they are dying down in early summer. Groups of three to a dozen, depending upon the size of the border, are effective.

A choice, late-flowering bulb for the very front of the border is *Sternbergia lutea*. Although not botanically related to crocuses it looks more like one than does any other flower—like a glowing, golden yellow crocus with blooms of more substance than those that bloom in spring. This species begins to flower in mid-September and continues to be attractive for a few weeks, for its blooms withstand with impunity weather that damages the more fragile colchicums and true crocuses that also flower in autumn.

For mid-August display be sure to plant the so-called hardy amaryllis, *Lycoris squamigera,* which is often known in catalogs as *Amaryllis Hallii.* It bears a close resemblance to the true amaryllis, *A. Belladonna,* but not to the indoor hippeastrum that is commonly called amaryllis.

*Lycoris squamigera* is much hardier than *Amaryllis Belladonna,* a bulb that is really suitable for mild climates only. The lycoris produces great masses of strap-shaped, bluish green leaves in spring; these fade and disappear by mid-June and then, two months later, stout naked scapes push themselves out of the ground and attain a height of two or three feet in a matter of days. Each stem bears from its apex up to nine lily-like flowers of superb fragrance and lovely lilac-pink coloring. The display of bloom lasts for several weeks. *Lycoris squamigera* thrives in full sun or in light shade. Because it is bereft of foliage at blooming time, for good effect it must be planted with carefully selected companions that make good this deficiency. One of the most satisfactory plants to use with it is the gray-foliaged artemisia "Silver King." Other appropriate associates are the yellow bedstraw, *Galium vernum,* plantain-lilies, and ferns.

ON FACING PAGE: *Dwarf dahlias are easy to grow. They bloom profusely throughout the entire summer and early fall. This planting at the base of a bird bath illustrates how they may be used effectively.*

A little-known fall-blooming squill, *Scilla chinensis,* is a charming item for planting among a patch of creeping thyme or other lowly groundcover right at the front of the border. In late August and September it produces generous quantities of six- to nine-inch stems with starry, soft pink flowers clustered along their upper parts.

Another rather unusual item is the only hardy bulbous begonia, *Begonia Evansiana.* This native of China lives outdoors over winter in sheltered places in New York City and perhaps farther north. It is a good border plant for partly shaded locations and is easily increased by means of bulbils that form freely on its foot-tall leafy stems. It has attractive foliage and, in the typical kind, clear pink flowers; a pure-white-flowered variety of this species, named *alba,* is equally attractive.

Where climate permits the year-round cultivation of more tender bulbs the assortment of summer- and fall-bloomers that may be used as permanent features in borders is increased. Among the more useful of such additions are montbretias, alstroemerias, oxalises (notably *Oxalis Bowieana*), zephyranthes, cooperias, agapanthuses, crinums, and calla-lilies.

## Tender Bulbs for Summer Borders

Tender bulbs that in most parts of the country must be stored indoors over winter can be used to great advantage to add brightness and interest to mixed borders in summer and fall. Gladioluses planted in groups of from six to a dozen or more assure gay though comparatively short seasons of color. By choosing appropriate varieties and planting dates flowers may be had at any desired period from early July until frost. Use glads to give a lift to the border at times when there are not too many other flowers in evidence. Just when that will be depends, of course, on the particular selection of plants you grow. Just remember that glad varieties differ in the lengths of time they need from planting to bloom; the earliest varieties flower in fifty-five to sixty days, others take as long as ninety days. Dealers' catalogs indicate the approximate number of days from planting to bloom.

Glads may be had in a tremendous variety of heights, flower forms, and colors. Selections may be made to fit any color scheme. For border planting the smaller-flowered types and the softer colorings are exquisite. Because their swordlike leaves are carried nearly vertically gladioluses have little horizontal spread; they are therefore ideal for interplanting with annuals and perennials that are too closely spaced to permit of more spreading plants being set among them.

Montbretias, which is the most popular name for a group of fine South African

bulbs that the botanist now includes with *Crocosmia,* are close relatives of gladioluses and may be used similarly. Their color range is more restricted, being confined to warm tones of yellow, apricot, copper, and rich orange-red, and they are more airy and graceful. Because of this they should be planted in groups of at least twelve to twenty-five, with the bulbs set more closely than those of gladioluses. From Philadelphia south montbretias are generally winter-hardy.

Tigridias or Mexican shell flowers are at least as hardy as montbretias. If you have a really sunny border and your soil is on the sandy side, plant them in small groups right near its front and enjoy vivid accents of exotic color in high summer. How beautifully formed and charmingly marked are these shallow, broad, upturned "shells," each with three flat spreading wings. Each lasts only a day, but fortunately there is a day-to-day succession of new flowers for some time. The flower colors include soft creamy yellow, buff, orange, and red. The centers of the blooms are richly spotted with darker hues.

Summer-hyacinths or galtonias bear little resemblance to real hyacinths—at least that is true if we compare them with the popular spring-blooming kinds. Their flowers are nodding white bells arranged in handsome, loose racemes along the upper parts of three- to four-foot stalks. Planted toward the rear of the border in groups of five to nine they are of high decorative value in late July and August. Because their ample, broad, floppy leaves need a fair amount of

*For formal bedding effects the small-flowered tuberous begonias are excellent where summers are not too warm. Here an apricot-colored one is thickly massed beneath tree heliotropes.*

space, plant these in fairly open spots where they have room to grow un-
hindered and where the soil is well drained and the position sunny.

Ismenes, basket flowers— or Peruvian daffodils, to give them their up-to-date
botanical cognomen—*Hymenocallis calathina,* and its hybrids are valuable for
summer show because of their extremely handsome large blooms, pure white
or pale yellow and deliciously fragrant. They are seen to best advantage toward
the fore of the border, near masses of heliotrope or richly colored petunias perhaps.

Tuberoses, both single flowered and double flowered, can be used effectively
—but not too close to a window or sitting-out place where their heavy, pene-
trating scent may be disturbing. Plant them well back in a border that is seen
from some little distance away and where you may visit them or avoid them at
your pleasure. You will appreciate their fragrance more if it is adequately reduced by being wafted across a breadth of lawn or garden before it reaches you.
Tuberoses have white or creamy white flowers in rather stiff spikes that attain
a height of three to four feet.

Modern dahlias afford a wealth of varieties suitable for border work. Ordinarily the huge-flowered exhibition types that the connoisseur of these handsome plants so often favors are least suitable for associating with other hardy
flowers, but among less gross dahlias are many that may play not inconse-
quential parts in the summer border.

*To relieve the flatness of summer bedding
arrangements clumps of cannas may be
used effectively. Here they are planted
with geraniums and sweet alyssum.*

*Yellow-flowered* Sternbergia lutea *and lavender-pink colchicums are among the most splendid of fall-flowering bulbs. Because their colors do not go together especially well it is wiser to plant them apart than together as has been done here.*

Select varieties from among the singles, collarettes, pompoms, decoratives, and other types that will not look foreign among other plants. The taller varieties are effective when planted in threes or pairs or even singly well back in the border. Their masses of foliage give a solidity that is valued, and their blooms, perhaps viewed against a background of evergreens or shrubbery, will be appreciated and will follow each other in long succession.

Neat, inconspicuous staking is absolutely essential. Nothing detracts from a border more than lengths of broom-handle-like supports sticking out like beanpoles, painfully evident and obviously installed in optimistic anticipation of some dahlia's future. Stakes of suitable length, one and a quarter inches square, set perfectly vertically and one to a plant, are the best solution. Tie the plants so that their natural habits are preserved; avoid bunching them like sheaves of wheat.

Low dahlias including mignon or dwarf types such as the "Coltness" and the "Unwin" hybrids are invaluable for front-of-the-border display. They need no supports and even those of intermediate height get along with none more sturdy than other border plants of like stature require.

The lower dahlias may be planted in groups of half a dozen or more. Often colors will vary within a group because these types are frequently raised from seeds in the manner of annuals. The seedlings will usually have open flowers at setting-out time and so you can easily group colors according to your preferences. When it comes to named varieties the kinds of dahlias are legion, and new ones in great numbers appear each year. When making selections for border planting choose, if possible, from kinds you have seen growing. This is so much more satisfactory than depending upon catalog descriptions or selecting from blooms seen at flower shows. Catalogs and flower shows emphasize perfection of individual blooms—other factors such as habit of growth and carriage of the flowers are of importance in the border.

Cannas, like dahlias, are more neglected than they should be as possibilities for the mixed border. Planted in groups of three to five (or, in large borders more), they are spectacular sure bloomers that can be used effectively for summer and fall color. Their foliage is handsome. It's high time to put aside silly prejudice against these fine plants and to introduce modern varieties into the mixed border with confidence and good taste. It can be done.

Tuberous begonias, particularly the multiflora types which are less susceptible to sun-scorch than the larger-flowered kinds, can be used in interesting patches at the front of lightly shaded border planting; the larger-flowered types are "naturals" for shaded locations.

There are a few other possibilities among tender bulbs for the summer and fall border. Acidantheras, with fragrant, purple-blotched, gladiolus-like flowers, may be used in the same manner as gladioluses where the growing season is sufficiently long for them to bloom before frost. *Oxalis Bowieana,* with its bright pink flowers in late summer, makes a charming display planted in small patches at the very front of the border. Gloriosas are elegant twiners that have beautiful red and yellow down-turned flowers measuring fully four inches across. They are best supported by five- or six-foot-tall "teepees" of brushwood made by sticking three or four pieces in the ground in a two- or three-foot-wide circle and tying their tips together. The gloriosas attach themselves by tendrils.

# 5 NATURALIZING BULBS

⸗⸗⸗⸗⸗⸗⸗⸗⸗⸗⸗⸗⸗⸗⸗⸗⸗⸗⸗⸗⸗⸗⸗⸗⸗⸗⸗⸗⸗⸗⸗⸗⸗⸗⸗⸗⸗⸗⸗⸗⸗⸗⸗⸗⸗⸗⸗⸗⸗⸗⸗⸗⸗⸗⸗⸗⸗⸗⸗⸗

Naturalizing plants simply means establishing them in places where they do not grow natively and with such success that they will maintain themselves in competition with local vegetation. It does not refer to the *arrangement* of the plants. Thus daffodils planted in straight rows in a grassy orchard and fending for themselves are just as truly naturalized as if they were growing in a similar location in casual drifts and groups and giving the impression that they were native to the site. However, because plants that are naturalized are commonly arranged informally, the word "naturalize" has come to imply informal arrangement generally in its garden usage. Most naturalized plantings are also naturalistic plantings.

Naturalized plants require minimum care. They are not weeded in the ordinary sense of the word, although some effort may be needed to curb extremely vigorous and invasive species to prevent them from overpowering their more stay-at-home neighbors. Nor do many other garden routines such as staking and cultivating receive a great deal of attention. The philosophy behind this type of gardening is the assumption that vigorous plants, happily located, can successfully fight most of their battles, and, within limits, this is borne out in practice. The limits are established by the kinds of plants that can be so grown. These vary from location to location.

Among plants suitable for naturalizing are many bulbs, both native and foreign. Selections may be made that are suitable for planting in lawns and meadows, under shrubbery, beneath solitary trees, and in wooded areas. By their careful use, delightful garden pictures can be created, pictures that will be repeated year after year with a minimum cost for garden maintenance.

Naturalized bulbs are usually set out in a naturalistic fashion. They are disposed in the landscape to appear as if they had arisen from chance-sown seeds and from natural offsets. To heighten this effect, it is normal to select types that will not be too obviously foreign in the landscape and that are not too highly developed horticulturally. It is usual to prefer single flowers to double ones for

*Blue grape-hyacinths, naturalized in great abundance beneath these birch trees, seed themselves and increase in numbers yearly.*

naturalistic plantings, but this is not an inviolable rule. Some double-flowered narcissuses can be used with good effect, and magnificent results have been secured by naturalizing great areas with the double-flowered bloodroot. Tulips, except for a very few of the species, one of which is *Tulipa Clusiana,* are not generally suitable for naturalizing. Most do not persist long enough under American conditions, and most simply do not look right when set out naturalistically—they fail to convince one of their possibilities either as wildlings or as established immigrants. And this brings us to the only real rule apart from a consideration of the bulbs' ability to establish themselves permanently that can be applied in deciding which are suitable for planting naturalistically. The rule is: if they will look as though they belonged and will thrive with minimum attention, they are acceptable.

Now let us consider a few of the possibilities, and in doing so let us remember that it is not necessary to plant great quantities of bulbs to achieve satisfactory naturalistic effects. Thousands of narcissuses besprinkling a meadow or strewn along the margins of a lake are glorious indeed, but not less lovely are a scant two or three dozen springing up in ones and twos and in small clumps from the grassy floor beneath a white-stemmed birch. A hundred or two hundred crocuses, especially of a golden yellow kind, will bring sunshine to a slope of lawn that is close backed by shrubs or evergreens. A few tufts of snowdrops planted near a beech are charming; but their charm is not increased proportionately by increasing their numbers.

*Even in the small garden narcissuses can be naturalized effectively. Here, small irregular clumps are planted at the fringe of a woodland. They contrast sharply with the formally planted tulips in the bed in the foreground.*

*The double-flowered bloodroot is not common. Here it is naturalized in broad sweeps in a shaded location. It is most effective when in full bloom.*

When bulbs are naturalized in small quantities it is almost always wise to relate them closely to an important shrub or tree or rock evergreen. The two or three dozen narcissuses that are so delightful beneath a birch would be "lost" and ineffective in an open meadow; the one or two hundred crocuses would mean little in a lawn unless they were backed by evergreens or shrubs. It needs a beech, or other featured tree or shrub, to give reason for the few clumps of snowdrops and to direct attention to them.

Bulbs can be naturalized near the house as well as in more remote parts of the garden. It is especially desirable to use the early-flowering kinds there. Some may form part of the foundation planting; others may be established under shrubs and trees and in lawns where they will be seen from the principal windows of the house and from the path leading to its door.

Any planting near a house and particularly near a doorway should have restraint and dignity, qualities that are easily lost by the too-extravagant use of bright color. This must be considered when bulbs are selected for using with foundation shrubbery. If azaleas form a prominent part of the scheme, a companion planting of bulbs that flower at the same time as the azaleas is likely to be overpowering, even blatant; in such circumstances use only those bulbs that are well past flowering before the azaleas come into bloom and those you are sure will combine satisfactorily. For foundations favor low bulbs; long-stemmed narcissuses, summer snowflakes, and the like are ungainly in such surroundings.

There are many smaller kinds that are very lovely for the purpose. What is more pleasing to discover beneath the winter-bronzed foliage of a mahonia or a leucothoë that forms part of the foundation shrubbery than the first bright yellow winter aconites nestling in their ruffs of fresh green leaves? Or what is

*For places in light shade where the soil is fairly moist and cool snowdrops are excellent. They bloom in early spring before the last snows have melted.*

more welcome than the pendant green-tipped glistening-white flowers of the first snowdrops springing up in not too widely scattered groups in the shelter of evergreen shrubs—perhaps appearing through the last remnants of snow? Scillas or colorful crocuses may be used with good effect in patches on the sunny side of a mugho pine or a yew. Grape-hyacinths seem more choice when set close to *Pieris japonica*. Chionodoxas, the blue flowered and white flowered mixed, may carpet the ground effectively near azaleas.

In spring, more than at most seasons, there is emphasis on parts of the garden that are seen from the house windows. Attention is then directed to renewed activity outdoors. Trees and shrubs are principals in the drama of awakening nature in which they play prominent parts. The beauty and effectiveness of many can be greatly enhanced if bulbs are planted naturalistically in association with them.

The Cornelian dogwood (*Cornus mas*) is one of the first small trees to bloom. Its clusters of tiny yellow flowers are doubly beautiful when hundreds of deep yellow crocuses carpet the ground beneath it. Forsythias are suddenly covered with myriads of wide-open yellow flowers that complement the early blue of grape-hyacinth "Heavenly Blue." A slightly earlier yellow and blue combination may be had by planting *Chionodoxa Luciliae* beneath pale yellow corylopsis. Try this chionodoxa, too, below *Magnolia stellata*—one of the showiest of spring-flowering shrubs or small trees—or plant sweet-scented white narcissuses near a flowering almond or Japanese cherry. Plant second-season hyacinth bulbs of white- and pink-flowered varieties or the white-flowered *Scilla sibirica alba* to bloom with fragrant lavender-pink *Daphne Mezereum*. Under *Viburnum fragrans*, which has flowers the delicate color of trailing arbutus, establish colonies of blue *Scilla sibirica* and of its white variety *alba*.

If, across the lawn, there is a flowering dogwood, white-stemmed birch, a sturdy oak, gray-barked beech, or other featured tree of character, strew crocus bulbs generously beneath it and set them where they fall.

In modern home grounds, closely clipped lawns that surround the home often merge into grassland that is mowed only two or three times during late spring and summer. Such grassland is an ideal place in which to naturalize certain bulbs. Narcissuses top the list of spring-blooming kinds useful for this purpose. Suitable varieties are commonly sold in mixtures especially for naturalizing, but for the best results it is usually best to purchase named varieties separately and to plant them in colonies each consisting mainly of one kind—though gradually intermingling with adjacent colonies at their margins. To see thousands of narcissuses covering a slope open to the sun, carpeting the sides of a grassy glade under scattered trees, or blooming beneath flowering apples,

LEFT:   *For the rock garden wild species crocuses are preferred to the stouter garden varieties. This is a variety of the Cloth of Gold crocus,* Crocus susianus. *It is planted among a dwarf groundcover.*

RIGHT:   *Dutch crocuses are splendid spring-flowering bulbs for naturalizing in grass or beneath shrubs. This is the variety Striped Beauty.*

is an unforgettable experience. These displays should always be visible from a much-frequented vantage-point, if possible from the house windows or from a terrace adjacent to the house.

Spanish bluebells (*Scilla hispanica* or *S. campanulata*) and English bluebells (*S. nonscripta* or *S. nutans*) are superb for naturalizing in the same manner as narcissuses and thrive in shadier locations. They prosper in partial shade and will bloom even where they get no direct sun. They are not really plants for full exposure although they grow under such conditions if the soil is not too dry. Spanish bluebells and English bluebells deserve greater popularity. Plant the blue-flowered and white-flowered ones freely but give more thought to locating the pink-flowered variety: you may not like its bluish hue. Spanish bluebells are more vigorous and increase more rapidly than the English kind. These blue-bells are well adapted for naturalizing in woodlands—as are many native American bulbs, notably trilliums, bloodroots, and jack-in-the-pulpits, as well as others mentioned in the discussion of bulbs for woodland gardens in the next chapter.

Camassias particularly lend themselves to naturalizing in moist soils in par-tial shade. Summer snowflakes are excellent in grassy areas in light shade or full sun. Beneath shrubs and trees that border lawns most of the spring-bloom-ing smaller bulbs—glory-of-the-snows, crocuses, snowdrops, puschkinias, and low-growing scillas—can be used effectively as well as the fall-blooming col-chicums, the latter grateful for part-day shade. In meadows among low shrubs and at the margins of woodlands many lilies can be made at home. They will delight you in summer with their forms and fragrances. Casual plantings of *Lilium canadense, L. tigrinum, L. philadelphicum, L. umbellatum, L. pardali-num, L. chalcedonicum,* and *L. regale* can be used with fine effect in open meadows and at the edges of woodlands; but *L. Hansonii, L. Henryi, L. specio-sum,* and *L. superbum* are better suited for part-day shade at the woodland edge.

Several alliums are well worth naturalizing. Even common chives, upon which botanists have pinned the somewhat unwieldy name *Allium schoeno-prasum,* is splendid when so used, but not more so than *A. Moly, A. Rosen-bachianum,* or *A. tuberosum,* to cite but a few of the possibilities that these flowering onions offer.

Summer-hyacinths (*Galtonia*) in July send up most un-hyacinth-like flower scapes to a height of three to four feet. Each bears numerous fragrant white flowers. This plant is fine for naturalizing and is seen to excellent advantage when interplanted with yuccas.

In late summer, when it is completely naked of foliage, *Lycoris squamigera* blooms. This too is a good subject for naturalizing in an open or very lightly shaded location. Of this bulb it is necessary to remember (as it is of colchi-cums) that it produces ample foliage in spring which is apt to look messy when it is dying in early summer. Locate these kinds where you can visit them when in bloom and ignore them when leaves are yellowing.

We have not exhausted the possibilities. In some sections of the country brodiaeas, colochortuses, and erythroniums can be successfully naturalized; in others zephyranthes and cooperias, and there are many others. The criterion is: will the bulbs that it is proposed to naturalize establish themselves, flower each year, and perhaps increase with little care from the gardener?

## Planting and After Care

When bulbs are to be set out naturalistically, their placement calls for no mean skill. It is easy to get them in studied patches, groups, and rows; but it seems so difficult to plant them as nature does in an arrangement that seems effortless. Some bulbs are best naturalized in small clumps and as individuals—lilies in a meadow, for example—but even then there should be no regular pattern. In one place two or three or four may be planted closely together; elsewhere single bulbs may be scattered. The distances between individuals and between

*Here, late-flowering narcissuses bloom profusely in association with the non-bulbous Virginia bluebell,* Mertensia virginica.

*Glory-of-the-snows and daffodils naturalized near the base of a tree present a charming spring picture.*

groups is always varied so that the result is a spacing as casual as that of the stars in the sky—and in some areas in the meadow there should be no "stars" at all.

But most bulbs that are naturalized are planted more densely than this—narcissuses in grassland, crocuses in a lawn, Spanish bluebells in open woodland, grape-hyacinths beneath shrubbery, for example. In such cases distribute the bulbs unevenly by strewing them by handfuls in long sweeping motions so that they fall in elongated drifts and in greater density at one end of each drift than the other. Allow the planting to thin out here and there to areas without bulbs. See that the drifts and the bulbs are more widely spaced near the extremities of the area that is planted. This is a satisfactory method of copying nature's planting, examples of which can be seen in meadows where wildflowers grow profusely, in communities of trees in woodland—even in the way marsh grasses grow on the sand dunes along the coast.

Because naturalized bulbs remain on location for long periods without disturbance, it is essential that the soil in which they are put be suitable for their particular kind or that it be made so before planting is undertaken. The bulbs must, of course, be set at correct depth and it is simply asking for failure to make holes through three or four inches of topsoil and entomb good bulbs in an underlying stratum of cold clay or impossible subsoil. The kind of soil beneath bulbs is always more important than that above them, so before naturalizing bulbs, make sure the soil is deep, fertile, and, for most kinds, well drained. Planting may be done with spade, trowel, or a special bulb planter. It is important that the bulbs be placed at the bottom of the holes and that the soil be in firm contact with them all around when planting is completed.

At the beginning of this chapter it was emphasized that naturalized bulbs need a minimum of care. This is true. Some kinds in some situations bloom regularly for decades with no attention at all, but all benefit from an annual application in early spring of a complete fertilizer and, if planted in grassless places under trees or shrubs, from a light mulch of compost, leafmold, well-rotted sawdust, or peatmoss in fall. Bulbs that must compete with the roots of trees for food and moisture also benefit greatly if they are watered liberally during droughts that occur while they are in leaf. Never remove foliage until it has died. Naturalized bulbs that become crowded to the extent that the number of flowers they produce is lessened should be dug up, separated, sorted to size, and replanted in newly prepared ground as soon as their foliage has turned brown and before it disappears.

*Eranthis Tubergenii is one of the finest winter aconites. It may be used effectively for naturalizing. It needs a woodsy soil and light shade.*

TOP: *Colonies of snowdrops planted among grass or among low-growing rock plants are effective in the rock garden.*

BOTTOM: *The fragrant* Iris reticulata *is one of the earliest bulbs to bloom. This colony would be seen to better advantage if it were planted among a low evergreen groundcover such as creeping thyme.*

# 6

## BULBS FOR ROCK GARDENS AND WOODLAND GARDENS

Rock gardens are here to stay. They are delightful and appropriate features in many American home landscapes and afford opportunities to create charming pictorial effects as well as to grow a wide variety of plants, including many bulbs, in a comparatively small area. The latter advantage provides attractive possibilities to the gardener who is by nature a plant collector.

As understood in this chapter, a rock garden is an area with conspicuous out-croppings of rock and appropriate vegetation similar to that found on moun-tainsides and in valleys where rock masses protrude from the ground and where plants normally grow in intimate association with them. The outcrop-pings in a rock garden may be natural or ingeniously constructed of imported rock to simulate native formations.

In most cases a rock garden should be segregated from the rest of the garden by a screening of trees and shrubs unless the contour of the land makes this unnecessary; but tiny, pocket-handkerchief-size "rock gardens" consisting of a few rocks let into the soil of a bank or along a path margin can be altogether charming and afford homes for small bulbs.

Details of rock garden construction are discussed in treatises on the subject. Consult a good text before planning a rock garden of any size.

It is of major importance that rock garden plants have an adequate depth of suitable soil—and for bulbs this means at least a foot of good topsoil underlaid by a foot of porous subsoil. Natural pockets or hollows in rock formations are unfit places in which to set bulbs unless they extend downward to suitable depths or are connected with crevices so that the roots have an opportunity to stretch into good deep earth and are assured adequate drainage.

In rock gardens the kind of soil provided is commonly varied to meet the special needs of particular plants. Its character changes from place to place so that specimens growing a few feet apart may be in entirely different soils.

67

*Leucojum vernum carpathicum has snow-drop-like flowers tipped with yellow. Here, it is planted in association with up-turned glory-of-the-snows and deep blue Siberian squill.*

Most plants suitable for rock gardens are low in stature and are natural species and varieties that grow wild in some part of the world and that have not been "improved" by plant breeders. Here belong many bulbs, including *Hyacinthus azureus* (or *Muscari azureum*) and other wild hyacinths, crocus species from Mediterranean lands, "botanical" tulips (so called because they are usually known by the Latin names used by botanists rather than by common names), and tiny narcissuses exquisite in form and sometimes delightfully fragrant.

Despite this preference for natural species and varieties of plants, a few man-developed kinds are accepted for rock garden planting and are included even in the gardens of connoisseurs. The narcissus varieties "Queen of Spain" and "Raindrop" and "W. P. Milner" come to mind as examples. Provided they do not look out of place in naturalistic surroundings, few will quarrel about the admittance of such plants. Stalwart bedding hyacinths, obese garden crocuses, bedding and border tulips, and the large-flowered developments of narcissus hybridizers are generally not for the rock garden. Just which bulbs other than natural species and varieties may properly be planted is largely a matter of taste, but one thing is certain: they should be reminiscent of wild types and should not suggest their garden origins.

In the rock garden more than anywhere else, bulbs must be cleverly related to their immediate surroundings, to neighbor plants, and to rocks close by. A

*Erythroniums or Trout-lilies are among the choicest native American bulbs for planting in the woodland.*

*Trillium grandiflorum is one of the finest native trilliums. It appreciates a moderately moist, rich soil and a lightly shaded place in rock garden or woodland.*

*The native bloodroot bears handsome white flowers in early spring. The new leaves spear through the ground while the flowers are at their maximum development.*

LEFT: Tulipa tarda *is a neat low species from Turkistan. Established bulbs normally produce several flowers, yellow with the petals edged and tipped with white. This tulip is often misnamed* Tulipa dasystemon.

RIGHT: *The large, water-lily-like flowers of* Tulipa Kaufmanniana *expand in warm spring sunshine even before the winter covering of salt hay has been removed from the ground.* Tulipa Kaufmanniana *may be used effectively with other bulbs at the front of the mixed perennial border.*

rock garden should present a series of intimate pictures—a succession of plant close-ups that can be enjoyed and studied at near range. The larger, over-all picture of the garden is important, but always in the finest examples this will be found to consist of numerous lesser views worked out in fine detail. The designer of rock gardens does not use as bold a brush to paint his landscapes as does the creator of perennial borders.

Set rock garden bulbs in naturalistic, informal groups. Let the individuals within each be spaced irregularly so that they rise from the ground as casually as if they originated from chance-sown seedlings. In one spot they may be close together, in another more scattered, and occasional outlying individuals may suggest offspring that have grown from seed transported by wind or running water. The number of individuals comprising a group may vary from as few as two or three to hundreds.

Because bulbs are without foliage for part of the garden season, it is important to set them among plants that cover the ground when the bulbs are leafless. There are numerous rock garden plants that serve this purpose—creeping thymes and veronicas, *Mazus repens* and acaenas, trailing hypericums and *Lotus corniculatus,* for example. The list is long and well worth exploring for variety.

See that the groups of bulbs vary in size in different parts of the garden and, when more than one patch of the same kind is used, that these patches vary in size also. Small groups of choice bulbs such as dwarf narcissuses, rare brodiaeas, and species tulips may be used effectively near walks where their individual beauty may be enjoyed easily, while larger drifts of commoner kinds such as grape-hyacinths, scillas, snowdrops, and crocuses may be located farther back.

For sunny places, select tulip species (those that the catalogs term "botanical"): for instance, *Tulipa Clusiana,* striped red and white like peppermint candy, the waterlily tulip, *T. Kaufmanniana,* which comes in many distinct and beautiful varieties; *T. tarda,* with golden-centered pale yellow blooms, usually several from each bulb; and such magnificent species as brilliant red *T. Greigii* and *T. Eichleri.* Crocus species—including fragrant, golden-flowered *Crocus chrysanthus,* early *Crocus susianus,* and *Crocus tomasinianus,* with rosy

*Puschkinias are less well known than scillas and are of less intense coloring. They need the same care and are attractive for spring bloom in the rock garden.*

*Hyacinths are not generally considered suitable for rock garden planting but the amateur sometimes uses them to good effect. Here they are planted with grape-hyacinths and narcissuses and with violas of various kinds.*

lavender flowers—are also good for sunny locations. The last named self-sows freely and if you are careful not to weed out the grasslike seedlings, in a few years you will have a blow of hundreds where you planted perhaps a dozen. Not all crocuses bloom in spring. The flowers of *Crocus speciosus* and its many varieties expand in October and there are other fall-blooming kinds.

In sunny places, too, set gorgeous fall-blooming *Sternbergia lutea*, as well as *Hyacinthus azureus*, *Iris reticulata* and its varieties including the clear blue

*Here the white-flowered variety of the guinea-hen-flower* Fritillaria meleagris, *blooms in association with dwarf non-bulbous irises.*

*The spring star-flower* Brodiaea uniflora *is one of the few bulbs native south of the equator hardy at New York City. Here it is blooming in association with* Puschkinia *and with white-flowered grape-hyacinths.*

*Ornithogalum nutans is of refined appearance and lends itself particularly well to planting in shaded places in woodland gardens.*

"Cantab," brodiaeas, and the smaller alliums such as *senescens glaucum, pulchellum, flavum,* and the blue-flowered *Beesianum, caeruleum,* and *cyaneum.* For a particularly happy combination, plant *Allium cyaneum* close to or among dwarf *Achillea tomentosa* and in June delight in a display of blue and gold.

*Scilla chinensis* (sometimes called S. *japonica*) thrives in sun and increases from self-sown seeds. Like *Scilla autumnalis,* it flowers at a season when squills are least expected (in this case in August) and displays pink flowers clustered along six- to twelve-inch stems. There are many other squills, the majority being spring-bloomers. Most, if allowed, self-sow as freely as *Scilla chinensis.* Glory-of-the-snows are excellent under conditions that suit these scillas.

Grape-hyacinths thrive in sun and are well known. No rock garden should be without a few of the rarer ones. Be sure to include *Muscari moschatum* or one of its varieties such as *majus* or *flavum.* Although the flowers are not showy, they will enchant you with their fragrance, especially after rain. Other sun-loving bulbs for the rock garden are zephyranthes, cooperias, oxalises, and calochortuses, as well as bulbocodiums and leucocrinums.

In locations that are shaded for part of each day but are exposed to sun for at least a few hours, many bulbs recommended for sun will thrive. Here you may also plant bulbs that prefer part-day shade such as puschkinias, *Ornithogalum nutans,* snowdrops, colchicums, cyclamens, camassias, and choice narcissus species. Among the latter, *Narcissus Bulbocodium* and its varieties are "musts," for who is not charmed by the slightly upturned hoop petticoats they display in earliest spring? *Narcissus cyclamineus,* a diminutive one that lays its petals back like the ears of an angry horse, is excellent; so, too, is that three- to four-inch daffodil—the earliest of all to flower—*Narcissus minimus.* Other good narcissus species for the rock garden are *N. juncifolius, N. triandrus* and its varieties, and *N. calcicola,* the last named known to be native in only one locality in Portugal but easily raised from seeds and very adaptable in American gardens. These bulbs for part-day shade prosper also where a not too heavy canopy of trees creates a dappled shade throughout the entire day.

Bulbs for shaded spots in the rock garden should be chosen from among low-growing kinds that like woodland conditions. This brings us to a consideration of woodland gardens and of bulbs suitable for planting in them.

The woodland garden may be large or small, flat or hilly, heavily or lightly shaded. Its soil type and the kinds of trees that dominate it will affect its char-

*The winter aconite,* Eranthis hyemalis, *is a choice plant for early spring bloom in the rock garden.*

*Bulbous oxalises are excellent for summer bloom in the sunny rock garden in milder parts of the country.*

Cyclamen neapolitanum *is one of several hardy kinds that are choice as rock garden plants.*

acter and its possibilities. For the best results the woodland itself must be controlled. Unwanted trees and underbrush must be cleared, low-hanging limbs that serve no useful purpose removed (for dappled shade or good side light is much preferable to dense shade), the soil prepared by forking it deeply and by incorporating into it generous amounts of organic matter, compost, leafmold, or peatmoss. Each fall a mulch of leaves or compost should be spread to protect and nourish plants in woodlands.

In a patch of tended woodland many bulbs will thrive—fewer if the shade is dense than if a little sunshine filters in from top or sides, but a surprising number in any case. Many of the best are native Americans such as trilliums, bloodroots, jack-in-the-pulpits, Dutchman's-breeches, squirrel corn, spring beauties, wood anemones, and dainty rue-anemones. Here belong, in dampish soil, camassias and deadly zygadenuses. Among Americans, also, are certain erythroniums, fritillarias, and dainty hepaticas that welcome shade and woodsy earth.

Important as native bulbs are, they are not the only ones for woodland landscapes and shaded rock gardens. Spanish and English bluebells revel in such an environment and multiply from year to year if given congenial conditions.

LEFT:  Allium Moly *is one of the few flowering onions that thrives best in partial shade. After it has finished blooming its tops and foliage die away and are not seen again until the following spring.*

RIGHT:  *For the shaded border where the soil is not too dry colchicums (autumn crocuses) are splendid. They make a brave display of bloom in early fall.*

Their blue- and white-flowered forms are lovely. Plant them generously wherever you have space. The pink-flowered forms are often disappointing because the pink is too bluish to suit most people's taste. Some of the European anemones are delightful and are suitable for shaded areas: *Anemone blanda, A. nemorosa,* and easy-to-grow and entirely charming *A. ranunculoides* belong here. Give them choice positions where they do not have to meet strong competition from the roots of vigorous neighbors. Winter aconites and snowdrops go well together in well-thinned woodland where shade is not dense. Also under such conditions you may successfully grow summer snowflakes and hosts of narcissuses, and in a moistish spot the lesser celandine (*Ranunculus Ficaria*) and its copper-colored and double-flowered varieties.

Colchicums appreciate the very lightest shade and rich porous earth. The large white, lavender-pink, pink, and rosy violet flowers of kinds usually grown make brave displays in August and September. The flowers come up in groups, many from each old bulb, and quite naked of foliage. In spring large coarse leaves appear and are attractive until June, when they die down and for a period assume sear-brown hues that seem out of place in midsummer, but less out of place at the fringe of a woodland or in other "wild" landscapes than they would be in the tidier environment of more formal flower borders.

There are true lilies that either need or tolerate some shade, but none are plants of deep woodland and all need good light although not necessarily much

LEFT AND TOP OF FACING PAGE: *Spanish bluebells are easy-to-grow bulbs that thrive without difficulty in shade. They may be had in lilac blue, white, and pink. The first two are usually preferred.*

direct sunshine. *Lilium Hansonii, L. testaceum, L. elegans, L. superbum, L. canadense, L. philadelphicum,* and the somewhat difficult *L. Grayi* are all worth considering.

The placement of bulbs in a woodland garden calls for much the same skill as planting a natural rock garden. It is based on an appreciation of nature's patterns, yet not a slavish imitation of them. In any patch of planted woodland there are likely to be many more different kinds of plants than there would be in a similar natural area, yet the effect should appear natural and convincing.

Avoid overplanting. Remember that under woodland conditions individual

*The double-flowered Bloodroot is an exquisite plant for a choice spot in the shaded rock garden. Here it grows in association with a trout-lily and a pink-flowered primrose.*

plants and groups of plants need more space between them than do those that grow in the open. The forest floor in temperate regions is rarely as crowded with vegetation as the meadows and open fields; a feeling of restraint characterizes woodlands. To achieve conviction, try to locate each kind of plant where it is likely to prosper. Thrifty plants that increase moderately and bloom freely are the best advertisement of a gardener's skill in planting. If most of the bulbs in your woodland garden are really doing well, it is more than likely that their arrangement will be pleasing.

*For moist soil and partial shade try camassias. These native bulbs grow without difficulty and bear elegant spikes of blue or white flowers.*

# 7 BULBS
# FOR CUT FLOWERS

There should be flowers in every home, and a special cutting garden is the answer to a constant supply without sacrifice of border display. Even a small, not too conspicuous spot will yield quantities of cut flowers, and utilizing an end of the family vegetable patch, a sunny space behind the garage, or some odd-shaped corner to grow flowers for the house is frequently practical. Perennials and biennials chosen for easy culture and adaptability pay off handsomely, supplying flowers from frost to frost. Not the least attraction of a cutting garden, where labor is limited, is the fact that two or three times as many flowers planted in rows can be grown with the same expenditures of effort as when they are cared for in informal groups in borders.

Bulbs offer wonderful possibilities for cutting and their flowers follow one after another from late winter until well into fall. The small, early kinds, such as snowdrops, grape-hyacinths, glory-of-the-snows, and squills, so choice for intimate arrangements by a much-used easy-chair or the bedside table of a special guest, can be gathered from bulbs planted under shrubs or in a grassy area. A good handful will never be missed where they come up in hundreds. Try lifting a clump of crocuses or snowdrops with a bit of surrounding turf and fitting it into a plain flattish container. It has just the air of informality for a late-winter breakfast table.

Daffodils and other narcissuses can often be picked from naturalized plantings without noticeable loss of floral effect, but if they are not naturalized lavishly in your garden by all means include some in your cutting compound. From tulip time on, the cutting garden should be the main source of cut flowers —and it is a real luxury to cut just the right flower stalks without concern for detracting from any decorative outdoor display. The quantity of each variety grown should be adequate for any possible indoor need.

The arrangement of the cutting garden should provide for a section devoted to perennials and a section to such short-term crops as annuals and biennials. In the first part plant lilies, tulips, eremuruses, and other bulbs that remain in the ground from year to year; in the second, those such as gladioluses and dahlias that are dug at the end of each growing season and are planted anew each spring. Just which kinds are treated as hardy perennials will depend to some extent upon where you live. From Philadelphia south montbretias may safely be left in the ground all winter; in colder climates they should be lifted and stored. In California tender agapanthuses and calla-lilies are hardy outdoors but not, of course, in Michigan and like areas.

Where space permits, plant in rows with sufficient space between to allow for stirring the surface soil with a cultivator during the growing season. If space is very limited, more flowers can be obtained from a given area by planting the bulbs comparatively thickly in beds five or six feet wide with paths two feet wide between. This necessitates hand weeding, but need for this can be reduced by mulching the ground with peatmoss, buckwheat hulls, old sawdust, or other suitable organic material that discourages weeds.

Nor need all bulbs occupy exclusively the area in which they are planted. Lilies benefit from having their roots and the lower parts of their stems shaded; they may with advantage be planted midway between rows of lower-growing perennials, such as peonies, that retain their foliage throughout the summer but do not spread rapidly. Daffodils, narcissuses, and other early-bloomers that lose their foliage by early summer may be lined out similarly between rows of perennials that do not make much foliage until spring is well advanced. Perennial babys-breath and monkshoods belong here.

*Foxtail-lilies are excellent cut flowers where stately subjects are needed. This is* Eremurus himalaicus.

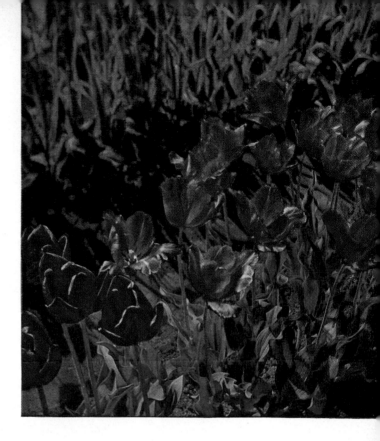

*A few rows of tulips in the vegetable garden provide a great many cut flowers. The flowers should be cut before they open as far as these.*

In the annual section of the cutting garden intercropping can also be practiced with advantage if space is short. Later-planted gladioluses set between rows of early annuals before the annual flowers are cut will follow along and provide welcome second bloom from the same piece of ground. In rows midway between, where lines of dahlias are to be planted later, hardy annuals may be sown in early spring to provide a crop of bloom before the dahlias occupy all the space allotted to them.

### Kinds to Grow for Cutting

In selecting bulbs for the cut-flower garden two things must be borne in mind: first, the kinds and colors you can use to advantage; second, the quantities you need. In the latter matter be generous, particularly with bulbs that have foliage on their stems that is cut with the flowers, as is the case with lilies. The removal of leaves weakens bulbs; if you plant plenty it will not be necessary to cut flowers from all every year and the individuals from which you do not cut will have an opportunity to build up strength.

When it comes to choosing kinds and colors much depends, of course, upon individual taste and preference. The style and decoration of your home should be the guiding factor. Many contemporary interiors dictate the use of stylized arrangements of flowers and foliage which lack frilliness and intricate detail. Crisp, formal arrangements of gladioluses with their sharp bladelike foliage and massive cannas or cool calla-lilies combined with caladium leaves are examples. Traditional rooms are more often an ideal setting for more intricate arrangements which may have greater variety of form and color. Combinations of gladioluses, celosias, and zinnias; narcissuses with grape-hyacinths and just the right twigs from a flowering cherry; Dutch irises, day-lilies, and clematises; dahlias, tritomas, and autumn foliage lend themselves to harmonious relationships. If specific colors for individual rooms can be selected, so much the better. It is an interesting undertaking to plan a continuity of flowers to complement color schemes throughout the house. Selections may even be made for favored containers which have added beauty with just the right flowers.

Many consider those narcissuses with short cups most useful for cutting but all varieties can be used effectively and it is important to grow a diversity of types to ensure a long season of bloom and a variety of form. Consider therefore the bunch-flowered kinds as well as those that bear but one flower on a stem. Plant the large trumpet daffodils as well as the poet's narcissus. . . . Include triandrus hybrids and even some of the double-flowered varieties.

Tulips with sturdy stems are best for cutting; those that have "weak necks," as have most parrot varieties, are less usable. Long-stemmed varieties are generally preferred to those of shorter growth although the early singles and early doubles, which are naturally low, are appreciated because of the promise they bring of a more lavish tulip season to follow. Most May-flowering tulips are excellent cut flowers. The interesting lily-flowered and peony-flowered varieties are well worth planting. For earlier color some of the taller species including *Tulipa Greigii, T. Marjolettii,* and *T. Clusiana* may be used in addition to the early garden varieties. Plant tulip bulbs eight or ten inches deep in the cutting garden to reduce the tendency bulbs have when planted shallowly of splitting up into smaller bulbs that fail to bloom at all or bear only small flowers.

The first spring after their purchase good quality, large-size hyacinths produce flower spikes too massive to be of much use in flower arrangements. In succeeding years their stalks of bloom are lighter, looser, and more graceful. It is good practice to use first-year hyacinths for formal effects in display beds and to transfer them to the cutting garden afterward or to purchase smaller-size bulbs to provide cut flowers. In the southern states Roman hyacinths, which have sparser-flowered spikes than the Dutch types, are hardy and are ideal for cutting.

To follow tulips closely plant Spanish and Dutch irises. Their bulbs are smaller than those of tulips and are much less expensive. Each produces on a tall wiry stem a solitary, lovely bloom and they are ideal for cutting. Colors include white, cream, yellow, bronze, lavender, blue, and purple. You must not confuse these irises with more common types that do not grow from bulbs. They are very different, less leafy and, as cut flowers, longer lasting. Although not as hardy as tulips they survive outdoors in sheltered locations in the vicinity of New York City if well protected over winter.

Most important of the winter-hardy bulbs that bloom in summer are the true lilies. Such variety exists that one hesitates to make specific recommendations, but a selection is surely a must for every cut-flower garden. The easiest to grow

—and ease of culture is most important in a cutting garden—include the regal lily with white trumpet flowers flushed wine on their outsides and yellow in their throats, the tiger lily with recurved petals of orange-red that are spotted black, and Henry's lily with flowers that have orange-yellow, turned-back petals. The botanical names of these are respectively *Lilium regale, L. tigrinum,* and *L. Henryi.* A beautiful softer-colored hybrid of *L. Henryi* called "T. A. Havemeyer" is as easy to grow as its parent. Its flowers are buff-yellow.

The pure white Madonna lily that blooms in early summer cannot be omitted, and *L. speciosum* and its deep-pink- and white-flowered varieties which supply such grand cutting in August should find a place in every cutting garden. There are many, many more that call for consideration, most notably some of the splendid hybrid types that have been raised by American breeders in recent years. Only a comparatively few years ago scarcely any hybrid lilies were known; today there are hundreds and the end is by no means yet in sight. Each year new and finer varieties are introduced. It is worth-while watching bulb catalogs of reliable dealers for these.

The stately spires of foxtail-lilies are lovely indeed for cutting. Those of stout-growing *Eremurus robustus* and *E. himalaicus* may be too massive for small homes but *E. Bungei* and its varieties and hybrids are elegant indeed and something a little different. Each three- or four-foot stalk terminates in a long tapering cone of hundreds of starry yellow or orange-yellow flowers. They need rather special planting conditions and protection against late frosts.

There are several other hardy bulbs well worth growing for cutting—a few of the flowering onions, for example (especially *Allium albopilosum* and *A. tuberosum*) and alstroemerias if they will winter outdoors with you (they scarcely will in New York City even in sheltered places). *Lycoris squamigera,* which is often cataloged as *Amaryllis Hallii,* is one bulb you will not harm by cutting too much foliage along with its flowers—for it has no leaves at blooming time: its flower scapes rise naked from the ground. Grow for arranging with it perennial artemisia "Silver King"—the lavender-pink lilies of the lycoris and the silver-white foliage of the artemisia are marvelous when combined. *Ornithogalum nutans* is a charming gray-green flower that you may wish to grow in modest numbers to cut for unusual arrangements, and perhaps you would like a few plants of the pineapple flower (*Eucomis*) to furnish the unexpected when midsummer has passed. Camassias are other hardy bulbs that might fill a very modest amount of space in your cutting garden. There will be others, of course, in regions of mild winters, including such very well-worthwhile items as "St. Brigid" anemones and tuberous ranunculuses.

Of bulbs to plant in spring to give summer cut flowers gladioluses and dahlias are undoubtedly most important, with montbretias (where it is too cold for them to remain out over winter), tuberoses, and cannas playing lesser roles. Where frosts are delayed until late fall, acidantheras are welcome additions and you may find it helpful to have Peruvian daffodils, summer-hyacinths, gloriosas, and tigridias in modest quantities.

Gladioluses almost span the spectrum in their color range and, including the smaller-flowered varieties, offer considerable diversity of form. Very often those varieties which have flowers not too large and not too closely set on the spikes have greater artistic merit in arrangements than the more spectacular ones. Order gladioluses in named varieties in colors and types that please you. Plant them in double or triple rows spaced two to three feet apart with the two or three lines of bulbs that form each row six inches apart and with about four inches allowed between the bulbs in each line.

Sturdy stakes pushed in every few feet along either side of each row and connected by one or two strings drawn taut are the only support that is likely to be needed and even this may not be necessary if the bulbs are planted fairly deeply (about 6 inches). Plant gladioluses at about two-week intervals beginning when the trees first start to leaf in spring and continuing until the latest date that will leave the needed number of growing days (which varies for different varieties and is usually given in catalogs) before fall frost is expected.

Dahlias come in a great variety of forms and colors and new ones are offered annually. For cutting purposes long, strong stems are important. Consider this when selecting kinds to grow. Giant flowers are of little value for cutting: they wilt too soon. Much more practical are medium-sized blooms of decorative and cactus dahlias as well as those of the pompoms, singles, colarette and other smaller-flowered types. Individual staking of all but the dwarf dahlia plants is essential.

*Tulip Princess Elizabeth is a favorite cut-flower variety.*

*This collection of narcissuses indicates some of the variety which is to be found in this group of bulbs, so grand for providing cut flowers.*

Montbretias are treated exactly like gladioluses except that the bulbs are set more closely together. The rows may be eighteen inches to two feet apart, and the bulbs in them are two or three inches apart spaced over the flat bottom of a four-inch-wide drill. Under cutting garden procedure other summer bulbs are set out in rows at distances suggested in the cultural notes given under their alphabetical listing at the end of this book.

## The Soil

The soil in a cutting garden should be prepared and maintained as for a good vegetable patch. It should have sharp underdrainage and be reasonably deep. Free it of perennial weeds and bring it into a mellow, fertile condition before planting. Nearly all bulbs resent fresh, rank manure but none object to the presence of some which is old and well decayed. Use manure that has rotted to a black, nourishing amorphous mold, or rich compost that has decayed to the same degree, in generous quantities to build up the organic content of the soil. If these materials are not available substitute commercial humus or peatmoss. Bone meal is an excellent fertilizer to incorporate with the soil before planting and it is safe and desirable to give an annual dressing of a regular vegetable garden fertilizer to those bulbs grown in the cutting garden. Be careful when using fertilizers containing quickly available nitrogen. These *can* be used effectively but the amount that bulbs can be given at one time without harm is less than for many other garden plants.

Above all remember that bulbs root downward from the level at which they are planted (stem-rooting lilies root from *above* the bulb also) and therefore it is of the utmost importance to have a good depth of kindly, fertile soil underneath them. The undersoil is of even more importance than the covering layer.

## Care and Cutting

The routine care of bulbs in a cut-flower garden is not markedly different from that which they need when grown elsewhere. The provision of ample supplies of water during dry periods that occur while they are in leaf (both before and after flowering) is extremely important. The application of dilute liquid manure water or liquid fertilizer at weekly intervals beginning with the appearance of the flower spikes and continuing until the first buds begin to open makes for larger stems and finer blooms. Timely attention in the matter of staking prevents crooked flower stalks; take care to keep stakes sufficiently far away from the stems that they are not thrust through the bulbs. Shading the blooms of tulips and gladioluses with heavy cheesecloth (or with the special cloth that cut-flower growers use for cloth houses) helps them retain their colors better and prevents them from passing by so quickly.

The removal of foliage while it is yet green interferes, in direct proportion to the amount removed, with the ability of the bulb to manufacture the food it needs to store for the following year's effort. Never lift bulbs or clear away their leaves unless they have ripened and died naturally or have been killed by frost.

When cutting bulb flowers you must make a choice. If you take leafy stems as long as possible, cutting them almost at ground level, then the bulbs almost surely will not bloom the following year and they may be killed. On occasion, if the longest possible stems are important to have, you may be perfectly willing to face this loss—with gladioluses, Spanish irises, tulips, and other kinds that can be inexpensively replaced, for instance—but it is less likely that you will be willing to seriously harm or lose more expensive or rarer bulbs such as those of lilies. In all cases it is practicable to take a little foliage when cutting without serious damage, but this should be kept at a minimum and should not exceed a sixth or eighth perhaps of the total leaf area. Stems that are without leaves as, for instance, daffodils, should be cut as low as possible.

Cut nearly all bulbs when their buds first open . . . in the case of those (such as gladioluses and lilies) that have several flowers on a stem, when the first two or three buds open; the others will expand in water. Exceptions to this rule are May-flowering tulips. These should not be cut until the flowers attain almost full size; if taken too early the blooms remain comparatively small. Very early morning is the best time for cutting, the next best time being evening. Handle each flower carefully for crushed or bruised petals cannot be repaired. Slice firm stems such as those of gladioluses slantwise. Unless they are needed at once, stand the freshly cut blooms in deep containers of water in a cool dark cellar out of all drafts for ten or twelve hours before arranging them in the house or using them in other ways. If you wish to keep flowers that are opening in the garden, they will last longer cut and in water in a dark cool place than in warm sunny weather outdoors.

## In Cold Frames and Greenhouses

A cold frame is a great asset in a cutting garden. In it can be grown bulbs that are not quite hardy enough to winter outdoors; from it can be had flowers both earlier and later in season than outdoor beds will supply. It can be a simple affair—a rectangular box of stout planks covered with removable cold-frame sash of standard six-by-three size. The back of the frame should be nine inches or a foot higher than the front so that the glazed sash will shed water. A suitable height for the front is twelve inches. Provision should be made to increase the height of the entire frame by a foot or more on occasion so that flowers that have attained considerable height can be accommodated. This is easily done by setting a removable extension frame on top of the first, securing it, and placing the glass sash on top of this.

Locate the frame to face south in a sheltered, sunny position where good drainage is assured; avoid low spots where water may collect. Extra coziness can be assured in winter by banking soil or cinders against its outer walls. In very cold weather the sash may be covered with heavy mats, blankets, or with a layer of salt hay or straw. The soil inside the frame should be light and fertile, and the bulbs planted as closely as possible, according to kind, so that maximum flower production from a limited area is assured. This means planting considerably closer than is usual outdoors.

In cold parts of the country such beautiful spring- and early-summer-flowering bulbs as ranunculuses, anemones, Dutch and Spanish irises, alstroemerias, and even ixias, sparaxises, and watsonias may be successfully grown in cold frames even though they are unreliable or impossible in the open garden. They supply grand cutting.

Perfectly hardy bulbs such as tulips and narcissuses may be had in bloom two to four weeks earlier from a frame than from the open ground. The same is true of summer-flowering gladioluses and montbretias; plant the last named in a frame three or four weeks before it is safe to plant them outdoors and you will cut your first blooms considerably earlier. The frame may be used in fall to protect from early frosts the flowers of late-flowering gladioluses and montbretias.

The management of a cold frame calls for an understanding that its purpose is to protect bulbs that are *nearly hardy* from severe weather; it is not to provide them with unusually "soft" conditions. On all days when the temperature is above freezing ventilate it thoroughly. On mild days in spring and fall remove the sash entirely, replacing it at night if freezing temperatures may occur.

It is beyond the scope of this book to enter deeply into greenhouse culture, yet it would be remiss to pass without mention the possibilities that even a small greenhouse afford for producing cut flowers from bulbs. The two great groups that attract attention are: first, the "forcing" bulbs which are handled as advised for their pot culture in Chapter 10, except that instead of being

LEFT:  *Scarlet Leader* (*Division II, Large Cupped*)

RIGHT:  *Actea* (*Division IX,* Poeticus)

*These pictures illustrate narcissuses that may be grown with advantage as cut flowers. They require little care and bloom repeatedly year after year, the bulbs increasing in number each year.*

RIGHT:  *Damson* (*Division II, Large Cupped*)

LEFT:  *Geranium* (*Division VIII,* Tazetta)

planted in pots and pans the bulbs are set closely together in four-inch-deep flats (wooden boxes); and, second, the cool-temperature freesias, watsonias, "baby" gladioluses, and others that need similar growing conditions, that are often planted directly in beds of soil in greenhouse benches but otherwise are grown in the same way as when they are cultivated in pots. Calla-lilies, Easter lilies, gloriosas, and some other kinds are a few of the possibilities that the greenhouse affords. In the small greenhouse these will usually be grown in pots.

# 8 FLOWER ARRANGEMENT
## *by* ANN HAGAN

There is a popular misunderstanding that arranging flowers is a difficult and complex art to be explored and understood only by the middle-aged endowed with leisure and mild eccentricities. The fallacy of this myth is apparent, but enough of a mist lingers about it to intimidate busy young people into believing that they lack the time or the touch to arrange their own flowers. Arranging flowers can be a nervous domestic responsibility, a private pleasure, or a creative expression, all depending on one's point of view.

Forget about rules, begin arranging flowers with a viewpoint. You are not competing in a flower show or interested at the moment in becoming a virtuoso. You like flowers growing in the garden, you want them about your house for the personal pleasure they give you and your family; they bring a room alive, change its flavor with the seasons, add gaiety and variety to the luncheon and dinner table. Flowers in your house should be personal—your house and your flowers are subject to endless variations and exceptions, and for that very reason it is difficult to give beginners a neat handbook on just how to arrange their flowers. Boil an egg for ten minutes and at the end of that time you have a hard-boiled egg, despite the intensity of the heat or the size of the egg or the pan. But place six Darwin tulips in a glass vase and you may or may not make an arrangement.

But then, how does one begin composing arrangements rather than putting flowers in water? Where does one start? Start with the flower.

In a broad general way a flower arrangement might be divided into five parts: the *flowers;* the *container;* the *location,* where the arrangement is to be placed; the *mechanics,* how the flowers are kept in place and alive; and last the *arranging,* or putting together of the flowers and container. Let's take each division and look at it separately.

92

## The Flowers

One may see a flower for years without ever looking at it. This may seem very elementary, but the first process in arranging flowers is to *look* at the flower. Study the flower as if you had never seen it before. Look at a tulip growing in the garden, examine it with the care of a scientist and the eye of an artist. What shape is the blossom? Bell, ball, or circle? What texture have the petals? Are they one or three colors? How thick or thin is the stem? Does it support the flower with ease or as a burden? How are the leaves arranged? Do they grow out of the stem or seemingly from the ground? How is this flower placed or related to the other flowers and plants around? This is an exercise to apply to any flower you are working with. Make little back-of-the-head notes on the way nature arranges flowers . . . a gray mullen hugging a gray stone wall, wonderful combination of color and texture . . . yellow dandelions shouting on a green lawn. Look at nature closely not so much to imitate as to learn about combinations of color, form, and texture.

## Containers

Train yourself to be open-minded about what constitutes a container, yet critical enough to avoid what is forced or obviously contrived. A silver water pitcher, a wicker bread basket, a pony brandy glass, an earthenware crock are as acceptable containers for flowers as the classic urn and vase. Reserve frying pans and teapots for their original functions.

The relationship between flowers and containers is fundamental, for the container is half of the arrangement even if hardly any of it is seen in the finished composition. A delicate flower does not automatically have to be arranged in a fragile container. Its very delicacy can be emphasized by the contrast of a coarse, rough-textured container. Testing and experimenting will establish this perception of where a contrast is more exciting than a similarity. However, heavy long-stemmed flowers and branches need sturdy containers to keep their practical balance. An arrangement that is top-heavy and looks ready for collapse at a slight nudge is disturbing.

Build your collection of containers gradually. Let it grow along with your knowledge, otherwise it will be cluttered with too many passing fancies. Keep all your containers in one place so that, when you are in a hurry, you can sweep your eye across the shelf or cupboard and select the right container for the flowers in hand.

GLASS:  Look for goblets, small, medium, and large, clear glass and colored—Mexican aqua, sea-green, pink, mauve, ruby, Bristol blue, milk-white. Chemical beakers are magic for simple arrangements—flasks, retorts, and cylinders in all sizes. Highly decorated glass or pottery can be too busy and distracting; use them with caution.

POTTERY, CHINA, EARTHENWARE:   Look for pitchers, all sizes and shapes and textures, casseroles, bean pots, jelly molds, soup tureens, and bowls—there's an endless variety to explore.

METAL:   Silver, tin, lead, copper, brass, even iron . . . the kitchen shelves and a second-hand shop may provide you with real treasures. Remember the price of a container has nothing to do with its value for flower arranging.

WICKER, WOOD, LEATHER:   Investigate berry and fruit baskets; French and Italian bread baskets, round, oval, or long as French bread; market baskets of split hickory, willow, rattan, and rush. There's a basket to match every kind of flower and period of decoration. Collect wooden mortars, large and small, grain measures, leather boxes, baskets, and buckets. Baskets, wood and leather, and plaster containers require metal liners for water. A tinsmith will make them on order. Often a hardware store will have pails, pans, or buckets that can be adapted. Line an open lacy wicker basket with sheetmoss before putting in the water tin. It adds a pleasant garden quality as well as concealing the liner.

## Location

Where the flowers are to be placed has an important influence on the size and shape of an arrangement. There are times when you'll work in reverse, make an arrangement and then look for the place. It's less logical, but if it's more

*Public rooms need mass bold arrangements. Don't overlook the dramatic strength of the gladiolus.*

LEFT:  *A few flowers, such as these six tulips and four poeticus narcissuses, can generate a cordial welcome on a hall table.*

RIGHT:  *Homey, at-ease arrangement of massed lilac, assorted tulips, and English bluebells.*

spontaneous for you to work that way don't discourage yourself by trying to be logical.

Remember, placed in front of a mirror the back side will be part of the arrangement. On a mantel the arrangement is usually above eye level and is seen from the front and both sides. On a coffee or dining table it will be below eye level and seen all around. Whether it is placed against a figured wallpaper or a white painted wall or pine paneling are outside conditions which influence the quality of the arrangement when it is placed. Make a note of all the places in the house where flowers might be used: the front hall, mantels, buffet, dining table, end and coffee table, desk, chest, lowboy, window seat, stair landing, floor, bedroom, kitchen.

Watch that your arrangements don't become obstacles for the young and old and for family pets. If your two-year-old is determined to demolish all coffee-table arrangement, keep the table free until he is older. Test one arrangement in three or four places. If it seems crowded, you know it is too large for the space; if it seems lost and insignificant, it is too small. Right then take time and make an arrangement scaled to fill a particular space. A small coffee table overwhelmed with a large bouquet loses its purpose; the flowers confuse instead of decorate.

Arrangements for the dining table are a separate study. Think of table flowers as a decoration rather than a centerpiece, for the arrangement may not be one piece and may not even be placed in the center. Experiment with arrangements at the side or end, especially if you have a large table for only two or three people. Play with fruits, flowers, and ornaments. Vary the table decoration with your mood, the seasons, and your company.

## Mechanics

Holding an arrangement in place is particularly important to the novice. With experience one learns to establish a natural balance between flower and container, to select a container that will not require a holder, but for a beginner it is very reassuring to have the support of a holder and to know that a flower is firmly anchored where it is placed.

Learn to work with chicken wire. It is invaluable because it is pliable and adjustable to large, small, and medium containers. It is available by the yard at hardware stores. Use a lightweight gauge that is flexible and of a coarse one- or two-inch mesh. For the average container allow the piece of wire to be twice the size of the opening. Cut it with wire shears or pliers. Don't be afraid to push it around and make it work. In a shallow container the wire will slip unless it is fastened. Tie it to the container with a wire or light cord, across the sides and ends as you would tie a package; then cover the mechanics with your arrangement. Avoid using chicken wire in glass where it shows and is distracting to the finished arrangement.

Pinpoint holders are excellent for shallow bowls. You can buy them in all sizes and weights. Remember a small holder will not balance a large bouquet. An interesting piece of fruitwood or driftwood makes a natural holder; combine it with spring branches and flowers as part of the completed picture. Use a solid rugged container, submerge and wedge one end of the wood in the container, let the other end become part of the arrangement, and build around it with your dogwood and tulips.

Discover "Snowpac" at your florist. It is a spongy, moisture-retaining white plastic material in brick form, which can be cut into squares, pyramids and balls. Cut with a paring knife the form you wish to work with, soak it in water until saturated, cover it with waxed paper, and decorate it with short flower heads, ferns, and ribbon. Be as fancy-free in trimming it as when decorating an Easter egg.

Sheetmoss is almost as useful to the flower arranger as aluminum foil is to the cook. Cover a coffee tin with it and you have an enchanting container for short bunches of spring flowers. Tie it cornucopia-fashion around little bunches of snowdrops and scillas and arrange the bunches in a brown mug or weathered basket. Use it as a decorative lining in open-weave wicker baskets or as a garden carpet to trim and finish basket arrangements of hyacinths and cottage

tulips. Readily obtained at nurseries and florists, it is a material that flower ar-
rangers will cherish.

## Simple Arrangements

Think of arranging flowers at first as quietly and as simply as possible. Think of
it as if you were playing the scale of C with one hand only. Don't worry about
your inability to reproduce a Flemish masterpiece immediately. Who ever
played a Beethoven concerto the first month they studied the piano? Work first
with one kind of flower. Take six tulips, all cut the same length, all the same
color, and try them in six completely different containers. Try them with a
holder and without. Decide for yourself which container is best for the flowers.
Do you really need a holder to keep them in place?

Next, shorten to assorted lengths three or four of the stems, mix the colors to
half pink and half red, and arrange these in the same containers. What difference do the shortened stems and color change make? Do you still find the
same container as pleasing?

Next, experiment in placing the arrangement. Set it on a coffee table, desk,
buffet, window ledge, or dining table. Ask yourself why it looks more attractive
in one place rather than another. Does it seem too high on the dining table? too
crowded on the desk? too small in the hall? faded in the window? This kind of
exercise or experiment takes both time and patience, and yet it is the most direct way to learn how to arrange flowers for your house.

Once you have developed ease in working with one variety, a sense of balance and proportion between flowers and container, a freedom to cut the stems
short or long and match them either way with a suitable container, take another step. Work with two contrasting flower forms of the same color, say three
pink hyacinths and six pink cottage tulips. Again you will want to test containers for this new grouping. The character of your material has changed and
it requires to be looked at and studied freshly. Try arranging them as if they
were growing beside each other in the garden. Use a low tureen or basket, pack
it with chicken wire, place your flowers, and cover the surface with damp sheetmoss. The moss heightens the spring-garden quality of the arrangement and
hides the mechanics of the wire. Continue to experiment . . . discard the wire
and moss, substitute a low squat earthenware pitcher as container, shorten the
stems of two or three tulips, add three red-black tulips, and analyze the result.

Don't be in haste to dash on to arrangements of three varieties of flower until you feel very confident and at ease working and playing with two forms.

It is sometimes helpful, when beginning to work with three varieties, to consider the third flower as a filler or bridge that combines and harmonizes the
contrasting flower forms. Soft, bouncy, feathery flowers such as alyssum, candytuft, sweet rocket, and gypsophilia are good to test as a blending third flower.

Bunching is a simple, charming—above all, foolproof—way of making a
bouquet. Its size is controlled by the supply of flowers at hand and the stretch
of one's hand. A bunch of violets is a complete bouquet. Three bunches, each

in a separate low bowl, placed in a line down the middle of a table make a complete luncheon table decoration.

Make your bunch in many ways . . . all of one variety or of several varieties, collared with leaves or without. Small spring bulbs usually have only green splinters of foliage; ivy, cyclamen, and geranium leaves supply pleasant ruffs. Try bunching as they come in flower such plants as snowdrops, scillas, "Paper White" narcissus, valley, Roman, and grape-hyacinths.

Try this bunch experiment. Place in a small wicker basket one bunch of violets, one of forget-me-nots, and one of grape-hyacinths. The violets will be overpowering, so divide and form them into two bunches, removing two or three leaves if they seem clumsy and heavy. Then work these four bunches into an integrated composition. When you are satisfied with it take it apart, cut the strings, and make a hand bouquet with the same material. Arrange it child-fashion, holding the flowers in your left hand. Place the hyacinths in the hand, as if they were small blue plumes, circle them with the violets, circle the violets with the forget-me-nots; then ruff with violet leaves, bind the stems securely with raffia or cord, and place in a footed goblet. If you have four different colored goblets, test how the color of each flower seems to fade or brighten depending on the goblet in which the bouquet is placed.

Massed arrangements are merely many bunches grouped together, either short or long stemmed. It is best to keep all short bunches in one arrangement, the long in another. They can be mixed but it involves mechanical difficulties that are better left for another year. Massed arrangements have an extravagant, free-handed character. They are an unlabored way for a beginner to create a bold effect. But remember they require a generous supply of flowers. Bunch separately ten stems of pink-edged white tulips, ten medium pink tulips, and ten black-purple and let them arrange themselves in an ironstone pitcher. Try the black-purples high and at the back of the container, then shorten the rest perhaps two inches and place it in the front of the arrangement. Do you see any difference? Then, if you have the patience, loosen the bunches and distribute the colors up and down and all over. Which arrangement seems the boldest?

Stylized arrangements are frankly artificial, all for show and effect. They contradict all the laws and ways of nature. They are gay and amusing as party decorations but rather tiresome to live with day in and day out. In stylized arrangements you consider the flower not as a flower but as a piece of material with color and form. A simple stylization is to mass or form a number of identical flower heads into one exaggerated blossom. Because the weak stem of the "Fantasy" tulip makes it a rather unreliable general arrangement flower, massing is a fine way to use it effectively. Take a dozen, cut the stems from three to seven inches (the length is arbitrary and will vary depending on the size and quality of the flower), and mass them into one giant rounded flower head. When finished it should look like an exotic, exaggerated rhododendron blossom. It is surprisingly easy to construct. Take a finger bowl and pack it firmly with chicken wire, tying it in place if it moves about. Then mound the flowers in

LEFT: *Combine daffodils with everyday spring flower branches, such as Norway maple.*

RIGHT: *Experiment with exotic tuberous begonia, massed on driftwood or in a mound on an ironstone compote.*

this and place them closely together, touching each other. They should completely hide and cover the bowl. Next place the bowl and flowers on a small cake or fruit compote, the flowers coming to the edge of the compote so that all the mechanics are invisible. Experiment in the same way with Dutch Iris . . . use one color for an arrangement—all yellow, or white, or blue—rather than mixing the colors. Try them mixed and see if you don't prefer the solid color.

After you feel completely at ease making simple arrangements, then investigate—if it interests you—the intricacies of line, point, and period arrangements. But, above all, continue to practice and experiment, asking yourself questions incessantly.

**BULBS FOR BOXES**

**AND TUBS**

Boxes of wood or metal supported upon or suspended below window ledges and planted with gay flowers are familiar in many places. These unpretentious little gardens, enjoyed from the living room as well as from outside, are a European heritage that should have wider popularity, particularly where space is not available for real gardens. Similar boxes have long been favorites on porches.

In contemporary home and office buildings, built-in boxes are often incorporated as part of the architectural design. These boxes, when properly made, are in close harmony with the building, introduce no suspension problems, and have drainage provided by concealed plumbing.

Box gardening has extended from such simple beginnings to more elaborate installations. Today entire gardens made of a series of boxes at one or more levels and in varying sizes are often featured on terraces and roofs. Such gardens are especially adaptable to city conditions. In this chapter we are concerned with the uses of bulbs in such boxes as well as in tubs, pots, and other large containers used outdoors.

## In Window Boxes

Because window boxes must be narrow, there is not enough space to permit planting for succession flowering—and so spring-planted bulbs in them must be taken out before summer plants are installed. In this respect they are handled like bulbs used for spring bedding rather than like those planted in permanent flower borders.

Many combinations of bulbs and of bulbs and other spring flowers are practical and beautiful. A single variety of daffodil or narcissus—not the tall kinds—is splendid when combined with forget-me-nots, chionodoxas or trailing myrtle. Tulips and hyacinths are choice and are usually more effective in solid plantings of one color than when more than one variety is used in the same box.

100

Hyacinths ordinarily look best planted rather closely together and alone, but tulips can be combined with pansies, English daisies, forget-me-nots, and other low seasonal flowers to achieve most charming effects. If an edging is desired for a box of hyacinths the double-flowered variety of perennial white-flowered *Arabis albida* is excellent.

Tulips of the early or single or double types are delightful blooming at the window sill. For a later show, double-, peony-flowered varieties can be used. The taller May-flowering tulips are not suitable for window boxes because their height is too great.

Hyacinths are old favorites. The flower spikes that bedding-size bulbs develop are not as heavy as those produced by exhibition grades, but are preferred for window boxes because they withstand winds and rain better. Even these require thin, inconspicuous stakes.

If you wish variety in your window box, groups of the lady tulip (*Tulipa Clusiana*) may be planted alternately with clusters of *Scilla sibirica* at the back and with snowdrops and glory-of-the-snows set rather thickly in front. Or for color in a shady spot, snowdrops and winter aconite have charm planted in groups with ferns and primroses. Many other combinations can be worked out and such mixed plantings are of great interest to watch from the inside of the window.

Three bulbous plants stand out above all others as being useful for planting in window boxes for summer bloom: they are fancy-leaved caladiums, tuberous begonias, and dwarf dahlias. All have their limitations. Caladiums will not stand strong sun or whipping winds, begonias resent bright sun and excessive heat and are easily broken by strong winds, dahlias wither under parching heat that comes from bright sun reflected off nearby surfaces. If you cannot provide the conditions these plants need, it is better to fill your window boxes with annuals in the summer than to depend upon bulbs.

## In Garden Boxes

Boxes used to form a garden on a roof or terrace offer greater possibilities for varied planting than do window and porch boxes. They can be deeper and wider and thus provide more root room and more accommodation for larger plants.

The boxes may be of different sizes and can be arranged to give style and lend composition to the garden picture. They may be used effectively in a double series—those in back being planted with evergreens where climate permits these to remain outdoors throughout the winter or, in sections where evergreens are not practicable, with privet and other deciduous shrubs. Any of the bulb combinations suggested for window boxes as well as those mentioned in Chapter 3 as suitable for spring bedding will be attractive in the foreground boxes. A few well-branched plants of English ivy or creeping myrtle spilling over the front relieves the starkness of box fronts.

# HYACINTHS

Dutch hyacinths are among the most stately of spring-flowering bulbs. They are well suited for outdoor flower beds and for forcing indoors. Here is a selection of some of the best varieties.

1                                    2

1. *Hyacinth L'Innocence*

2. *Hyacinth Myosotis*

3. *Hyacinth Grand Maitre*

4. *Hyacinth Bismarck*

5. *Hyacinth City of Haarlem*

6. *Hyacinth Lady Derby*

7. *Hyacinth Jan Bos*

8. *Hyacinth Pink Pearl*

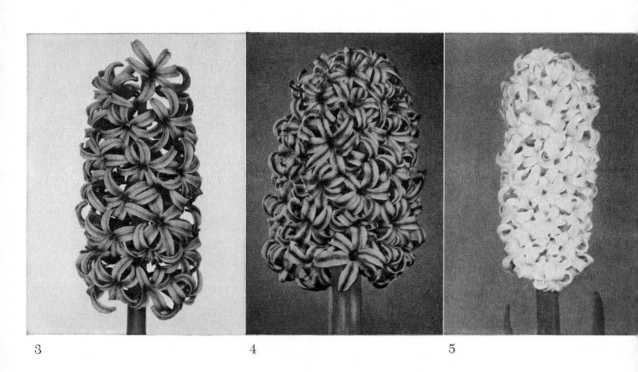

3            4            5

6            7            8

For accents, groups of boxes of varying sizes may be built to comprise units —a larger square box containing an evergreen shrub with two lower boxes of just the right size fitted against it to hold bulbs and other flowering plants is a useful combination . . . a triangular-shaped cluster of boxes may form a planting unit for a corner . . . a more complicated pattern of boxes to feature plants in the center of a terrace. There is great opportunity for creating imaginative box gardens for adaptable locations where beds and borders may not be practicable.

In addition to bulbs favored for window boxes, others of greater stature may be employed in boxes set at or near ground or floor level. For spring display the taller "Darwin" and other May-flowering tulips are unsurpassed; such items as Spanish bluebells and camassias may be used if the location is shady.

For summer bloom there is a wealth of possibilities in addition to the three items—caladiums, tuberous begonias, and dwarf dahlias—mentioned as most suitable for window and porch boxes. Gladioluses, montbretias, tuberoses, Peruvian daffodils, tigridias, summer-hyacinths, and even lilies come to mind as good possibilities. Indeed with a little ingenuity there is no reason why you cannot grow in plant boxes almost any of the bulbs that are suitable for outdoor beds and borders. You can plant them in groups among long-flowering annuals to add interest. Oxalises in variety, notably the large pink-flowered *Oxalis Bowieana,* are exceedingly useful for edgings because they are attractive in foliage and flower and keep blooming for a long time.

Built-in plant boxes constructed as part of buildings vary greatly in size and possibilities. Very often it is advisable to use permanent evergreen shrubs toward the back of them, leaving a space in front for other plants to be added for seasonal color. In spring these may be hyacinths, tulips, daffodils, and other kinds of bulbs as well as non-bulbous spring-bloomers; in summer they can be arranged in similar fashion to ordinary window boxes.

Built-in boxes and raised beds of masonry constructed away from the building as part of a landscape plan are sometimes used to accommodate potted plants which are changed to provide for a constant colorful display, but this kind of gardening is expensive because it calls for many plants and much growing space to grow them to flowering size. On an extensive scale it is best adapted for stores and commercial and public buildings; in a modest way it can be used by the home owner.

As a matter of fact, to prolong the flowering season with bulbs in a box garden, it is possible to use boxes supplied with good drainage and filled with peatmoss into which potted bulbs in bud or full flower may be plunged deeply enough to obscure the pots. This ensures a continuous display, color combinations can be changed at will, and plants that have faded flowers or that have been damaged can easily be replaced with fresh ones.

By plunging the pots the soil in them is retarded from drying. It is easily possible to design a box garden that depends for its color on a display of potted plants—a succession of flowers may be continued until frost without the necessity of taking the plants from their pots, but again it is a little extravagant of plants.

Boxes to be planted directly with flowering plants or boxes in which potted plants are to be displayed must be well constructed. Although many materials have been used, wood is the most popular because of its appearance and comparative lightness, and because it insulates the roots from extreme heat.

Lumber should be at least one inch thick and of a moisture-resistant kind such as redwood or cypress. Even so, it should be treated with a preservative and the boxes should be fitted with removable liners of zinc that have heavily soldered corners and provision for drainage at the bottom.

Cleats are important on the bottom of boxes intended to set on a level surface to permit the drainage and air circulation that prolongs the life of boxes. Where soil-filled boxes are to be left outside over the winter in the north, one side of each box should be slanted to allow for soil expansion caused by frost. There must, of course, be a sturdy means of support for suspended boxes because even a small box is heavy when filled with soil.

Wherever boxes are used, shun that dreadful shade of green paint often used for garden furnishings which is so out of harmony with garden foliage and so beloved by those responsible for the management of many public parks. Most green paints are unsuitable; try neutral tones of other colors.

## Culture of Bulbs in Boxes

The cultural requirements of bulbs planted in boxes are essentially the same as for bulbs planted in pots. Free drainage must be assured, a fertile and porous soil provided, and at no time may the bulbs be permitted to suffer from lack of moisture in the soil. Summer bulbs benefit from weekly applications of dilute fertilizer after they are well established and have filled their soil with roots. Careful staking may be needed to anticipate storm damage. Faded flowers should be removed promptly. A layer of peatmoss an inch or two thick spread over the soil surface at the beginning of hot weather will keep the roots cool and prevent excessive loss of moisture.

Special provision must be made to prevent boxes planted in the fall with tulips, hyacinths, daffodils, and other hardy bulbs from freezing solid and remaining frozen for long periods in the winter. This does not occur when bulbs are planted several inches beneath the ground outdoors, but it happens easily in a box insulated from the warmth of the lower soil layers and exposed at its sides and tops.

One way of assuring protection is to stand the boxes together on the ground and cover them with a four-inch layer of sand, fine ashes, or sifted earth. If earth is used spread an inch of sand over the boxes before you apply it; this will make it easy to clean off the covering layer in spring without disturbing the soil in the boxes.

Don't bury the boxes too deeply . . . otherwise the bulb shoots will be too

*This gay window box is filled with a variety of bulbs that have been grown in pots and when in bloom buried in the window box in peatmoss. This method permits the box to be kept continuously in bloom by simply taking out potted plants that have faded and replacing them with new ones.*

long and will break when you attempt to remove the soil covering from them. If the boxes are on a roof, use peatmoss for covering instead of sand, cinders, or soil—it is lighter.

An even better method than burrying them with soil is to place the newly planted boxes in a root cellar or unheated (but nearly frostproof) cellar. Failing this, you may excavate a hole six inches deeper than the boxes in a well-drained place in the garden and place the boxes in this. Cover it with planks, and, when the ground freezes, add a foot or so of leaves or straw. This method may involve more work at planting time than simply covering with soil, cinders, or sand, but it certainly makes it easier to remove the boxes of bulbs in spring without damage to either boxes or bulbs.

If your plant boxes are of such a quality that you do not wish to bury them over the winter and if you cannot conveniently store them in a suitable cellar, the best plan is to construct one or more inexpensive wooden boxes that will fit inside the regular ones, plant the bulbs in these, and bury them over the winter as previously suggested.

One word of warning regarding mice should be given. They are very fond of tulips and some other bulbs (but not of daffodils and narcissuses). It may,

therefore, be well to tack small mesh-wire netting over the boxes before putting them in their winter quarters.

Plant the bulbs in the fall at the same time as you would plant the same
kinds in the outdoor garden. If they are to be buried outdoors choose a site
on the north side of a building or hill so that they will not be encouraged to
sprout prematurely. After the surface soil has frozen cover the box with several
inches of loose straw, salt hay, or leaves. In early spring uncover it carefully
and gradually.

The bulbs you plant in the fall to bloom in spring are less fussy than most
plants about soil fertility. The texture of the soil, however, is of considerable
importance. Don't expect them to flourish in clay or subsoil that packs so hard
that air can scarcely penetrate.

A reasonably good topsoil that contains enough sand and enough organic
matter (peatmoss, leafmold, humus, or compost) to prevent it from becoming
a hard clod when you squeeze a handful in just-moist condition is satisfactory.
A scattering of bone meal worked into it is helpful.

For summer bulbs a more nutritious earth is needed. They must manufacture
from the soil the foodstuffs they need for their development and growth
(most of the food necessary for the production of spring flowers is stored in
the bulbs at planting time).

Let the soil for summer bulbs consist of good topsoil, coarse sand, and leafmold, humus, or peatmoss, in about equal proportions. Add one eighth part by
bulk of dried cow manure and, to each bushel, a pint of bone meal and a
quarter as much 5-10-5 garden fertilizer or one of somewhat similar analysis.

If possible the soil in plant boxes should be changed completely each year.
This is rarely practicable in city gardens and not always in the country if a
box garden is extensive. However, it *is* the best plan, and it is particularly important for small boxes that hold but little soil.

If the soil cannot be renewed each year try to change one third of it. Do
this by removing *all* the soil from one end of the box, leveling down the re-
mainder, spreading the new soil on top, and mixing it thoroughly with the old.

Old soil left in place more than one year should be improved each spring by
the addition of peatmoss or humus, dried cow manure and fertilizer, and by a
liberal sprinkling of lime, all mixed in thoroughly. After mixing leave the
surface rough and exposed to the air for a few days before planting.

## In Tubs and Pots

Flower boxes planted and cared for like miniature gardens are not the only
plant receptacles used outdoors. Large pots and tubs containing (usually) individual plants are often employed to beautify patios, terraces, steps, entrances,
and formal gardens. Among the plants adaptable for such purposes are a number of bulbs that have foliage and flowers sufficiently bold and massive to in-
vest them with a certain "architectural" character that is desirable in specimen
tub and pot plants that are used to add accent and dignity to formal surround-

ings. Bulbs suitable for this purpose are of kinds that retain interest for a relatively long period and are decorative even when out of flower.

Unexcelled for planting in large tubs and pots is the lily-of-the-Nile, or *Agapanthus*. It comes in several varieties and blooms for a fairly long period. Its deep green strap-shaped leaves are plentiful and are gracefully disposed. From among them in early summer arise wandlike stems, each tipped with a pointed bud and each attaining an eventual height of three to four feet. The buds open to release a multitude of star-shaped blue or white flowers disposed in globular heads. The blue-flowered kinds are more pleasing than the white.

Equally as decorative as the lily-of-the-Nile but, because of its earlier blooming season, less adapted to northern gardens are clivias. These have spectacular rounded flower heads of glowing orange which just clear the masses of dark green leaves that are shorter, broader, and stiffer than those of the lily-of-the-Nile. No better foils exist against which to display clivias than those suggested by McKenny and Seymour who recommend they be "grown in sea-green pots against screens of ivy." They complete their suggestion by saying, "used with orange and blue-green tables and chairs, no other blooming plant is needed on the terrace."

Certain crinums are well worth cultivating in large tubs for blooming outdoors in summer, notably *Crinum longifolium, Crinum Moorei,* and *Crinum Powellii.* These noble plants are three or four feet tall in bloom. They have bold foliage and clusters of handsome flowers, pink or white according to variety; they flower over a long season and are well suited for standing on steps or terraces and for associating with other architectural features.

The beautiful bigeneric hybrid between *Amaryllis* and *Crinum* that is called *Amarcrinum,* but should more properly be named *Crinodonna,* resembles a choice crinum. It has the same decorative value but blooms later, in the North often not opening its beautiful pink "lilies" before an early frost nips the garden. For outdoor display it gives its best service in gardens where winter comes late.

The spider-lily, or *Hymenocallis,* afford a few kinds adaptable for our purpose. These have good foliage and stout two- or three-foot stalks that carry umbels of richly fragrant, spidery narrow-petaled white flowers. Kinds to try include *H. Harrisiana, H. littoralis, H. rotata,* and *H. galvestonensis.*

Rare *Elisena longipetala* from Peru closely resembles its near relatives, the spider-lilies. It has good-looking foliage and, topping eighteen-inch stems, umbels of deliciously fragrant, fine white narrow-petaled flowers that are attractive over many weeks at high summer.

Although seldom planted in other than garden borders the fragrant Peruvian daffodils or ismenes (which botanically are *Hymenocallis* and thus belong with the spider-lilies) make fine specimens when accommodated several together in large pots or tubs—and, because this method of cultivation does not necessitate disturbing the roots at the end of each growing season (the pots are stored over the winter), the bulbs thrive and flower more certainly than under the plant-each-spring-dig-up-each-fall schedule that border cultivation demands.

The summer-hyacinth, *Galtonia candicans,* responds to the same treatment as Peruvian daffodils and carries stems bearing twenty to thirty pure white bell-shaped flowers to a height of from three to five feet.

If you crave unusual plants for outdoor summer bloom try the curious pineapple-flower (*Eucomis*) which produces two-foot cylindrical spikes of pale green or almost white starry flowers in July and August. Each cylinder of bloom is surmounted by a crown of green leaves after the fashion of the fruit of a pineapple, which accounts for the common name of this plant.

For a shaded terrace where summer nights are not too warm, by all means grow tuberous begonias in seven- or eight-inch pots. They will give a steady display of gorgeous blooms in a wide variety of colors and forms from June or July until frost.

Not to be overlooked as a decorative tub plant is the snake-palm (*Hydrosme*). The malodorous bloom of the arum relative is borne early in the year, lasts a few days, and is followed by the production of a handsomely marked, attractively divided, solitary umbrella-like leaf that stands on a three- or four-foot stem and spreads its top over a circle that equals in diameter the length of its stem.

## Care of Bulbs in Tubs

All the bulbs mentioned as specimens suitable for cultivation in pots and tubs for outdoor summer use must be protected from frost by wintering indoors in all but the warmest sections of the country. With the exception of tuberous begonias all may remain in the same containers, without repotting, for many years. Each spring they should be top-dressed with rich soil. The begonias are handled in storage and are replanted exactly as they are when they are grown in pots for indoor decoration as described in Chapter 11. The others are simply stored in the receptacles in which they are growing in a frostproof but cool shed, cold frame, greenhouse, or cellar. Those that retain green foliage, such as agapanthuses and clivias, must have good light at all times; those that lose their leaves must have light from the time new growth begins in spring. The latter, if stored in a suitably cool and not excessively dry location, will not need watering while dormant. Bulbs that retain their foliage should be kept on the dry side while in storage but should be watered often enough to keep the leaves from wilting or dying.

# DUTCH IRISES

Dutch irises are a group of hybrids that resemble Spanish irises but are sturdier and bloom earlier. They are splendid for garden decoration and for cutting.

1                                   2                                   3

1. *Iris White Excelsior*

2. *Iris Imperator*

3. *Iris Yellow Queen*

4. *Iris Wedgwood*

4

# 10 FORCING BULBS INDOORS

Forcing bulbs into bloom ahead of season is one of the simplest arts of gardening and one of the most delightful. By its practice we anticipate spring and are able to decorate our homes with some best-loved garden flowers at times when indoor posies are most appreciated. From November until April forced bulbs may be had in bloom. Though snow flies and all outdoors is cold and bleak, the greenhouse, sunroom, and window garden can present in procession from fall to spring a kaleidoscope of colorful narcissuses, daffodils, hyacinths, tulips, irises, lilies, crocuses, snowdrops, grape-hyacinths, squills, glory-of-the-snows, and other favorites.

The florists of the country force millions of bulbs into early bloom each year. Many amateurs force some, but more should try their hands at this phase of bulb culture. As a hobby its reward consists not alone of end results; there is a deep-seated satisfaction in watching and tending the developing plants.

Because results are achieved with considerable certainty and relative quickness, planting bulbs and bringing them into early bloom indoors is a highly interesting and distinctly educational activity for children. If you have youngsters purchase a few bulbs for them each fall and let them get their fingers in the soil and become acquainted with the joys of indoor gardening.

Bulbs suitable for forcing are nearly all of kinds that are hardy outdoors, although a few such as the narcissuses "Paper White," "Grand Soleil d'Or," and "Chinese Sacred Lily," Roman hyacinths, and Easter lilies are not reliably so in the North. After they are through blooming forced bulbs are of no further value as pot plants. They will not force satisfactorily a second year, but in many cases they can be salvaged for use in the outdoor garden.

Although fashions in indoor plants change, it seems certain that forced bulbs will always be popular. They appeal because the period between planting and flowering is short and because their blooms make gay displays when flowers are especially welcome. Some such as hyacinths, lilies, and certain narcissuses are wonderfully fragrant. Chances of failure are slight if a few simple rules are followed.

## General Culture

Because individual pots of forced bulbs do not remain in bloom long—usually for not more than ten days to three weeks—they must be brought into flower in planned succession to ensure continuous bloom.

The planning that precedes bulb forcing should be based not only upon the desire for a progression of bloom through winter and spring but also upon a consideration of the places in the home where pots of bulbs may be used effectively. Thought must be given, too, to locations where they are to be grown until they come into bloom. Nearly all need to be kept for some weeks after planting in a dark, cool place. Unless good root growth is made under such conditions before they are placed in forcing temperatures they will not flower satisfactorily. "Cool," for this purpose, means a temperature above freezing but not greatly exceeding forty-five degrees. The conditions we attempt to approximate are those to which bulbs planted a few inches deep out-of-doors are subjected; this means darkness, even moisture, and fairly low, reasonably stable temperatures.

One satisfactory way of assuring such conditions is to bury the pots, after planting, outdoors under an eight-inch covering of fine ashes, sand, or peatmoss. A variation is to place the potted bulbs in a large ventilated box or bin arranged in such fashion that at least six inches of peatmoss is between the sides of the box and the pots and so that eight inches of peatmoss covers them. The box should be located in a shaded place outdoors. If burying in ashes, sand, or peatmoss is not practicable, the pots of newly planted bulbs may be kept during their rooting period in darkness in a box or closet in a cool frost-proof cellar, sun porch, attic, or similar location.

Usually six to ten weeks of this treatment will be needed before the bulbs are ready to be brought into the light and greater warmth. Transfer the bulbs from darkness before shoot growth is three inches tall but not before healthy white roots crowd the pots.

When first moved the shoots will be pale. Shade them from direct sunshine until they assume a healthy green; then expose them to all possible sun. Lack of sufficient light and too high temperatures are responsible for many failures with forcing bulbs. A night temperature of fifty to fifty-five degrees with a daytime rise of five to ten degrees is ideal for most kinds. This is not always easy to provide in a dwelling house but even in a warmer room you may find that temperatures within this desired range prevail close to a window that has no radiator beneath it. Keep a thermometer near your developing bulbs so that you know to what temperatures they are subjected.

After the bulbs are brought into light plenty of moisture is needed. The root-ing medium must never be allowed to dry. It is difficult to give too much water to well-rooted bulbs planted in well-drained containers with holes at the bot-tom but it is easily possible to overwater those planted in vermiculite, peatmoss, or other soil substitutes in undrained receptacles. Endeavor to keep such mate-rials evenly moist but not constantly saturated. In the case of bulbs planted in pebbles and water, or in plain water in special hyacinth glasses, keep the water level about even with the bases of the bulbs.

Bulbs that have been forced are of no further value for indoor cultivation but if kept watered and growing under sunny conditions until their foliage dies down naturally they may be removed from the soil and be planted in the outdoor garden as soon as the weather is warm enough or after a summer of storage in a dry, cool airy place. Almost all will recover and bloom satisfactorily outdoors in future years.

Fall is the time to plant bulbs for forcing. In most cases the best results are obtained when this is done as early as good bulbs are obtainable from dealers. But in a few instances—for example with "Paper White," "Grand Soleil d'Or," and "Chinese Sacred Lily" narcissuses and with hyacinths—several plantings may be spaced at two- or three-week intervals to provide a succession of bloom-ing plants.

Forcing bulbs may be planted in soil, in which case the containers must have holes at the bottom to ensure drainage, or in a sterile rooting medium such as vermiculite or "bulb fiber." Bulb fiber is a mixture of peatmoss, oyster shell chips, and chopped charcoal. These ingredients are mixed in the proportions of about two quarts of each of the latter to a bushel of the former. Bulb fiber or vermiculite should be used for bulbs planted in undrained containers unless they are planted, as some few kinds may be, in pebbles and water or, as hya-cinths sometimes are, in plain water to which a few lumps of charcoal have been added. There is no doubt that the best results are assured by growing bulbs in soil in regular clay flowerpots or in the shallow flowerpots that florists call pans.

Because forcing bulbs contain at planting time in undeveloped form all the flowers that they will produce and because they have within themselves much of the food material needed for the development of their leaves and flowers, especially rich soil is not necessary. Nevertheless they should be given earth of good texture and reasonable fertility. Do not expect results if you plant them in a sticky, infertile clay. If possible obtain topsoil—the kind that would grow good vegetables or satisfactory flower-garden plants. Add to it about one third by bulk of peatmoss, leafmold, or compost and, if it tends to be heavy, an equal amount of coarse sand or fine cinders. Mix in bone meal at the rate of one pint to each bushel. Have the soil in a just-moist condition at planting time—not so dry that it is dusty, not so wet that it sticks to the fingers.

Most bulbs are planted several in a container, spaced so that they almost touch each other. With the exception of stem-rooting lilies, which are planted

*These bulbs are growing in fiber in undrained receptacles. Great care must be taken when watering not to apply too much.*

low in their pots and are top-dressed later, set the bulbs so that their tips just show at the soil surface which should be an inch or so below the rim of the pot to allow for watering.

Prepare each pot for planting by placing over the hole in its bottom an inch or so of coarse cinders, bricks broken to the approximate size of marbles, or crocks (pieces of broken flowerpot). Cover this layer with dead leaves, moss, or straw to keep the soil from washing down and clogging the drainage. Fill with soil to a suitable level and press it lightly. Do not make the soil beneath the bulbs firm or the downward pressure of the developing roots will lift the bulbs right out of their pots. On the other hand, the soil on top of the bulbs (the surface soil) should be made quite firm by pressing it with the tips of the fingers. This firm-at-the-surface, loose-underneath arrangement minimizes the danger of the bulbs lifting. After potting, water thoroughly and place the pots where they are to stay during their rooting period.

The technique of planting in bulb fiber is somewhat different. Moisten the fiber thoroughly and squeeze out all surplus moisture. Fill the container with fiber and press it down firmly leaving its finished surface almost or quite level with the rim. With the fingers scoop a hole in the surface and plant one bulb. Pack fiber around it and repeat this until the container is filled; then put it in a dark cool place for rooting. Undrained containers must not be put outdoors; they must be kept under cover so that rains will not fill them with water.

If vermiculite is used as a rooting medium, simply pour it into the container to a suitable level, set the bulbs upon it, and add more vermiculite until only the upper halves of the bulbs show. The surface may be level with the rim of the receptacle. Don't press or pack vermiculite. After planting apply enough water to moisten the vermiculite but not to make a pool in the bottom of the container.

Bulbs planted in pebbles and water are normally set so that their lower half only is below the surface of the pebbles. Water is then poured in until its surface is about level with the bases of the bulbs.

Only first-quality bulbs are worth buying for forcing. Second grades, which may be usable for outdoor planting, are less likely to be satisfactory indoors.

LEFT:   *In this greenhouse tuberous begonias of the hanging types are grown suspended from the roof and the erect, large-bloomed double-flowered kinds are on the greenhouse benches.*

RIGHT:   *Even a tiny greenhouse gives opportunity to grow a great variety of bulbs. Here daffodils and grape-hyacinths are in bloom long before they come into flower outdoors.*

Top-quality bulbs always give finer flowers, and in some cases, as for example with narcissuses, more flowers per bulb are had from them than from inferior grades. When selecting bulbs for forcing (this particularly applies to narcissuses, tulips, and irises) choose varieties that are known to be especially suitable for the purpose; this is particularly important in the case of bulbs that are to be brought into bloom well in advance of their normal outdoor season. For later forcing, to have flowers three or four weeks only before the same varieties flower outdoors, the selection of special forcing varieties is of much less importance. Catalogs of specialists indicate the best forcing varieties.

### Containers to Use

To achieve the finest decorative effects with bulbs forced indoors it is necessary to consider where in the home they can be displayed to best advantage and to give thought to the types of containers to use. From an aesthetic point of view the best results and the greatest enjoyment may come, not from keeping them in a window, but from moving them when in bloom to places where they may be appreciated more intimately, where they make a more dramatic appeal, or where they fit most pleasingly into the general decorative scheme.

By all means select containers which will not look out of place. Clay pots may be unobtrusive on an enclosed terrace, sitting on a tile-top table, arranged on a plant stand, or standing at floor level, but if bulbs are to be used on dining tables, coffee tables, chairside or bedside tables, more refined containers are usually preferred. For such locations the best answer may be a glazed jardiniere into which regular clay pots can be set, but jardinieres for this purpose are not easy to find. More often than not they come in shapes that either leave half an inch or more of clay pot protruding above their edge or are too ungainly to be attractive. Why jardinieres are so seldom proportioned to fit the standard clay pots and pans of the florist is something of a puzzle.

For bulbs that are to be grown in containers without holes in the bottoms there are numerous solutions. Glazed receptacles are available in any number of shapes and sizes—varying in price and quality. For bulbs which do not have to be buried outdoors after planting, such as "Paper White" narcissuses and Roman hyacinths, you may use beautiful handmade bowls in neutral colors. But when the containers must be plunged outdoors, the danger of breakage must be considered and only clay pots or inexpensive glazed containers should be employed. Chinese pewter, antique bronze, and specially constructed boxes of wood masonry or metal with removable liners may also be used. For special indoor display sizeable built-in boxes are good, pots of bulbs already in bud or flower being set in them in moist peatmoss deeply enough to hide their pots. If the boxes are wide enough, a few carefully selected foliage plants may be used as background and a trailing vine such as English ivy may be employed to soften the front. The influence of changing design on contemporary homes affects the use of plants as it affects furniture trends. Displaying plants attractively indoors is an art that challenges one's creative ability.

## Kinds to Grow

If we accept November as the beginning of the forcing season, among the earliest bulbs to be had in bloom are three similar narcissuses: the "Paper White" with clusters of white flowers, "Grand Soleil d'Or" with golden-cupped yellow flowers, and the "Chinese Sacred Lily" with flowers that have yellow cups and creamy white petals. All are sweetly scented. Because their flower stems are eighteen inches to two feet high and their foliage ample and of nearly the same height, they are most suitable for setting on low stands. Select

LEFT: *Planted in soil or fiber hyacinths are easily grown and bloom with certainty indoors if given a fair chance.*

MIDDLE: *Crocuses in varied hues are excellent for forcing early indoors in shallow pans. They must be grown in a cool temperature.*

RIGHT: *In special hyacinth glasses, hyacinths may be brought into bloom in water.*

for them containers at least three or four inches deep and broad enough to accommodate five to seven bulbs without touching. Early-planted bulbs of these narcissuses may be had in bloom by Thanksgiving. Successive plantings will provide flowers well into the new year.

Roman hyacinths, often sold as "French Roman hyacinths," may be had in bloom as early as these first narcissuses. They have small bell-shaped flowers in a looser, more graceful arrangement than the large show varieties; they

LEFT: *Spanish bluebells make attractive subjects for forcing into bloom early indoors.*

MIDDLE: *Daffodils are prime favorites for forcing into bloom in the greenhouse and window garden.*

RIGHT: *No bulbs are easier to grow indoors than Paper White narcissuses. They may easily be had in bloom well before Christmas.*

produce several flower spikes from each bulb, but they come in white only. Prepared hyacinths, sometimes called "Dutch Roman hyacinths," are similar and are available in pink and blue as well as white. They cannot be had in bloom quite as early as the French Romans but even so they may be flowered before Christmas. Bulbs of both the French Romans and of the prepared hyacinths that are intended for early flowering must be planted as soon as they are received for retail sale in August or early September—and good results are possible when bulbs are grown in pebbles or fiber. These are more usable for dinner and luncheon table decoration than are large-flowered hyacinths.

Lily-of-the-valleys are easy to grow. They are not true bulbs, but the single crowns or "pips" from which they grow are treated much like bulbs for forcing purposes and are offered in the catalogs of bulb dealers. The "pips" are available from late fall until early spring. They are suitable for small deep bowls filled with fiber or for growing in soil in regular flowerpots. Straight-sided bowls are better than those with slanted or curved sides because root growth is heavy and the plants stand up stiffly. The pips flower in about four weeks from the time they are planted.

Except for specially prepared (precooled) daffodils and tulips that need very special temperature control from the time they are received and are suitable for greenhouse cultivation only, it is well into the new year before most other forcing bulbs can be had in bloom. Hyacinths are among the earliest. When grown in flowerpots in soil or in bowls in fiber they have great decorative value. Unlike most bulbs hyacinths look well when grown singly in small pots, and you may find more places in your living rooms appropriate for such examples than for large bowls that display a number of large-flowering spikes. Nevertheless, bowls planted with several bulbs make gorgeous feature pieces when suitably located. Because hyacinth varieties may not bloom together even though given the same treatment, plant only one variety in each container.

Colors include pink, rose, scarlet, yellow, lavender, blue—from light to very dark—purple, and white. Depth of color will hold better if the bowls are removed from full sun during the brightest part of the day. Because the perfume of hyacinths is heavy they will be more appreciated if there are only a few in the house at a time.

Hyacinths are as easy as "Paper White" narcissuses to grow in water if you use high glasses designed for the purpose. These glasses are about seven inches tall and are pinched in near their tops and flared sufficiently above the pinch to permit setting a bulb in the cup so formed so that the roots that develop from the bulb can extend down into the water. Hyacinths grown in such containers have the added attraction of visible root development as the plants mature, but are somewhat awkward in appearance. Bulbs grown in clay pots or deep bowls have greater decorative value and usually yield larger flowers.

All varieties of narcissuses and daffodils should be planted several together in pots, pans, or bowls, using one variety to a container. The larger varieties grow from eighteen inches to two feet high and have an abundance of long, decorative leaves. When the bulbs are in flower, the containers are bulky and have considerable weight; they can best be enjoyed below eye level as seen from a sitting position. Low stands or stools are serviceable to set them on, provided they are of the right height. But if you wish to arrange groups of bulb bowls in front of a window that extends nearly to floor level, a better plan is to acquire a set of blocks either of solid wood or of hollow structure—such as those used for store window display. These blocks can also be used for displaying pots of bulbs against a space of free wall very effectively. Such displays with spot lighting can be very dramatic after dark. Glass bricks or building blocks may be substituted for the wood blocks but are not as satisfactory.

Tulips are a little more difficult to force in the house than hyacinths and narcissuses because they are best grown in a moderate temperature in an airy but moist atmosphere, which is difficult to provide without a cool greenhouse. Because they are more temperamental, selections should definitely be made from among well-proven varieties, which means generally those of the single early and early double types.

Unless tulips are to be displayed considerably below table level indoors, only the shorter-stemmed ones will be easy to use. Some of the tall May-flowering tulips are richest of all in color, however, and should by all means be considered if cool growing conditions can be provided and if they can be displayed to good advantage. Staking will likely be necessary and heavy wire or very thin bamboo stakes should be used for support—the stems being tied with lightweight green thread or narrow pieces of raffia as inconspicuously as possible. Stakes set around the outside of pots with string stretched between pulls the plants together too much and detracts from their natural beauty. Pots should not be planted with less than five or seven tulips; some of the shorter ones look very well in pans.

Among other bulbs suitable for forcing are a number of the smaller-flowered ones that are especially valuable for growing in shallow bowls and in bulb pans, which are like ordinary clay pots but not as deep. Simple, unpretentious containers are in the best taste for these small bulbs. Crocuses, grape-hyacinths, and certain scillas are the easiest to force. Any of the grape-hyacinths and any of the crocuses make delightful subjects. Of the squills, the species *Scilla biflora* and *Scilla sibirica* and the splendid variety "Spring Beauty" are recommended. Snowdrops, winter aconites, and *Iris reticulata* and its delightful varieties may also be successfully forced although they are inclined to be less dependable. All these small bulbs and some of the others mentioned here must be allowed to root well under cool conditions before being brought inside, and even after they are indoors they must not be subjected to much warmth. A night temperature of fifty degrees that is not increased to over sixty degrees during the day is ample but may be difficult to provide in the house.

Other standard forcing bulbs are lilies—particularly Easter lilies, which are brought into bloom in such great quantities for the Easter season—and irises of the Wedgwood types, which may be had in bloom from Christmas onward. The latter provide splendid cut flowers. None of these is suitable for growing in the house; they are essentially plants for greenhouse cultivation. Recommended procedures for growing them in greenhouses are given under the entries *Lilium* and *Iris* in the alphabetical listing in the latter part of this book. In that listing too will be found the cultural needs of yellow callas and some other bulbs that are sometimes thought of as forcing items.

# NARCISSUSES

Narcissuses (which included daffodils) are classified into eleven divisions and several subdivisions based on the form of their flowers and the species from which they have been derived. This selection of varieties illustrates some of the divisions.

1       2       3       4

5       6

DIVISION I (Trumpet)

1. *Narcissus Spring Glory*

2. *Narcissus Mrs. Ernst H. Krelage*

3. *Narcissus Unsurpassable*

4. *Narcissus King Alfred*

5. *Narcissus Magnificence*

6. *Narcissus Beersheba*

DIVISION II (Large-Cupped)

7. *Narcissus Mrs. R. O. Backhouse*

8. *Narcissus Tunis*

9. *Narcissus Fortune*

10. *Narcissus Helios*

7       8       9       10

11. *Narcissus Dick Wellband*

12. *Narcissus Scarlet Elegance*

11                  12

13         14        15        16

17         18        19        20

21            22            23

DIVISION III (Small-Cupped)

13. *Narcissus Princess of Wales (Mrs. Barclay)*

14. *Narcissus Lady Moore*

15. *Narcissus La Riante*

16. *Narcissus Verger*

DIVISION IV (Double)

17. *Narcissus Inglescombe*

18. *Narcissus Cheerfulness*

19. *Narcissus Texas*

20. *Narcissus Mary Copeland*

DIVISION V (*Triandrus*)

21. *Narcissus Thalia*

DIVISION VII (*Jonquilla*)

22. *Narcissus Trevithian*

DIVISION VIII (*Tazetta*)

23. *Narcissus Actea*

24. *Narcissus Scarlet Gem*

25. *Narcissus Geranium*

DIVISION IX (*Poeticus*)

26. *Narcissus Laurens Koster*

24            25            26

# 11    PERMANENT INDOOR BULBS

In the preceding chapter we discussed bulbs that are forced into bloom ahead of season and that, after flowering once, are discarded as indoor plants. Here we will consider kinds that may be grown indoors year after year and that are bloomed annually at or about their normal flowering season without "forcing." There are a great many of these that are suitable when grown in pots and tubs to brighten the window garden, sun porch, and greenhouse. Some are useful for outdoor terraces in summer; some provide flowers for cutting.

By making a judicious selection it is possible to have a display of bloom at all times of the year. These bulbs differ considerably in their cultural needs and in their adaptability for special uses.

Bulbs that may be grown indoors permanently are mostly not winter-hardy outdoors in the colder parts of the country. They fall into two distinct groups: the first consists of freesias, lachenalias, tuberous begonias, caladiums, gloxinias, and all others that have annual roots only; and the second includes all perennial-rooted kinds such as amaryllises (*Hippeastrum*), agapanthuses, crinums, haemanthuses, and nerines.

## Bulbs With Annual Roots

Annual-rooted bulbs die down completely at the beginning of their resting season and are without tops or roots while dormant. They must then be kept quite dry. They may be stored during dormancy undisturbed in the pots of soil in which they grew. Or, they may be taken out, cleaned, and kept until the beginning of the next growing season in open-topped paper bags, shallow trays, or even suspended in old nylon stockings, in a dry, airy place where they are protected from direct sunshine and widely fluctuating temperatures.

Because, when the end of the resting season comes, bulbs left in pots of soil may start into growth unnoticed, it is usually wiser to remove them from their pots as soon as their foliage has died and to store them without soil where

124

they may be inspected at intervals. In any case they must be replanted in clean, well-drained containers of new soil at the beginning of each growing season.

The water requirements of these bulbs follow a seasonal rhythm. Immediately after planting they are well watered, but additional moisture is supplied sparingly for a few weeks afterward—though with increasing generosity as roots develop. When the pots are well filled with roots the soil is kept constantly moist and this condition is maintained until, after flowering, yellowing of the foliage indicates unmistakably the approach of the resting season. When that occurs, intervals between waterings are gradually lengthened and finally, when the foliage has completely died, water is withheld and another season of dormancy begins.

No one time of the year is right for replanting all the various annual-rooted bulbs. Many, notably kinds that are native to South Africa, begin their growth cycle in fall and are repotted then. These rest in summer. Others such as gloxinias, fancy-leaved caladiums, and some oxalises are dormant in winter and start into growth in spring, at which time they must be provided with new soil and with moisture. Details of culture for each particular kind is listed under its name in alphabetical sequence in the second part of this book.

## Bulbs With Perennial Roots

The pot culture of bulbs that have perennial (permanent) roots differs markedly from those that have annual roots. They are not replanted each year. Often they live for many years in the same container with nothing more than a top-dressing applied at the beginning of each growing season. Top-dressing means that as much of the surface soil as can be loosened with a pointed stick without damaging the roots is taken off and is replaced with rich earth containing fertilizer. Just before this is done, the plant is removed from its pot and its

*Gloxinias are favorite plants for greenhouse cultivation; many people succeed with them as window garden plants. The center picture represents a gloxinia of the slipper type, the others choice hybrid kinds.*

*Achimenes are choice relatives of gloxinias and require about the same cultural care. They come in pink, red, white, blue, purple, and intermediate shades.*

roots are carefully examined to make sure that the drainage is not clogged and to check whether repotting is necessary. This latter operation (except in the case of young bulbs that are being grown on rapidly and that are repotted every year or two) receives attention infrequently. Intervals of four or five years between pottings are common . . . and large specimens of clivias, agapanthuses, and some other kinds are not disturbed as often as that.

Most perennial-rooted bulbs have a dormant season during which their tops die down completely. A few, such as clivias, agapanthuses, eucharises, and certain crinums, are evergreen. The evergreen ones obviously require moisture at all times, but much less when they are semidormant (even bulbs that do not go completely dormant have a season of partial rest) than when they are actively growing. Bulbs with evergreen foliage must never be allowed to dry completely.

The leaf-losing kinds that have perennial roots, such as amaryllises, nerines, haemanthuses, and eucomises, are kept almost completely dry during their season of dormancy, although the soil is not permitted to become so devoid of moisture that the roots shrivel. Under good storage conditions (as when the pots are turned on their sides under a greenhouse bench or in a not too hot and dry cellar) there is usually sufficient moisture in the atmosphere to prevent excessive drying, but in a very dry atmosphere there is danger of desiccation and it may be desirable to soak the soil about once a month during the storage period.

## Repotting Bulbs That Have Perennial Roots

Repotting perennial-rooted bulbs is a simple operation. It is done at the beginning of the growing season. Twenty-four hours before repotting immerse the pot containing the bulbs in water for five to ten minutes and then let it drain.

Prepare the potting soil. Because this will not be renewed for several years it should be fertile and of coarse texture so that it will not pack tightly as a result of repeated watering and thus prevent the free passage of air. A rich loam is the best basis for such a soil. Grass sod taken from a fertile field and piled in a stack until its roots are dead but are still clearly visible as fibrous material is ideal. If this is unavailable rich garden topsoil from well-cultivated ground is a satisfactory substitute.

Add to the soil an equal bulk of coarse leafmold, compost, or peatmoss; half as much coarse sand; and half as much gritty material of a rougher character such as coal cinders (but not fine ashes), old broken brick, or crushed oyster shells. This gritty material should pass through a half-inch mesh and should be free of fine dust. For each bushel of ingredients add one quart of dried cow manure, one pint of coarse bone meal, and one pint of unleached wood ashes. Mix the whole thoroughly while it is in a just-moist but not wet condition and you will have a potting compost in which any permanent bulb will thrive. The moisture content of the mixture at mixing time is important. If it is dusty dry sprinkle a little water into successive layers as you turn it over; if it muddies your fingers spread it out and let it dry before mixing.

Begin the repotting operation by removing the plant from its pot. Next carefully pick out the old crocks (drainage material) from among the roots at the bottom of the root ball. If the plant is in need of dividing attend to this now in the manner described in Chapter 12. If not, pick away from the top of the root ball as much earth as you can remove with a pointed stick without damaging the roots. If you can pick any soil from the sides of the ball without harming the roots do so. The new soil will adhere more intimately to the root ball and new roots will develop faster if the sides of the ball are somewhat rough rather than smooth at potting time.

The pot into which the bulb is set should be clean and dry, but if it is a new one immerse it in water until bubbles cease to come from it; then let it dry.

If you do not do this you may have difficulty removing the plant from its pot at some future time because moist soil sticks to kiln-dry pots.

Adequate drainage is important. Place an inch of crocks over the drainage hole in the bottom of a five-inch pot, proportionately more in containers of larger diameter. Cover this drainage with coarse leaves, moss, or hay to prevent the soil from washing down; then throw in a little soil and make it firm. Now set the plant to be potted in position. It should be centered and at such a level that when potting is completed its old root ball will be covered with a quarter- to a half-inch of new soil and the new soil surface will be sufficiently below the rim of the pot to allow for watering. This means about three quarters of an inch below in the case of a five-inch pot, more for those of larger sizes.

The new pot will ordinarily be about an inch larger all around than the old container. Only in the case of very large specimens should it be as much as two inches bigger all around. If the roots are few and in poor condition it may be desirable to pot the plant into a receptacle of the same size as the one from which it was taken or even into a smaller one. This is called "reducing." If reducing is necessary, remove all dead roots and as much of the old soil as you can conveniently pick away and then transfer the plant to a container just large enough to hold the roots that remain, with a little space allowed all around for new soil.

Whether the plant is reduced or promoted, the next move is to fill the space between the root ball and the new pot with prepared soil and to ram it with a lath or shaped potting stick. A good potting stick may be made by shaving down the lower eight inches of a foot-long piece of broom handle so that it has two flattened sides and is about three quarters of an inch thick along the shaved-down portion; the rounded upper end serves as a handle.

*Hybrid amaryllises are among the choicest bulbous plants for growing in the greenhouse or window garden. They are justly popular.*

*Freesias in many colors and in white may be grown in a cool, sunny greenhouse. These fragrant flowers are extremely useful for cutting.*

Ram the soil firmly but not really hard; it should be packed so firm that even by exerting pressure it is not possible to indent its surface noticeably with the finger. Finish the potting by making the surface level and roughening it slightly so that no potting stick or finger marks show.

It is usually well to delay watering for twenty-four or forty-eight hours and then to soak the newly potted plant thoroughly with a fine spray. If the bulb has foliage at potting time, keep it out of direct sunlight for two or three weeks afterward and spray the foliage daily with water. Avoid watering more often than is necessary to keep the soil just moist until roots have taken possession of the new soil. Give no fertilizer until the plant has filled its new pot with healthy roots.

## Repotting Bulbs That Have Annual Roots

Some annual-rooted bulbs such as tuberous begonias and gloxinias are potted singly, while others including freesias, oxalises, achimenes, and lachenalias are planted several together. Recommendations for each kind are listed under their names in alphabetical sequence in the second part of this book; so too are the special soil preferences of each.

Most annual-rooted bulbs that are normally planted several to a container are set in their final pots at planting time; they are not transferred to larger receptacles during their growing season. For these bulbs a nutritious soil must be supplied from the beginning. Annual-rooted bulbs of kinds planted singly are most often started in small pots and are repotted into larger ones as growth proceeds. These may be started in such a medium as peatmoss and be transferred to progressively richer soils at each potting.

The treatment of freesias well illustrates the procedure adopted with most annual-rooted bulbs that are planted several together. Achimenes and some of their relatives are exceptions to this procedure and for them special recommendations are given in the cultural directions in the second part of this book. The treatment of tuberous begonias illustrates the method of handling annual-rooted bulbs that are potted singly.

For freesias a soil consisting of mellow loam (topsoil), coarse sand, and leafmold or humus mixed in such proportions that the result is porous and rather sandy and will pass water readily is best. It should not contain so much organic matter that it is likely to remain wet and spongy. Bone meal added at the rate of a pint to each bushel of the mixture is advisable. The pots or pans are drained by placing an inch of crocks in the bottom of each and covering these with a layer of rough leaves or moss to keep the soil from washing down. An inch of dried cow manure may be placed on top of the drainage with advantage. The freesia bulbs should be set with their tops half an inch below soil level, and half an inch of space should be left between the soil surface and the rim of the pot to allow for watering.

The planting procedure consists of filling soil into the container, firming it with the fingers, and leveling it at a suitable distance below the rim. The bulbs are then spaced on this at appropriate distances and are covered to the required depth with soil packed with the fingers.

After planting, the soil is soaked with a fine spray of water and the pots are placed in a cool and light, but not sunny, place. The soil must never be permitted to dry but great care must be taken not to sour it and spoil its texture by overwatering, which is easily done until roots have ramified through it. One excellent method of avoiding the necessity for frequent watering is to cover the newly planted pots with an inch or two of moss and to keep this in position until new shoots push through.

Tuberous begonia bulbs are best started by planting them fairly closely together just below surface level in a pan or shallow box containing a loose mixture of peatmoss and sand or leafmold and sand. This should be kept moist but not saturated. In a temperature of sixty-five to seventy-five degrees roots soon begin to grow. When a good mass of these one to two inches long have developed, each bulb is potted into a well-drained pot just large enough to hold it comfortably with a reasonable space around it for new soil; this usually means a container four or five inches in diameter.

The soil used at this potting should be rich in organic matter, loose, and spongy, one tenth to one eighth of its bulk consisting of dried cow manure, the rest of loam, peatmoss or leafmold, and sand. A pint of bone meal to each bushel should be added, as well as a good sprinkling of chopped charcoal. The latter is of great aid in preventing soil that contains a good deal of organic matter from becoming sour under the influence of repeated watering.

The soil should be packed only moderately firmly and immediately after potting it should be watered thoroughly with a fine spray. A warm and humid atmosphere favors rapid establishment of the newly potted plant. As soon as the roots begin to mat around the outside of this first pot, transfer the plant to one an inch larger all around (that is, to one that measures two inches more in diameter). This may be the "final" pot or it may be desirable to repot it once again into a still larger container, but under no circumstances should potting

*In the North alstroemerias grown in the cool greenhouse provide quantities of beautiful cut flowers.*

be done so late in the season that there is no opportunity for roots to fill the pot before the end of the growing season. Use a soil similar to that used for the earlier potting but of coarser grade. Do not sift it through a fine sieve. Take great care not to disturb the roots when repotting during the active growing season. Keep the newly potted specimens shaded and out of moving air currents until they "get over the shift," as gardeners say. Care in watering is especially necessary after each repotting until the new soil is permeated with roots, but extreme dryness must, of course, be avoided.

### Feeding Potted Bulbs

Like all pot-grown plants bulbs respond to intelligent fertilization. In general the particular fertilizer used is less important than how and when it is applied. The most satisfactory types to mix with soil in which bulbs are to be planted are slow-acting organics such as bone meal, cottonseed meal, hoof-and-horn dust, and tankage. Unleached wood ashes are also good. But for supplementary feedings that are applied to plants already potted, more readily soluble, quicker-acting fertilizers are preferred. There is little to be gained from sprinkling bone meal, for instance, on the surface soil of a potted bulb!

There are on the market many highly soluble complete fertilizers compounded especially for house plants. Any of these is suitable for feeding bulbs;

*In milder parts of the country tuberous begonias can be grown to great perfection in a lath house.*

*Calla-lilies in white, yellow, and pink are popular greenhouse plants and in favorable situations may be grown in the window garden.*

so too is a liquid made by steeping a burlap sack of cow manure or chicken manure in water for a week or ten days and then diluting the resultant liquid until it is only faintly odorous and is not darker in color than weak tea.

Important points to bear in mind are to use supplementary fertilizers in liquid form, to use them often during the season when the plants will benefit from them, and to use them weaker than generally recommended for pot plants. You will not go far wrong if you apply complete commercial fertilizers twice as often and twice as dilute as the manufacturers recommend.

Healthy, well-rooted, vigorous bulbs in pots will benefit from feeding twice a week during their active growing season.

There are a few other points to observe. Never apply fertilizer to a plant that has not filled its container with healthy roots. Never fertilize a bulb that is going to rest. Never fertilize a bulb that is decidedly dry. In the latter case soak the soil with water first and two or three hours afterward with the fertilizer solution.

## Permanent Bulbs for House and Greenhouse

One of the best-known permanent bulbs for indoor culture is the amaryllis (or *Hippeastrum,* to give its correct botanical name). Gorgeous hybrid kinds have been derived from species that occur wild in the warmer parts of South

America. They are massive in appearance, and well-grown examples will each year produce one or more stout, erect stalks each having up to four, and occasionally more, huge crimson, orange-red, red and white, pink, pink and white, or pure white flaring trumpets which remain attractive for a considerable period. A fine amaryllis, well grown, is decidedly a conversation piece.

Amaryllises are displayed to best advantage when placed so that their flowers are seen at about eye level. They are splendid for arranging in groups. Because their foliage is often sparse at flowering time (late winter and spring) it is helpful if ferns, asparaguses, or other light foliage plants are available for placing among them.

Much less conspicuous than amaryllises, and needing a cooler temperature, is another winter-bloomer, the South African veltheimia, which has a flower head that suggests the hardy poker plant but is of softer hue, while the plant itself is much less gross. Dusty pink perhaps best describes its flower color. It is charming in a sunny window.

Callas are better adapted to greenhouse cultivation than to growing as house plants, but the white and pink ones may be brought to bloom in a cool sunroom. The yellows are more difficult. Callas are chiefly winter- and springbloomers. They last well when transferred from the greenhouse to a sunny position in the home if the location is not too warm and dry. Only when their pots are set at floor level can the taller kinds be enjoyed at their best, but the baby calla, with white flowers, and the pink calla (the "pink" usually leans strongly to lavender) are short enough to be used at ordinary window height.

Early spring brings clivias in bloom. These are tricky to flower out of a greenhouse but it can be done, and it is certainly worth every effort to persuade these handsome South Africans to develop and expand their lovely heads of orange-yellow flowers, each head fully as large as that of a rhododendron. Clivias should be exhibited near a low window or in a sunroom placed slightly, if at all, above the floor.

*Caladiums come in a wide variety of foliage color and may be had at their best from late winter until well into the fall.*

*Tuberous anemones are excellent for cut flowers. The St. Brigid type is here pictured. In cold climates they must be grown in a cool, sunny greenhouse.*

In five- or six-inch pots—and highly creditable examples can be grown in such containers—tuberous begonias are desirable house plants for summer display, but, alas, they are not suitable for regions where scorching summers prevail. Even where nights are fairly cool they will probably respond best if you keep them on a cool, lightly shaded porch for most of the summer and bring them indoors on special occasions only. Perhaps you can grow sufficient begonias to permit a rotation system that gives each individual a couple of weeks' tour of duty in the house followed by a recuperation period of two to four weeks on the porch.

The flowers of tuberous begonias exhibit astonishing variation in color, form, and size. Even the poorest are lovely, but for indoor display—where each plant is scrutinized individually—select the finest. Bulbs are not usually sold in named varieties—the dealer ordinarily labels them according to general flower form and approximate color. Not until they bloom can you decide which are choicest—cherish the good ones and give them special care so that you may be sure to have them in succeeding years.

Fancy-leaved caladiums are among the most satisfactory plants to grow as summer decorations. They are easy to handle; they remain attractive over a long period; they are available in many distinct and beautiful varieties; and they may be used in containers of widely varying sizes, the bulbs being planted singly if the receptacle is five or six inches in diameter, two or more together if it is larger. For the best effect fancy-leaved caladiums should be grown in pans rather than in deep pots, those the florist calls "azalea pans" being eminently suitable.

The jack-in-the-pulpit-like blooms of caladiums are interesting but last briefly and are more or less hidden by the foliage. These plants are admired for their gorgeous leaves rather than for their flowers.

No consideration of summer-flowering bulbs suitable for cultivation in pots would be acceptable without mention of gloxinias. These are plants for the greenhouse, for choice positions in the home, and, in summertime, for locating on shaded, sheltered porches. Their foliage must be protected from getting wet. Their velvety trumpet flowers come in a rich array of colors and in white. They are displayed to perfect advantage above large, softly furry, dark green simple leaves. Gloxinias are choice flowers; there is an unmistakable air of quality about them.

Less well known than gloxinias and generally of more restricted usefulness, although not less beautiful, are some of their botanical relatives. Here belong achimenes, which have pretty flowers of lavender, purple-blue, white, red, and pink . . . flowers that somehow seem to remind one of pansies although they do not really look like them except for the fact that their faces are flat. Isolomas, or kohlerias, are kin of gloxinias. They are hairy plants with leafy stems two to three feet tall and have drooping, tubular, spotted-reddish flowers that possess considerable charm. *Corytholoma* and *Smithiantha* are the botanical names of other gloxinia relatives that older gardeners knew as gesnerias. These are plants for the advanced amateur rather than for the beginner; they really need a greenhouse for their successful culture. If you are adventurous and can provide the conditions they need by all means try them. *Corytholoma cardinalis* has bright green leaves and brilliant scarlet flowers in fall and early winter— just the right colors for Christmas and it can be bloomed then in the greenhouse! Well-known specimens are a welcome change from better-known "Christmas plants." *Smithiantha zebrina* and *Smithiantha cinnabarina* are summer-bloomers having large, richly colored, hairy leaves and handsome flowers.

The number of vines that grow from bulbs is limited and so we especially appreciate the glory-lily (*Gloriosa*) which can be trained to enframe a window, to clothe a trellis, or to attach itself to other suitable supports. Over a long summer season it delights us with its elegant, lively red and yellow flowers that are as useful for cutting as they are decorative on the vine.

A close relative of *Gloriosa* that will interest the plant lover even though it is not as showy is the yellow-flowered *Littonia modesta*. There is, by the way, also a beautiful buff-yellow-flowered variety of gloriosa that is rare and is well worth seeking; it is called *Golutea*.

September and October bring into bloom the first of the many winter-flowering bulbs that are natives of South Africa—the nerines. These are plants for the cool greenhouse. If you can provide such accommodation few bulbs give greater reward for less trouble. As cut flowers and as decorative pot plants for locating when in bloom on tables and at other vantage points they are superb.

Among bulbs that bloom in winter and spring are a group of South African natives that need decidedly cool conditions and the full exposure to sunshine. They are plants for the greenhouse or, if conditions are very favorable, for the slightly heated sun porch; they cannot be expected to thrive in living rooms.

Here belong fragrant freesias, that nowadays may be had in such a wonderful color range, and the closely allied baboon flowers (babianas) with cupped flowers in tones of lilac, violet, red, and yellow. Sparaxises, slender graceful ixias—which range in hue from near-white through yellow and orange to red and purple and, in the case of *Ixia viridiflora*, include a wonderful metallic green that reminds one of a color in a peacock's tail feather—tritonias, lach-

*Nerines are subjects for the cool greenhouse. They bear flowers of brilliant scarlet, pink, or white in fall and winter.*

Lycoris aurea *is a choice plant for cultivating in the greenhouse.*

enalias, lapeirousias, gladiolus-like watsonias, and montbretia-like chasmanthes belong here. So do "baby" gladioluses and gladiolus species (unimproved kinds from the wild), the best known of which is fragrant *Gladiolus tristis* which has tall spikes of soft-yellow flowers.

South Africans for spring bloom that are easier to grow in the home than some of those mentioned above are several oxalises, the most frequently seen of which are the clear-yellow-flowered one popularly called Bermuda buttercup (*Oxalis cernua*) and the pink, lavender, and white varieties of *Oxalis variabilis* that form the "Grand Duchess" series. These must have full sun and fairly cool conditions. They are excellent window garden plants.

This by no means exhausts the list of bulbs that may be successfully cultivated in pots in the greenhouse and home. If you crave greater variety, try *Ornithogalum arabicum*, which has tall stems topped by clusters of black-centered white flowers that smell richly of ripening apples . . . or the South African chincherinchee, the cut blooms of which last so long that shipments are made from its home country to the United States and the flowers remain attractive for weeks after arrival. The white-flowered flowering onion called *Allium neapolitanum* is dainty and easy to grow. If you can provide tropical greenhouse conditions by all means cultivate the Eucharis lily—it will reward you with two or three crops of sweetly fragrant, excellently formed pristine flowers each year. Seek out, too, some of the bulbs belonging in the genera *Vallota, Sprekelia, Leucocoryne, Acidanthera, Haemanthus, Hymenocallis, Hedychium, Habranthus, Crinum, Brunsvigia, Chlidanthus, Scilla, Arum, Alstroemeria, Dierama,* and *Crinodonna* (*Amarcrinum*). If your taste runs to oddities you will find them among *Amorphophallus, Hydrosme, Schizobasopsis, Sauromatum,* and *Urginea*. Among bulbous plants can be found kinds to satisfy all tastes.

# 12 PROPAGATION OF BULBS

Methods of increasing bulbs are of primary importance to the grower who raises them for sale and to the connoisseur who wishes to multiply rare specimens. They are of interest also to home gardeners who wish to obtain stocks inexpensively or who would like to try some of the fascinating ways by which bulbs may be propagated. This discussion does not concern commercial practices.

Bulbs are raised from seeds and from parts of other bulbs which are segregated from the parents and are grown as new individuals. This latter practice is termed "vegetative propagation." Only by vegetative propagation is it possible to multiply hybrids and highly developed horticultural varieties true to their types; seedlings raised ordinarily from such plants differ markedly from, and are often inferior to, their parents.

Seeds may be used to propagate natural species and most natural varieties (that is to say, kinds that are not highly developed horticulturally but which are cultivated in the same forms as they are found in the wild), to produce new hybrid and new cross-bred varieties and, in some cases, to raise worth-while mixtures in which varieties of color, form, size, or other factors are clearly evident and are not objectionable.

A gorgeous hybrid amaryllis or a variety of daffodil such as "King Alfred" or "Aerolite" will not reproduce true from seeds, but seeds of the regal lily or of the common grape-hyacinth (which are natural species) produce plants that duplicate their parents. If one intended to attempt to raise a hybrid between the regal lily and some other kind of lily the only way to go about it would be to pollinate the flower of one with pollen from the other, to obtain fertile seeds, and to raise from these the hybrid progeny. A gay swarm of tuberous begonias or of dwarf dahlias, none exactly like their parents nor any two precisely alike (at least genetically), are readily raised from seeds and are for many garden purposes as useful as selected varieties grown from vegetative propagations.

LEFT: *Clivias are choice evergreen plants adapted for greenhouse, conservatory, and sunroom.*

RIGHT: *The curious Jacobean-lily is related to the amaryllis (Hippeastrum) and requires the same general care but thrives in temperatures a few degrees lower.*

## Seeds

Seeds of hardy bulbs are usually best handled by sowing them in a cold frame either as soon as they are ripe or in early fall in a gritty well-drained soil that contains an abundance of leafmold or peatmoss. If the quantity is large the floor of the frame may be prepared as the seed bed; otherwise sow in flats, pots, or pans and keep these in the frame. Pots and pans should be buried to their rims in sand or cinders so that their contents do not dry too rapidly. Cover the seeds to two or three times their own diameter with soil. Shade the frame until germination takes place, which in most cases will occur the following spring but in some instances not until a year later, and keep the soil evenly moist but not saturated. Winter freezing benefits the seeds of hardy bulbs but excessive alternate freezing and thawing may disturb them more than is desirable; to circumvent this protect the seed bed with a light cover of salt hay, excelsior, or evergreen branches after the soil has frozen. Seeds of hardy bulbs may also be sown indoors in late winter, in well-drained flats or pots that contain a sandy, peaty soil. Keep the containers in a greenhouse where the night temperature is about fifty degrees.

Seeds of bulbs that are not hardy should be sown indoors in well-drained pots, pans, or flats. The best time to sow is a little before mature bulbs of the same kinds normally start into growth. Thus the seeds of freesias, sparaxises, and other bulbs that naturally begin growing in fall are sown in September, those of amaryllises (*Hippeastrum*) and tuberous begonias in January or February.

Seedlings of a few kinds grow rapidly—dahlias, for instance, are transplanted within a month of appearing above ground and are handled exactly as are petunias and tomatoes—but most bulbs do not make such rapid development in their young stages. In the vast majority of cases it is advisable to allow the young plants to complete their first season's growth without disturbance in the seed bed and to move them to new soil only at the very beginning of their second season of growth. A few bulbs benefit from being left for two seasons in the seed bed. Because of the long time that the seedlings are likely to remain undisturbed it is essential to sow thinly, to space the seeds so that the young plants will not be unduly crowded before they are ready for transplanting.

Nearly all bulb seedlings die down when the natural season of rest for their kind comes, but some (amaryllises, for example) may be prevented from going dormant if they are kept moist and warm . . . and this is advantageous because it considerably reduces the time that elapses before the first flower appears. After the first blooming normal resting periods are honored. Some bulbs bloom in as little as a year or eighteen months from the time the seeds are sown; others take several years.

## Separation of Offsets

Many bulbs increase naturally by the production of bulblets (small bulbs) and of new bulbs which develop alongside, near by, or in place of older ones. By separating these and planting them in favorable locations new stocks are easily acquired. Bulblets should not be removed until they have completed at least one full growing season attached to their parents. When they are separated it is advisable to plant them under especially favorable conditions where they will be encouraged to increase in size and attain maturity as quickly as possible. Depending upon their kind, this may mean accommodating them in a nursery bed, in a cold frame, or (in a greenhouse) community pots or flats; planting them individually in small pots is not generally advisable.

Bulblets should always be planted more shallowly and closer together than mature bulbs of the same kinds and always in sandy, light soil. A good general rule is to cover them to two to three times their own depth with soil . . . although some, such as amaryllises, are planted with their tops protruding. When they have grown to more mature size the young bulbs are replanted at a greater depth and with more adequate spacing. Gladioluses, crocuses, and other kinds that have bulbs technically known as "corms" produce in addition to new bulbs numerous "cormels" or tiny bulbs about the base of the mother bulb. These have very hard shells and new growth will develop from them evenly and quickly if they are soaked in water for several hours immediately prior to planting. They are planted or sown in spring in much the same manner as are seeds, after having been stored over winter in a cool, frost-free place mixed with barely moist peatmoss.

## Basal Cuttage

In Holland, where practically all large-flowered hyacinth bulbs are produced, these plants are propagated by injuring the bases of the bulbs in ways that cause each to develop a large number of bulblets. It is a method that can be applied to some other kinds of bulbs and is worth trying if rapid increase is desired and other techniques are not productive.

As applied to hyacinths, the bulbs are dug as soon as they are ripe in July and immediately three deep cross cuts (dividing the base into six wedge-shaped segments) are made with a sharp knife in the bottom of each or, alternatively, the entire base is scooped out leaving the interior of the bulb a hollow pointed dome. The injured bulbs are then spread out bottoms up, are covered with loose soil, and are allowed to remain for about three weeks while the cut surfaces heal and the cuts expand. They are next spread on benches or tables in storehouses where they remain until October, at which time they are planted in outdoor beds. The following June, when they are dug up, little or nothing remains of the mother bulb but as many as twenty or thirty sturdy small hyacinth bulbs are harvested.

Trilliums may be induced to increase by cutting a deep V-notch lengthwise along the upper side of the bulb and replanting it. This affords an effective means of propagating the double-flowered varieties.

## Bulbils, Tubercles, and Stem Bulblets

Some bulbs bear small bulbous growths on their stems above ground. These are known as bulbils or tubercles (depending upon whether they are technically tiny bulbs or small tubers). These form a ready means of propagation if they are planted at about the time they are naturally ready to fall from the stems. They should be covered to about twice their diameter with light soil. Among plants that bear aerial bulbils or tubercles are tiger lilies, *Begonia Evansiana*, and cinnamon vine.

A few plants that do not ordinarily produce bulbils can be induced to do so. If the stalks of certain stem-rooting lilies are severed just above the bulb and are potted and placed in a moist greenhouse they will develop them.

Tiny bulbs that form on the stems but below ground level, such as are produced by some lilies, are classed as bulblets although they have the same morphological origin as bulbils and may be used for propagation in the same way. The production of these stem bulblets by some lilies may be encouraged by jerking the stem from the bulb with a quick, positive twisting motion shortly after the flowers have faded and planting it at an angle of forty-five degrees

*The glory-lily is an excellent vine for the warm greenhouse or the window garden.*

with its lower twelve or fifteen inches buried in dryish soil in a location that is shaded from strong sun. By fall a crop of strong bulblets will have formed on the buried parts of the stems and these may then be removed and be planted in a nursery bed.

## Division

Division, which consists of cutting a single bulb or a clump of bulbs into two or more pieces each containing at least one bud or eye that is expected to produce top growth, is a popular method of securing increase of some kinds of bulbs. Dahlias, achimenes, cannas, and gloriosas are commonly treated in this way and tuberous begonias, gloxinias, caladiums, and some others may be. Division is done at the beginning of the growing season and it is usually best to subject the bulbs that are to be divided to sufficient warmth and moisture to induce the eyes to plump up and begin growing before actual cutting is done. This makes it much easier to carry out the operation without destroying eyes. Each division must consist of at least one strong eye attached to a good bulb or sizeable portion of a bulb. The cut surfaces should be dusted with powdered sulphur to discourage decay and the divisions should be planted immediately in loose, sandy, humusy soil that is kept moist but not wet, and be placed where the temperature is encouraging to growth and the atmosphere is agreeably moist.

## Bulb Cuttings

Bulb cuttings really represent a special type of division that can be used for many true bulbs (dahlias, cannas, begonias, etc., are actually tubers or tuberous roots) and is best known because of its employment in the propagation of amaryllises. The author has successfully increased the following bulbs by means of bulb cuttings and there are undoubtedly many more that are susceptible to this means of multiplication: *Albuca, Chasmanthe, Cooperia, Haemanthus, Hippeastrum* (amaryllis), *Hymenocallis, Lycoris, Narcissus, Nerine, Pancratium, Phaedranassa, Scilla, Sprekelia,* and *Urceolina.*

The bulb-cutting method consists of taking a mature bulb and quartering it lengthways with a sharp knife, then cutting each quarter lengthways into two or more wedges each including a portion of the basal plate of the bulb; these wedges are further divided by sliding a knife down between each third or fourth pair of concentric scale-rings of which the bulb is formed and cutting through the basal plate at the bottom. The resulting fractions are bulb cuttings. Each consists of segments of three or four scales attached to a small piece of basal plate.

The bulb cuttings are planted vertically in a mixture of peatmoss and sand with just their tips showing above the surface and are kept just moist and in a temperature that is somewhat warmer than that which mature bulbs of the same kinds require. In a matter of weeks, or at most a few months, small plump new bulbs will have grown from the basal plate portion and will be nosing out from between the segments of bulb scales and sending strong new roots from their bases. They may then be transferred to flats of light soil to continue their further development. The author's experiments with bulb cuttings have all been carried out in late summer, the cuttings having been made generally in August. Here is a good field for further experimentation regarding kinds that may be so propagated, times of the year that are most favorable, and the best methods of handling.

## Cuttings

Some bulbs may be propagated from cuttings consisting of pieces of stem with leaves attached, in the same manner as are geraniums and many other popular plants. Of these, dahlias and tuberous-rooted begonias are the kinds most commonly grown. The cuttings of these are usually made from young shoots that develop directly from the bulb. They should be taken off just as soon as they are long enough, which means when they are two to three inches long. It is better to use the entire shoot than to snip the top off a shoot that has grown too long and employ it as a cutting. On the other hand it is quite satisfactory to use the upper parts of the stems of achimenes as cuttings. In some cases—dahlias, for example—it is an advantage to take a sliver of the old bulb to form the base of the cutting. In all cases the base of the cutting should be prepared by cutting it cleanly across with a keen knife and this cut should be made, except where a sliver of the old bulb is retained, a short distance below a node (stem joint). The lowermost leaves (which on cuttings of young shoots arising from the bulb will be rudimentary) are removed and the cutting is planted in firmly packed sand or sand and peatmoss or in not firmly packed vermiculite, is well watered and is placed in a propagating case in a greenhouse, in a terrarium or other place where a humid atmosphere can be maintained. Here the cuttings remain until roots an inch or so long have developed; then they are potted individually, returned to a close atmosphere for a few days, and then gradually hardened to the conditions that established plants of their particular kinds favor. If the cuttings are provided with bottom heat (gentle warmth that keeps the rooting medium at a temperature five to ten degrees higher than it would otherwise be) rooting will be accomplished faster.

During their period of rooting the cuttings are shaded from strong sun but are afforded good light. It is important that cuttings be made sufficiently early in the growing season for them to form bulbs large enough to persist through

*Here is a good example of a modern gloxinia, one that is deep red and has an attractive white edge to its petals.*

the dormant season before this begins. It is perhaps worth noting that the author has successfully employed the leafy crown that tops the flower spike of *Eucomis* as a cutting. He does not recall having heard of this being done before.

## Leaf Cuttings

Certain bulbs are easily multiplied by using single leaves or portions of leaves as cuttings and by planting them under conditions recommended for regular stem cuttings. Gloxinias, achimenes, smithianas, isolomas, and others in the gesneria family belong here. In the lily family hyacinths, lachenalias, and probably some others freely reproduce from portions of leaves that are cut across horizontally and are planted with their lowermost inch in sand that is kept just moist but not wet. Undoubtedly there are others that will respond in similar fashion. Clivias are reported to respond to this method.

With the gesneriads it is advisable to use whole leaves as cuttings and to plant them at an angle of forty-five degrees with their bases half an inch deep in sand, a mixture of sand and peatmoss, or vermiculite. If stock is scarce it is often possible to obtain more than one offspring from each leaf by cutting the main veins across on the undersides of the leaf at two or three places and then placing the leaf horizontally underside down on a bed of peatmoss or peatmoss and sand. Each cut will generate a new young bulb. The small bulbs formed from leaf cuttings of these plants do not develop leaves until after their first dormant period; the bulbs only are produced the season the cuttings are inserted.

Cuttings of lachenalias and hyacinths should each consist of the upper few inches of a leaf. The bottom of each cutting should be cut squarely across. The cuttings are then inserted half an inch deep in a sand bed.

## Scales

In a sense scales are a type of leaf cutting, for scales are simply rudimentary leaves. It is in the propagation of lilies that they are chiefly employed, but fritillarias and other bulbs formed of scales that lap each other like shingles on a roof, can also be grown from scales. In this method parent bulbs are dug as soon as they are through blooming, the thick outer scales are pulled off entire, without breaking their bases, and are planted at once, before they have any chance to dry, in a bed of just-moist peatmoss and sand or in sandy soil in a cold frame or in flats that are kept in a cellar or other dry place until the young bulbs have formed. Excessive wetness will cause loss by rotting. The new bulbs will have developed nicely in from six weeks to three months and those planted in flats may then be set out in well-drained beds outdoors at a depth of about two inches. When winter comes they should be mulched heavily, the mulch being removed with the coming of spring.

# TULIPS

Tulips are classified into sixteen divisions based on flower form and growth habits. This selection of varieties illustrates some of the divisions.

1   2   3   4

DIVISION II: SINGLE EARLY TULIPS

1. *Olympiade*

2. *Ibis*

3. *Keizerskroon*

4. *De Wet*

5. *Prince of Austria*

6. *Couleur de Cardinal*

5          6

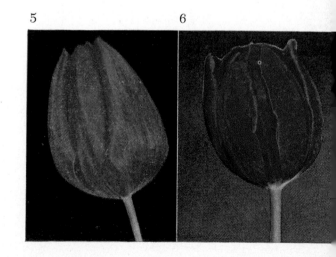

DIVISION III

DOUBLE EARLY TULIPS

7. *Marechal Niel (Marechal Neil)*

8. *Willemsoord*

9. *Dante*

10. *Orange Nassau*

11. *Peach Blossom*

DIVISION IV

MENDEL TULIPS

12. *Her Grace*

13. *Orange Wonder*

14. *Krelage's Triumph*

15. *John Gay*

16. *Van der Erden*

17. *White Sail*

7       8

9      10      11

12          13          14          15

16          17

DIVISION V

TRIUMPH TULIPS

18. *Korneforos*

19. *Elmus*

20. *Rhineland*

21. *Bandoeng*

22. *Telescopium*

23. *Glory of Noordwijk*

24. *Bruno Walter*

25. *Princess Beatrix*

18          19          20          21

22                    23                  24                 25

26                    27                  28                 29

30                    31                  32                 33

| DIVISION VI | DIVISION VII |
|---|---|
| COTTAGE TULIPS | DUTCH BREEDER TULIPS |

26. *Northern Queen*     34. *Tantalus*

27. *Advance*            35. *Louis XIV*

28. *G. W. Leak*         36. *Georges Grappe*

29. *White City*         37. *Indian Chief*

30. *Marshal Haig*       38. *Orange Delight*

31. *Mrs. Moon*          39. *Dillenburg*

32. *Princess Margaret Rose*

33. *Mother's Day*

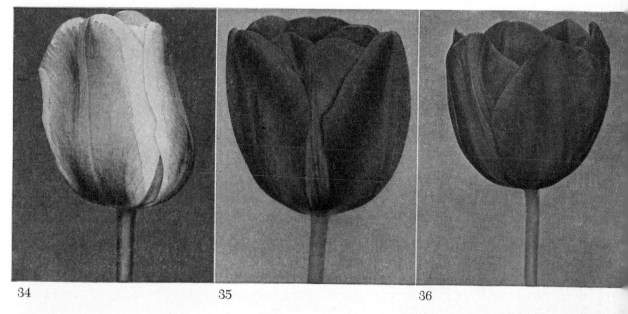

34          35          36

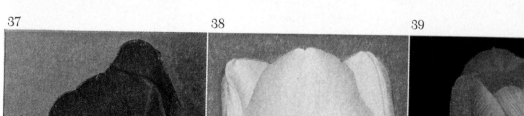

37          38          39

40          41          42          43

44          45          46          47

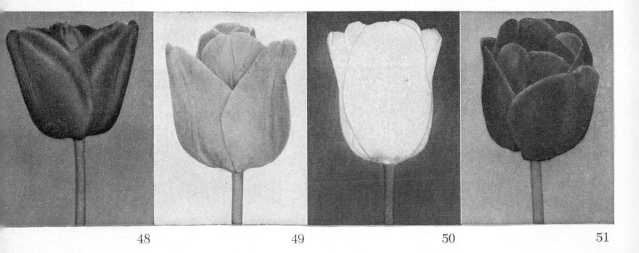

48          49          50          51

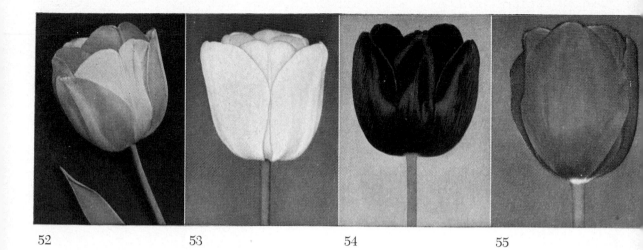

52                53               54               55

### DIVISION IX: DARWIN TULIPS

| | |
|---|---|
| 40. *Demeter* | 48. *Bartigon* |
| 41. *Peach* | 49. *Scotch Lassie* |
| 42. *Charles Needham* | 50. *Niphetos* |
| 43. *Smiling Queen* | 51. *Pride of Haarlem* |
| 44. *Aristocrat* | 52. *Insurpassable* |
| 45. *The Bishop* | 53. *Zwanenburg* |
| 46. *Golden Age* | 54. *Queen of the Night* |
| 47. *William Pitt* | 55. *Margaux* |

56           57

### DIVISION XII
### REMBRANDT TULIPS

56. *Cordell Hull*

57. *Montgomery*

DIVISION XIV
PARROT TULIPS

58. *Orange Favorite*

59. *Violet Queen*

60. *Therese*

61. *Fantasy*

62. *Blue Parrot*

63. *Sunshine*

58

59          60

61      62      63

64                      65                      66

67

# 13 KEEPING BULBS HEALTHY

>·)··)··)··)··)··)··)··)··)··)··)··)··)··)··)··)··)··)··)··)··)··)··)··)··)··)··)··)··)··)··)··)··)··)··)··)··)··)··)··)··)··)··)··)··)··)··)··)··)··)··)··)··)··)··)··)··)··)··)··)··)··)··)··)··)··)··)·

Poor health of bulbs in the home garden is more often caused by unfavorable soil or unsuitable location than by disease organisms or by insects or other small creatures. However, diseases and pests are sometimes troublesome and not all the latter are minute, unless mice and rabbits can be so termed. One thing is certain: bulbs planted in good, well-drained soil, in favorable locations, and well looked after in such matters as fertilizing, watering, mulching, and winter covering are much more likely to be healthy than are those less suitably located and less admirably tended.

It is a first responsibility of the gardener to detect signs of ill health early. It is useless waiting until an infection or infestation has done serious damage before doing something about it. Be curious. Be inquisitive. Examine your plants frequently and critically and at the first suspicion that something is amiss probe further. Correct diagnosis is of the utmost importance. It is a waste of time to spray insecticide on a plant infested with virus disease, to attempt to control nematodes with Bordeaux mixture, or to use rotenone dust trying to eliminate botrytis disease.

If a bulb is sickly and you are satisfied that it is not just yellowing naturally prior to going to rest and that the cause is not an obviously unsuitable soil or situation and if you cannot find, even with the aid of a hand lens, insects (interpreting the word in a broad sense to include other small animal life as well as true insects), then suspect disease. Diseases are usually more difficult for the amateur to identify than are insects. But be it disease, insect, or other unknown factor, if you cannot surely determine what is causing your bulbs to be sickly dig up a fair sample including roots, pack it carefully, and send it to the plant pathologist at your State Agricultural Experiment Station with a covering letter giving the name of the bulb, the culture it has received, and your observations of the symptoms which you believe indicate ill health. Ask for diagnosis and advice. You will receive a courteous reply and there will be no charge for the service.

When a disease or insect pest that requires more than simple control meas-

156

ures strikes, the home gardener will be wise to dig up the affected bulbs and burn them. Elaborate controls requiring special equipment are best left to the commercial bulb raiser who has a large investment in his stock. Good sanitation (the prompt picking and burning of dead leaves, the removal of weeds and trash in the vicinity of the garden, the early control of easy-to-handle pests, etc.) and the prompt elimination of affected individuals that are not likely to respond to treatment will go far toward keeping bulb plantings vigorous and thrifty.

Having determined what is wrong with sickly or damaged bulbs take vigorous measures to bring them back to health or destroy them. The commonest causes of trouble are here discussed.

## Insects and Other Small Creatures

Aphids or plant lice are soft-bodied slow-moving insects, green, brown, or whitish or blackish, with more or less pear-shaped bodies, slender legs, and with or without wings. They are easily visible and congregate on the young shoots and stems, on the undersides of leaves, and on the bulbs. They suck the plant's juices, cause debility and often distortion, and transmit virus diseases. They are easily eliminated by contact sprays and dusts and, in the greenhouse, by nicotine fumigation. Nicotine, rotenone, and pyrethrum used as sprays or dusts are effective.

Thrips are minute active insects barely visible without a hand lens. They are slender, short legged, and move with a peculiar weaving motion. They obtain plant juices by scraping the surfaces of leaves, petals, and other tissues with their mouth parts. This activity usually results in a streaky silvery, gray, brown, or other discoloration. Thrips hide beneath bulb scales, in flower sheaths and other out-of-the-way places. Search for them assiduously. They are especially likely to occur on amaryllises (*Hippeastrum*), gladioluses, hymenocallises, gloxinias, lilies, and dahlias. Effective control measures are repeated spraying with a DDT plant spray or a nicotine spray and, in the case of infected bulbs, by dusting them with 5 per cent DDT powder.

Mites are not true insects, a technicality that depends in part upon the fact that they have eight rather than six legs. They are white, yellowish, or reddish. Some are too small to be seen by the naked eye; others are just visible. The bulb mite, which is large enough to be seen, infests the bulbs of amaryllises, crocuses, eucharises, freesias, gladioluses, hyacinths, lilies, narcissuses, tulips, and other plants. It is most abundant on rotted bulbs and it spreads the rot infection. Recommended procedures are to destroy seriously infested bulbs and to treat suspected ones by immersing them when dormant for ten minutes in a nicotine sulphate solution (two teaspoons of Black Leaf 40 to a gallon of water) maintained at 122 degrees F., or by dusting them with a 2 per cent nicotine dust and keeping them in tightly closed paper bags for a few days. Some of the newer miticides (Aramite, Azo Fume, Dimite, Dow Metacide, Hexatox, Ovatram, and others) are probably effective. Cyclamen mites and broad mites attack cyclamens and sometimes other bulbs, causing puckering of the foliage and distortion of the flowers. They are too minute to be seen by the unaided eye and are nearly transparent, glassy white, or pale green. Dusting with Azo Fume, Dimite, and probably with some other modern miticides is effective. Badly infested plants should be destroyed. Red spider mites congregate chiefly on the undersides of leaves and can be seen with just the naked eye as they move and scurry along the slightly mealy cobwebs they spin. They are yellow-ish or reddish and cause the leaves upon which they feed to become yellowish or reddish in a peculiar "peppered" pattern. Red spider mites propagate rapidly when the atmosphere is hot and dry and where air circulation is poor. Modern miticides destroy them, spraying with nicotine insecticides eliminates them, and frequent spraying with clear water is a great deterrent, but the effective-ness of all of these depends upon applying them with sufficient force to break through the webby mats under which these pests hide and upon doing it with sufficient thoroughness to wet all the undersurfaces as well as the upper sur-faces of the leaves.

Mealybugs are easily visible, slow-moving insects of oval shape that are cov-ered with a white mealy or cottony covering. They tend to live in colonies and are most likely to be found on amaryllises, urgineas, calla-lilies, nerines, bulbs usually grown indoors; but they may also infest the bulbs of gladioluses and some other outdoor kinds. They are given to hiding among the bases of the leaves near the neck of the bulb and on the bulbs themselves, often concealed under loose skin. They cause distortion and discoloration of the foliage, weak leaf and shoot growth, and shriveling of the bulbs. The best treatment is to re-move the bugs by sponging the foliage, brushing out the leaf bases and clean-ing all loose scales from the bulbs. Dip the sponges and brushes in a nicotine insecticide and in severe cases soak the bulbs for two hours in water containing Black Leaf 40 at the rate of two teaspoons to the gallon, held at 100 degrees F.

Bulb flies give rise to maggots, those of the lesser bulb fly being grayish or yellowish, wrinkled, to half an inch long, and many together in each bulb . . . those of the narcissus bulb fly being white or yellowish, fat, wrinkled, and from half to three quarters of an inch long, and usually only one or two to a bulb. The grubs gnaw out the centers of narcissuses, amaryllises, galtonias, lilies, tulips, hyacinths, and some other kinds. Seriously excavated bulbs are lighter and softer than normal ones; they should be promptly destroyed. Commercial control is achieved by submerging the bulbs for two to four hours (depending upon their size) in water maintained at a constant temperature of between 110 and 111.5 degrees F.

Nematodes or eelworms are microscopic wormlike creatures that invade the roots, bulbs, and leaves of many species, causing foliage to be distorted and streaked and growth to be puny. Prompt destruction of affected bulbs and re-fraining from planting new bulbs in infested soil for two or three years or until it has been sterilized are the most practical controls for amateurs to exercise. Commercial growers use hot water immersion control as they do for bulb flies.

Soil may be sterilized by using chloropicrin, DDT, formaldehyde, or by baking or steaming.

Leaf hoppers, wedge-shaped insects that are easily seeable and that jump when disturbed, affect dahlias especially, causing them to "burn" in triangular spots at the ends of each leaflet and the leaf margins to roll inward and become brown. The plants are seriously stunted as a result and may not bloom. Spraying with DDT is effective.

Stem borers are grubs that tunnel in dahlias, gladioluses, and lilies causing considerable damage. By the time serious harm is done it is too late to save the stem. Keep a sharp watch for telltale frass ("sawdust") protruding from holes in the stems and kill the borer inside by running a wire through it or by carefully slitting the stem and knifing it. Eliminate thick-stemmed weeds such as burdock from the vicinity of the garden. Burn all old stalks of dahlias and other thick-stemmed plants in fall. Frequent dusting with DDT is a preventative.

Ants do not eat plant parts but they do carry aphids, mealybugs, and scale insects from place to place and sometimes they seriously disturb bulbs by tunneling among their roots. Chlordane used as recommended by the manufacturer and various commercial ant baits destroy these creatures.

Scale insects occasionally occur on the stems and foliage of bulbs including cannas, caladiums, hymenocallises, and gladioluses. They appear as small gray, brown, or black "bumps" that do not move. Repeated spraying with nicotine insecticides or with Melathion brings them under control.

Slugs and snails work at night eating shoots and leaves. They leave yellowish, silvery, or sometimes nearly colorless shiny trails where they have been. They hide during the day in dark, dank places, under leaves, planks, loose bricks, in loose stone walls, in the bottoms of hedges, etc. Clean out their hiding places. Use one of the commercial slug baits or trap them by leaving loose shingles on the ground each with a piece of lettuce beneath. Each morning they may be collected from under the shingles and destroyed by dropping them in a strong solution of salt and water.

The tarnished plant bug is a flattish, oval, quarter-inch-long creature of brownish "tarnished" appearance with a yellow triangle with a black dot on the lower part of each side. It causes the buds of dahlias, gladioluses, and other flowers to die or open imperfectly. Control is difficult. Remove and burn all trash in the fall. Keep weeds down. Dust repeatedly with DDT or tobacco dust, or spray repeatedly with a nicotine insecticide.

Caterpillars of various types eat the foliage of dahlias, cannas, hymenocallises, amaryllises, and some other bulbs. Dusting with lead arsenate or calcium arsenate at the first evidence of damage is effective.

Cutworms of surface types are sizeable, fat, slow-moving caterpillars, grayish, brownish, or greenish, that live in the soil and nip off the shoots of newly planted dahlias and other young plants at about ground level. They feed at night and remain coiled up just beneath the ground surface by day. Tar paper collars made to surround young shoots are on the market and are effective preventatives. Poison baits put out in the evening according to manufacturers' directions are also good.

Wireworms are smooth, brown, slow-moving, hard-skinned creatures, worm-like and from half an inch to one and a half inches long that live in the soil and feed on bulbs of dahlias, gladioluses, and some other plants. They are usually most prevalent in land that has recently grown grass. Wireworms may be trapped by planting half potatoes cut side downwards two or three inches in the soil and spaced about a yard apart. Take the potatoes up after about a week and destroy the wireworms adhering to them.

Millepedes are many-legged brown worms up to an inch and three quarters long that wrap themselves in tight watch-spring coils. They are found in rotting bulbs but apparently they eat only rotted parts and do not harm sound bulbs although occasionally they damage seedlings and young roots. They may be baited by spreading Paris green on cut potatoes and placing these under boards (to prevent birds from being poisoned), or by soaking the soil with a 1:1000 solution of deadly poisonous bichloride of mercury.

## Larger Creatures

Such rodents as squirrels, chipmunks, and mice that burrow or dig may cause a good deal of disturbance to bulbs, and mice even eat certain kinds including tulips. Moles rarely if ever eat bulbs but they disturb them and make runs along which mice travel in search of tasty morsels, which are very likely to be your choicest bulbs.

There are no easy ways of circumventing these creatures. Trapping, poisoning, and shooting (where these measures are lawful) help. The presence of an ambitious, not too well-fed cat around the garden has a discouraging effect. In extreme cases bulbs may be planted in baskets of fine-mesh chicken wire to prevent mice from getting them, or entire beds may be protected by enclosing them in a foot-wide strip of fine wire mesh sunk vertically along the bed margins in such a way that about two inches protrude above ground and ten inches extend below.

Rabbits eat the foliage of crocuses and some other bulbs. Fencing these creatures out of the garden is the best insurance against damage. Shooting or trapping, where permissible, are alternatives. Friend cat may have an inhibiting effect.

Birds sometimes destroy the buds of crocuses and other small spring-flowering bulbs. It is said that they do this when water is not readily available. The answer seems to be to provide them with drinking water, and it might help too to make sure that they are fed.

## Diseases

Virus diseases, several of which are serious, affect bulbs, notably lilies, amaryllises, narcissuses, tulips, and dahlias and in addition irises, calla-lilies, ornithogalums, galtonias, hyacinths, gladioluses, and lachenalias as well as others. Most are characterized by a loss of a green color in the foliage in a mottled or ring-spot pattern and by a stunting of growth and sometimes other distortions. Affected plants never recover. All vegetative propagations from them are infected and they act as sources of infection because these diseases are transmitted by insects puncturing a healthy plant after an infected one and by knives and other contacts that permit the sap of a diseased plant to enter that of a healthy one. Since there are no cures the control of viruses depends upon planting healthy stock, promptly removing and burning infected bulbs, keeping down thrips, aphids, and other insects that transmit these diseases and eliminating weeds that may be sources of infection.

Botrytises are a group of fungi that cause "tulip fire" and "narcissus fire" as well as "gray mold blight" on amaryllises, dahlias, gladioluses, lilies, eucharises, snowdrops, and other bulbs and the "leaf and stalk blight" of jack-in-the-pulpits. Botrytis diseases are most prevalent in wet weather and where air circulation is poor. Tulip fire manifests itself by the presence of malformed leaves and shoots and by the presence on the leaves of large light withered patches (do not mistake frost injury for these) upon which a gray moldly growth develops. Leaves and petals are marked with small white or brown spots. Control consists of picking off and destroying occasional leaves or petals that show infection and of removing seriously affected bulbs promptly and in such a manner that they are not shaken to disperse spores onto other plants. Spraying with Fermate is helpful. Narcissus fire causes spotting and rotting of the flowers and foliage. It is reported from the Pacific Coast only. Remove infected flowers and leaves. Spray early in the season with Fermate. Gray mold blight is best combated by sanitary measures, the prompt picking of all faded flowers and rotted or blighted leaves. Drop these as collected into a paper bag and burn them. If the rot affects the base of the stem or the bulb dig it up and destroy it. Provide good ventilation and appropriate temperatures in the greenhouse and avoid wetting foliage except on bright days when it will soon dry.

Other molds, rots, and blights may infect both the underground and aboveground parts of bulbs. These diseases are caused by fungi, bacteria, and other organisms. They are often most severe where soil or atmospheric conditions are too humid and too warm. Exposure of dormant bulbs to light and good ventilation and dusting them with sulphur or soaking them in Semesan may bring about control. Spraying or dusting foliage, at the first signs of infection, with Fermate or with Bordeaux mixture is often effective. In some cases, "gladiolus scab" for instance, soaking the affected bulbs for two hours in a 1:1000 solution of mercuric chloride (very poisonous) produces results. "Leaf spot" and "leaf blotch" diseases occur on calla-lilies, begonias, gladioluses, irises, eremuruses, and other bulbs. Symptoms consist of various foliage spottings and blotchings. Controls are spraying with Bordeaux mixture or Fermate, keeping the foliage dry, and picking and burning affected parts promptly.

# LILIES

Lilies are among the most stately and useful of summer-flowering bulbs. They may be had in great variety and are useful for a wide variety of purposes. Many are easy to grow; some need special locations or expert care. Here are a selection of natural species and hybrid kinds. All of those shown, except *Lilium longiflorum* (the Easter Lily), are reliably hardy in the North.

1. *Lilium Hollandicum*

2. *Lilium Davidii Willmottiae*

3. *Lilium canadense*

4. *Lilium Goldfinch*

5. *Lilium Tangelo*

6. *Lilium longiflorum* (Easter Lily)

7. *Lilium philadelphicum*

8. *Lilium Wallacei*, a hybrid

1  2

3

4

5

6

7

8

9                                        10

9. *Lilium regale*

10. *Lilium Orange Triumph*

11. *Lilium tigrinum*

12. *Lilium pumilum (tenuifolium)*

11                                        12

# ENCYCLOPEDIA
# OF BULB GARDENING

*In accordance with most greenhouse practice, all temperatures given in the cultural notes for growing bulbs indoors refer to night levels. Daytime temperatures should normally be 5°–10° higher, and in bright sunshine 15° or more higher. This daytime increase does not apply, however, to bulbs that are being held in a cool cellar or similar place during the early rooting period.*

# A

**ACHIMENES.** Summer-blooming gloxinia relatives with attractive, somewhat pansy-like flowers, for growing in greenhouses and window gardens, in pots, pans, and hanging baskets. Natives of the warmer parts of the Americas.

**Culture:** Plant rhizomes 1″ deep and 1″ apart in peatmoss and sand Feb.–April, night temperature 60°–70°. When shoots are 2″ tall transplant 3″ apart in well-drained 7″ or 8″ pans or baskets in rich, woodsy soil. Water moderately at first, freely when in full growth; at end of growing season, after flowering, dry gradually and store quite dry in soil during winter, temperature 50°. Pinch young plants to induce branching. Shade from strong sun. Give dilute liquid fertilizer regularly when in active growth. In early growth maintain close, moist atmosphere, more airy when flower buds show. Avoid wetting foliage.

**Propagation:** By seeds ⅛″ deep in light soil, Jan.–Feb., temperature 70°–80°; rhizomes into pieces at planting time; cuttings and leaf cuttings in spring and early summer.

**Kinds:** *coccinea*, 12–18″, crimson; *Ghiesbreghtii*, 12–18″, crimson-scarlet; *grandiflora*, 12–18″, red-purple; *longiflora*, 12–18″, violet-blue (white in variety *alba*); *patens*, 18″, red-violet with white throat; *pedunculata*, 24″, red and yellow; *tubiflora*, 12–24″, white, tubers solid and potato-like. In addition many fine named hybrid varieties are available and are described in dealers' catalogs.

**ACIDANTHERA.** African, gladiolus-like, late-summer- and fall-blooming cormous plants for beds, borders, and cutting garden where fall frosts come late; elsewhere for growing in pots and tubs plunged outdoors in summer and brought into a cool greenhouse or sunroom before frost.

**Culture** and **Propagation:** As for *Gladiolus*, but winter storage temperature should be higher, 55°–65°.

**Kinds:** *bicolor*, 12–18″, white blotched with purple, fragrant; *bicolor Murieliae*, similar but of stronger growth (*A. bicolor Murieliae* is by some botanists named *Gladiolus Murieliae; laxiflora*, 20″, cream.

**ADDERS-TONGUE.** *See Erythronium.*

**ADOBE-LILY.** *See Fritillaria.*

**AFRICAN-LILY.** *See Agapanthus.*

**AGAPANTHUS** (African-Lily, Lily-of-the-Nile). South African, fleshy-rooted, mostly evergreen perennials with strap-shaped leaves and many-flowered globular heads atop tall, stiff stems in early summer. Much cultivated in pots and tubs for summer use on terraces, patios, etc., and in beds outdoors in frostless and nearly frostless regions.

**Culture:** Soil—rich, loamy, well drained. Repot in spring just as new growth begins, large plants at intervals of several years only, small plants every two or three years. Avoid disturbing roots more than necessary. Pack soil firmly. Location—in full sun outdoors from date when it is safe to plant tomatoes outside until frost threatens; at other seasons in cool, light greenhouse, sunroom, or cellar. Night temperature Oct.–March, 32°–45°; March–May, 45°–55°. Water freely March–Oct., moderately Nov.–Feb. Apply dilute liquid fertilizers regularly to well-rooted specimens March–Sept.

**Propagation:** By division in early spring; seeds in spring.

**Kinds:** *africanus* (*A. umbellatus*), 36″, blue (its varieties *albidus*, white; *Mooreanus* (*campanulatus*), 12–18″, dark blue—the hardiest kind, wintering outdoors in sheltered places as far north as Philadelphia, deciduous; and *variegatus* with striped foliage); *caulescens*, 36″, dark blue; *inapertus*, 48″, deep blue; *longispathus*, 24″, bright blue; *orientalis*, 36″, blue (*albus* is a white variety); *pendulus*, 24″, purple.

**ALBUCA.** South African natives suitable for outdoor border cultivation in California and similar mild climates; elsewhere as pot plants in greenhouse, sunroom, and window garden. Flowers fragrant, in erect spikes, spring and early summer.

167

**Culture:** Soil—fertile, porous. Location—full sun. Night temperature, indoors, 40°–50°. Plant or pot in early fall; when grown indoors set with upper portion of bulb above soil. Repot at intervals of several years only; in intervening years top-dress in early fall. Water and feed freely during growing period; keep quite dry during summer dormant period.

**Propagation:** By offsets removed at potting time; seeds sown in early fall; bulb cuttings in Aug.; scales in Aug.

**Kinds:** *fastigiata*, 20–24″, white with green or brown tips on outsides of outer petals; *major*, 36″, pale yellow with green stripe down each petal; *minor*, 18″, pale yellow with green stripe down each petal; *Nelsonii*, 50–60″, glistening white with brick-red median ray.

**ALLIUM.** Late-spring- and summer-blooming bulbs, mostly hardy North. Of several hundred species that occur wild (mostly in the Northern Hemisphere) only a few are worthy of cultivation, but these are decidedly attractive. Most emit a strong, onion-like odor if bruised. Adapted for wild gardens, rock gardens, and borders; a few are used for cut flowers; one, the common chives, is both attractive in bloom and useful in the kitchen.

**Outdoor Culture:** Soil—well drained, preferably sandy. Location—for most full sun; *Moly* prefers light shade. Plant in spring or early fall, covering bulbs 2–3 times their own depth. Lift and replant when bulbs become crowded and flowers sparse.

**Indoor Culture:** *Neapolitanum* is excellent for a sunny greenhouse for late winter bloom. Soil—fertile, porous. Plant about ten bulbs in each well-drained 5″ pot in Oct., night temperature 40°–50°. Water sparingly at first, freely when in active growth; gradually reduce amount when leaves begin to yellow naturally; store dry through summer. Apply dilute liquid fertilizer regularly from time pots are filled with roots until flowers expand.

**Propagation:** Offsets at planting time; seeds sown indoors in late winter or outdoors in spring, in light, sandy soil; cover seeds 2–3 times their own diameter with soil.

**Kinds:** *acuminatum*, 6–10″, lavender, June; *albopilosum*, 12–18″, large heads, silvery lilac, June; *beesianum*, 9–12″, blue, Aug.; *caeruleum* (*azureum*), 12–18″, clear blue, June; *cyaneum*, 6–9″, blue or lavender, Aug.; *flavum*, 8–15″, yellow, July; *giganteum*, 60″, violet, July; *Moly*, 9–12″, yellow, June; *neapolitanum*, 12″, white, May (not reliably hardy North, but succeeds in sheltered places outdoors at New York City); *nigrum*, 24–36″, rosy purple, May; *pulchellum*, 12″, pink-lavender, July; *Rosenbachianum*, 36–48″, rose-purple, May; *schoenoprasum* (Chives), 9–12″, rosy violet, June; *senescens glaucum*, 6–9″, mauve, Sept.; *tuberosum* (often grown as *odorum*), 20–24″, white, fragrant flowers, June–July; *zebdanense*, 12–18″, white, May.

**ALSTROEMERIA.** Summer-blooming, tuberous-rooted South American plants, handsome for borders, beds, and as cut flowers. Not generally hardy north of Washington, D. C., although in sheltered positions, well protected, some live outdoors at New York City and perhaps further north. They may be grown for June bloom in cool greenhouses.

**Outdoor Culture:** Soil—well-drained, sandy loam enriched with peatmoss or compost. Location—sunny, sheltered. Plant in early fall; except in far South protect over winter with mulch of leaves. Fertilize in early spring. Water freely during dry spells when in active growth.

**Indoor Culture:** Soil—rich, porous. Location—sunny greenhouse. Pot in 8″ or 9″ pots or plant in beds or benches, Sept.–Oct. Water moderately at first, freely when growing actively; gradually dry off when leaves yellow naturally after blooming; keep quite dry in soil in summer. Fertilize regularly from Feb. until flower buds begin to open. Night temperature 45°–50°, 60° for *caryophyllea*.

**Propagation:** By division of roots at planting time; by seeds sown 1¼″ deep in sandy, peaty soil indoors Jan.–Feb. or outdoors in spring.

**Kinds:** *aurantiaca*, 36″, bright yellow, spotted brown, and some other color forms; *brasiliensis*, 24–48″, red-yellow to red; *caryophyllea*, 8–12″, scarlet, fragrant; *chilen-*

*sis*, 48″, rose or red; *haemantha*, 36″, red or orange-red, spotted; *Ligtu*, 24″, white, lilac, pink, or purplish (variety *Hookeriana*, 10″, is pink flowered); *Pelegrina*, lilac, spotted red-purple (white in variety *alba*); *pulchella* (*psittacina*), dark red tipped with green, spotted brown; *violacea*, 36″, violet.

**AMARCRINUM.** *See Crinodonna.*

**AMARYLLIS.** The common name of **Hippeastrum**, which see. *See also the two next entries.*

**AMARYLLIS** (Belladonna-Lily). A South African bulb that blooms in summer when devoid of foliage and somewhat resembles *Lycoris squamigera*. For beds and borders outdoors in mild climates but not generally hardy north of Washington, D. C. May also be grown in pots.

**Outdoor Culture:** Soil—deep, fertile, sandy loam. Location—sheltered, sunny. Plant 9″ deep, 12″ apart, in early fall. Water freely in dry weather when in active growth. Fertilize in spring. Mulch in fall.

**Indoor Culture:** As for *Albuca*.

**Kinds:** *Belladonna* (*Brunsvigia rosea, Callicore rosea*), 18–24″, pink, fragrant, Aug.–Sept. (several beautiful varieties of this species are known varying in color from white to deep pink). For the plant sometimes called "*Amaryllis Hallii*," see *Lycoris squamigera*.

*See also Hippeastrum.*

**AMARYLLIS, HARDY.** *See Lycoris squamigera.*

**AMAZON-LILY.** *See Eucharis.*

**AMIANTHIUM** (Fly-Poison). Hardy eastern North American bulbous plant closely related to *Zigadenus*. For wild gardens.

**Culture:** Soil—woodsy. Location—light shade. Plant in fall 6–12″ apart, 3–4″ deep. Leave undisturbed as long as doing well.

**Propagation:** By offsets at planting time; by seeds when ripe.

**Kind:** *muscaetoxicum*, 24–48″, white, summer.

**AMMOCHARIS.** South African bulbs for planting outdoors in the far South and for pots in cool greenhouses.

**Culture:** As for *Albuca*.

**Kinds:** *falcata* (*Cybistetes longifolia*), 5–10″, pink to red, fragrant; *Heterostyla*, 2–5″, pink with white stripe on back of petals, fragrant; *Tinneana*, 2–12″, pink to red with white stripe on inner surface of petals, fragrant.

**AMOLE.** *See Chlorogalum.*

**AMORPHOPHALLUS.** Tuberous-rooted plants of the arum family, natives of tropical Australasia. *Titanum*, from Sumatra, bears the largest inflorescence (not the largest flower) of any known plant. It was bloomed for the first time in the Western Hemisphere in 1937 at the New York Botanical Garden by the author, and by him, at the same garden, once later. The author also had in his care the magnificent specimen that flowered at the Royal Botanic Gardens, Kew, England, in 1926. This noble aroid has flowered in temperate regions on very few occasions; it is of practical interest only to institutions such as botanical gardens. Several smaller kinds are worth growing as curiosities.

**Culture:** Soil—rich, humusy, well drained. Location—moist greenhouse, night temperature 70°, or outdoors in summer. Pot when new growth begins in late winter or early spring in containers large enough to allow generous root room. Water freely during growing season; keep dry when dormant. Fertilize regularly when in active growth.

**Propagation:** By seeds sown when ripe, temperature 75°–80°; by bulbils formed on leaves of *bulbifer*, taken off when leaves die down and planted the following late winter or spring; less frequently, by rarely produced offsets.

**Kinds:** *bulbifer*, leaf 36″ tall, flower (inflorescence) 12–18″, green or yellow-green, spotted purple; *campanulatus*, leaf 20–30″ tall, flower (inflorescence) 9–12″, not ill-smelling. For another plant sometimes called "*Amorphophallus*," see *Hydrosme*.

**ANAPALINA.** A South African winter- and spring-blooming plant formerly known as *Antholyza*. For borders in mild climates, pots, and cut flowers.

**Culture** and **Propagation:** As for "baby" (*nanus*) gladiolus.

**Kind:** *revoluta* (*Homoglossum Watsonianum*), 24", bright red.

**ANEMONE** (Wind-Flower). Hardy and nearly hardy tubers adaptable for various purposes. Natives of Europe, Asia, and North America.

FOR BEDS, GREENHOUSES, AND
CUT FLOWERS

The poppy anemone in its many fine varieties is truly a magnificent garden plant, unfortunately not hardy in the northeast and north central states, but luxuriating in the Pacific Northwest.

**Outdoor Culture:** Soil—sandy, loam enriched, with well-decayed organic matter. Location—sunny. Plant in fall, 3" deep, 7–8" apart. Keep well watered in dry weather. Lift tubers when foliage has died after flowering and store in peatmoss in cool, dry place until fall planting season; alternatively leave undisturbed in the ground until crowding indicates the need for separating and replanting. In the North good results may be had by planting in fall in a cold frame which is well protected in the winter.

**Greenhouse Culture:** Soil—light, rich loam with liberal amount of organic matter. Location—sunny, airy greenhouse, night temperature 40°–50°. Sow seeds April–May and keep young plants growing without check; or plant tubers as early as they can be obtained in fall in pots, flats, or benches, spaced 8" apart. Water moderately at first, freely when in full growth. Apply dilute liquid fertilizer regularly from Feb. onward.

**Propagation:** By seeds in late April and early May; by offsets.

**Kinds:** Poppy anemones are varieties and hybrids of *coronaria*, *fulgens*, and *hortensis*. They come in a great variety of brilliant colors (except yellow and orange). Various fine strains have special names such as St. Brigid and Creagh Castle and de Caen; some individual kinds have been given varietal names such as The Bride, white; Mr. Fokker, blue; His Excellency, scarlet; and Sylphide, violet.

FOR ROCK GARDENS AND WOODLAND
GARDENS

A number of very good kinds are well worth growing; those listed are reliably hardy North with the possible exception of *fulgens* which, however, lives outdoors at New York City with winter protection.

**Culture:** Soil—gritty, humusy, cool, moderately moist, and—except for *quinquefolia*—with lime or limestone chips added. Location—lightly shaded, sheltered from sweeping winds. Plant 2–3" deep, 3–4" apart in early fall. Lift and replant only when obviously crowded.

**Propagation:** By seeds sown in light, woodsy soil in a cold frame or outdoors in early summer or fall; by offsets removed when foliage dies in early summer.

**Kinds:** appennina, 6", blue, rose, or white; *blanda*, 6", blue, violet, lavender, rose, and white; *fulgens*, 12", brilliant scarlet; *nemorosa* (European Wood Anemone), 6", white to violet and blue (several named varieties exist including *Allenii*, *grandiflora*, *Robinsoniana*, and double-flowered *alba plena*); *quinquefolia* (American Wood Anemone), 6", white or faintly tinged pink or blue; *ranunculoides* (Yellow Wood Anemone), 6–8", bright yellow (a double-flowered variety of *ranunculoides* occurs).

**ANEMONELLA** (Rue-Anemone). One dainty North American spring-flowering woodland plant related to *Anemone*. For woodlands and rock gardens.

**Culture:** Soil—rich, woodsy, fairly moist. Location—shaded, sheltered from sweeping winds. Plant in colonies in early spring or fall, 4–6" apart.

**Propagation:** By seeds sown in light, woodsy soil in cold frame when ripe or in fall; by division of tuber clusters, after leaves die down in early summer, or in early spring.

**Kind:** *thalictroides*, 3–6", white or delicate pink.

**ANGELS-TEARS.** *See Narcissus triandrus.*

**ANOMATHECA.** *See Lapeirousia cruenta.*

**ANTHOLYZA.** *See Anapalina, Chasmanthe, Curtonus, and Homoglossum.*

**APIOS** (Groundnut). Hardy North American summer-flowering deciduous vine for wild gardens, trellises, etc. Tubers edible.

**Culture:** Soil—rich, loose, fairly moist. Location—light shade. Plant in spring.

**Propagation:** Division of tubers in spring; by seeds sown in spring.

**Kind:** *tuberosa,* 96–120″, brown, with violet scent.

**ARISAEMA** (Jack-in-the-Pulpit, Indian-Turnip, Dragonroot). Deciduous, tuber-ous-rooted plants of wide natural distribution. Only kinds ordinarily cultivated are hardy natives, but there are several from the Himalaya and Japan—mostly less hardy than the native kinds—well worth attention. Tropical kinds require the same treatment as *Amorphophallus,* non-hardy temperate kinds that of tender arums.

**Culture (Native Kinds):** Soil—deep, woodsy, fairly moist. Location—shaded rock gardens, woodlands, and borders. Plant as soon as foliage has died or in fall, 5–6″ deep. Mulch in fall. Water freely during dry weather.

**Propagation:** By seeds sown when ripe; by division of tuberous roots in early fall or spring.

**Native Kinds:** *dracontium* (Dragonroot), 48″, green or greenish, red berries; *triphyllum* (Jack-in-the-Pulpit, Indian-Turnip), 12–30″, green striped with purple, red berries.

**Exotic Kinds:** *candidissimum,* 24–30″, white or tinged pink; *concinnum,* 12–24″, green or purple spotted with white; *fimbriatum,* 12–18″, brownish purple striped with white (needs tropical conditions); *Griffithii,* 24″, brown and green, violet markings.

**ARUM.** Tuberous-rooted relatives of the calla-lily, natives of Europe and Asia. For rock gardens, woodland gardens, and pot plants. The red berries are poisonous.

**Outdoor Culture:** Soil—rich, woodsy, fairly moist. Location—part shade. Plant in early fall or early spring, 4″ deep, 9–10″ apart. Protect in winter with mulch of leaves.

**Indoor Culture:** Soil—rich, containing liberal amounts of leafmold, rotted manure, or humus. Location—light greenhouse or sunroom, night temperature 40°–50°. Pot in early fall, covering bulbs to a depth of 2″. Water moderately at first, freely when in full growth, reduce supplies when foliage begins to die in spring and withhold completely during summer dormant period. Fertilize regularly when in full growth.

**Propagation:** By offsets at planting time; by seeds sown in woodsy soil when ripe. Seeds should be kept moist from time of gathering until sown.

**Kinds (Hardy, North):** *italicum,* 12–18″, creamy white; *maculatum* (Cuckoo-Pint, Lords and Ladies), 6–9″, yellowish green spotted with purple.

**Kinds (Tender, North):** *palaestinum* (Black Calla), 18–24″, yellow-green and purple. For other plants sometimes called "*Arum,*" see Calla, Dracunculus, Helicodiceros, Sauromatum, and Zantedeschia.

**ATAMASCO-LILY.** *See Zephyranthes.*

**AUTUMN-CROCUS.** *See Colchicum.*

**AUTUMN SNOWFLAKE.** *See Leucojum.*

**AVALANCHE-LILY.** *See Erythronium montanum.*

# B

**BABIANA** (Baboon Flower). South African corms that bloom in late winter and spring. Freesia-like flowers. Suitable for pots and pans in cool greenhouses or outdoors where winters are frostless or nearly so.

**Culture** and **Propagation:** As for *Freesia.*

**Kinds:** *disticha,* 9″, pale lilac; *plicata,* 6″, violet-blue, carnation scented; *stricta,* 12″, blue and white (varieties include *angustifolia,* blue and pink, fragrant; *rubro-cyanea,* blue and crimson; *sulphurea,* cream or pale yellow; and *villosa,* crimson).

**BABOON FLOWER.** *See Babiana.*

**BASKET-FLOWER.** *See Hymenocallis calathina.*

**BEGONIA.** Begonias that have tubers are nearly all South American species and their hybrids, all of which are frost-tender. The hybrids are given the group name *tuberhybrida* and are the most magnificent, most important, and best known of all tuberous begonias. The Chinese *Evansiana* and its variety *alba* are also tuberous; these are hardy outdoors in sheltered places at New York City and perhaps further north.

HYBRID TUBEROUS BEGONIAS
(B. TUBERHYBRIDA)
Useful for beds, borders, window boxes, pots, and hanging baskets. Summer-bloomers.

**Culture:** Soil—plentifully enriched with leafmold, compost, decayed manure, humus, or peatmoss, rather coarse, well drained, always fairly moist. Location—for tubers started early indoors, a warm moist greenhouse or equivalent in young stages, more airy conditions when half grown. Shade from bright sun, shelter from wind. They thrive best where summer nights are moderately cool and the atmosphere is humid. Plant tubers indoors March–April, 4″ apart, tops (hollow sides) level with surface, in shallow boxes of leafmold or peatmoss and sand. Keep moist but not sodden. Night temperatures 60°–70°, atmosphere humid. When masses of roots about 2″ long have developed pot individually in 4″ or 5″ pots, leaving as much of the rooting medium clinging to the roots as possible. Set with tops of tubers 1–2″ beneath the surface; avoid packing the soil very firmly. For outdoor planting gradually harden plants started early indoors and set them in their flowering locations when warm, settled weather arrives, choosing, if possible, a moist, dull period for doing this. Alternatively, plant unstarted tubers directly outdoors, 3″ deep, 10–12″ apart, as soon as the weather is warm enough to set out tomato plants. Tubers so treated produce plants that bloom 4–6 weeks later than those started indoors earlier. For pot cultivation repot from 4″ or 5″ to 6″ or 7″ pots when roots have fairly filled the smaller pots; later another shift to an even larger size may be desirable. Keep soil always moist but avoid constant saturation. When final pots are well filled with roots apply dilute liquid fertilizer once or twice a week. Stake and tie neatly. To obtain blooms of largest size allow central flower only to develop on each flower stem; remove side buds while tiny.

Just before hard frost lift tubers from garden with stems, foliage, and earth attached, keep in a dry, warm place 2–3 weeks, then clean tubers of soil and tops and store in peatmoss or dry sand, temperature 50°–55°, until planting time. Reduce water supply of pot-grown specimens when leaves begin to yellow naturally in fall, finally withhold entirely. When tops have died remove tubers from soil and store as advised for those lifted from outside garden.

**Propagation:** By seeds sown in fine sandy, woodsy soil but without soil covering, Jan.–Feb., temperature 70° (seedlings bloom first year); by careful division of tubers when new shoots are 1″ tall; by cuttings of young shoots inserted in propagating case, temperature 65°–75°, spring.

**Kinds:** *Tuberhybrida* includes many subgroups and varieties. They are 9–24″ tall and come in a wide range of colors including almost all except blues and purples; they range from pure white through pink to deepest crimson, through cream to bright yellow and orange. Pastel shades in unbelievable variety are common. In flower form they vary from singles to fully double flowers and include frilled, crested, and other interesting variations. Abroad they are offered in named varieties; in this country usually according to type such as single flowered, camellia flowered, carnation flowered, *narcissiflora* type, *cristata* type, and so on. Descriptions of these various types are given in catalogs of dealers. A drooping, pendulous type especially suitable for hanging baskets is known as *Lloydii* or *pendula;* the name *multiflora* is given to a type of compact growth that bears small leaves, a profusion of small flowers, and is particularly adapted for summer beds.

OTHER TUBEROUS BEGONIAS
As pot plants in greenhouses and window gardens; *Sutherlandii* for permanent planting outdoors in mild climates; *Evansiana* for permanent outdoor planting as far north as New York City in sheltered locations.

**Culture:** As for pot specimens of hybrid tuberous begonias, except that disbudding (removal of lateral flower buds) is not desirable and that *Sutherlandii* and *Evansiana* thrive in lower temperatures (50°–60°) indoors, lower outdoors. For permanent out-door planting of *Sutherlandii* and *Evansiana* provide well-drained but moist humusy soil, light shade, and protection from winds. Mulch in winter, plant in spring.

**Propagation:** As for hybrid tuberous be-gonias; *Evansiana* also by stem bulbils taken off in fall, stored and planted in spring.

**Kinds:** *boliviensis*, 24″, scarlet, summer; *Clarkei*, 24″, red or pink, summer; *Davisii*, 4–6″, red, fall; *Evansiana*, 24″, pink or white, summer; *Froebelii*, 9–12″, red, fall and early winter; *Pearcei*, 12″, yellow, sum-mer; *Sutherlandii*, 12–24″, orange-apricot, summer; *Veitchii*, 10–12″, red, summer.

**BELLADONNA-LILY.** *See Amaryllis.*

**BERMUDA BUTTERCUP.** *See Oxalis cernua.*

**BESSERA** (Coral-Drops). A Mexican summer-flowering bulb for outdoors in mild climates, elsewhere for indoor cultivation in pots. The author has grown this species suc-cessfully outdoors in New York City against a south-facing wall by protecting it in win-ter with a heavy covering of dry leaves.

**Culture:** Same as for *Albuca* except that bulbs in pots should be completely covered with soil.

**Propagation:** By offsets at planting time; seeds in early fall or spring.

**Kind:** *elegans*, 24–36″, orange-red banded with cream on inside of flower, pro-truding stamens with red filaments, green anthers.

**BLOOD-LILY.** *See Haemanthus.*

**BLOODROOT.** *See Sanguinaria.*

**BLOOMERIA** (Golden-Stars). Summer-flowering Californians allied to *Brodiaea*. For rock gardens and wild gardens in the West but not well-adapted to eastern con-ditions.

**Culture:** Soil—sandy, well drained. Lo-cation—full sun. Plant in fall. Where much frost is experienced mulch with leaves or similar protection over winter.

**Propagation:** By seeds in sandy soil; by offsets, slowly.

**Kind:** *crocea* (*aurea*), 18″, orange-yellow with darker stripings.

**BLUEBELL.** *See Scilla.*

**BLUE-DICKS.** *See Brodiaea capitata.*

**BONGARDIA.** Tuberous-rooted plant re-lated to Barberry. Native of Syria and Per-sia. Blooms in spring. Hardy in fairly mild climates and there suitable for rock gar-dens; also as a cool greenhouse or window garden pot plant.

**Culture:** Soil—light, sandy, fertile. Plant or pot in fall with top covered 2–3″ deep. Water freely when in growth. When foliage dies after flowering keep quite dry until growth starts naturally again. Indoor night temperature 40°–50°.

**Kind:** *Chrysogonum* (*Rauwolfia*), 6–8″, golden yellow, May.

**BOOPHANE.** *See Boophone.*

**BOOPHONE** (also called Boophane and Buphane). South African summer-bloom-ing bulbs requiring the same culture as *Albuca*.

**Kinds:** *ciliaria*, 6–9″, purple; *distachya*, 12″, pink.

**BOUSSINGAULTIA** (Madeira-Vine, Mi-gnonette-Vine). Perennial, Ecuadorean, tuberous-rooted, twining vine for porches, trellises, etc., naturalized in some parts of the South.

**Culture:** Soil—well drained, ordinary. Location—sunny. Is root-hardy to about Washington, D. C., further north with heavy winter protection; in colder climates dig in fall and store over winter like dahlias.

**Propagation:** By seeds in spring; division of roots in spring; tubercles taken from leaf axils in fall, stored, and planted in spring.

**Kind:** *baselloides*, 10–20′, flowers white, fragrant, fall.

**BOWIEA.** *See Schizobasopsis.*

**BREVOORTIA** (Floral Fire-Cracker). A summer-flowering Californian corm closely allied to *Brodiaea*. For rock gardens and wild gardens. Better adapted to western than eastern gardens. The author grew it successfully outdoors in New York City with heavy winter protection, but it did not prove long-lived.

**Culture:** Soil—deep, well drained, loose, woodsy. Location—light shade. Plant in fall, 3–4″ deep.

**Propagation:** By seeds when ripe; by offsets.

**Kind:** *Ida-Maia,* 12–36″, red and green (sometimes yellow), flowers long-lasting.

**BRODIAEA.** Chiefly western American corms that bloom in spring and summer. Most are less adaptable to eastern than western gardens, but a few persist and flower regularly in the East if happily located. Among these are *californica, capitata, grandiflora, ixioides, lactea, laxa, stellaris,* and *uniflora.* For rock gardens, wild gardens, cut flowers, and pot plants. Both in the garden and when cut the flowers are long-lasting. Another plant sometimes listed as *Brodiaea* is *Brevoortia.*

**Outdoor Culture:** Soil—gritty, fertile. Location—sunny. Plant in Sept., 3–4″ deep, in colonies with individuals rather close together, because brodiaeas are slender plants that do not need much lateral room. Because their foliage is scant and usually dies before the flowers are over they should be set among lower plants that furnish foliage. Where wet summers prevail it is well to lift the bulbs after the foliage has died and store in a cool, dry place until planting time, but this is not absolutely necessary.

**Indoor Culture:** Soil—fertile, sandy. Location—sunny greenhouse or sun porch. Night temperature 35°–45° until Jan., then 40°–50°. Plant several bulbs close together in well-drained pots or pans, Sept. Water sparsely at first, freely when in active growth. Reduce water when foliage begins to die; finally withhold and keep quite dry, either in pots of soil or stored free of soil, during summer dormant season. Fertilize sparingly during growing season. Repot in new soil each year.

**Propagation:** By offsets taken when foliage has died down; by seeds in sandy soil in spring.

**Kinds:** *Bridgesii,* 9″, pale lilac; *californica,* 12″, violet-purple; *capitata* (Blue-Dicks), 18–24″, blue; *coronaria* (*grandiflora*), 18″, violet-purple; *crocea,* 12″, bright

yellow; *Douglasii,* 24″, blue; *Eastwoodii,* 18″, white; *hyacinthina,* 24″, white to purplish; *ixioides* (Pretty Face), 18″, buff-yellow; *lactea* (Wild-Hyacinth), 18″, white or lilac; *laxa* (Grass-Nut, Triplet-Lily) 12–24″, purple or white; *minor* (Purdyi), 6–10″, violet-purple; *pulchella,* 36″, violet-purple; *stellaria,* 6″, violet-purple; *uniflora* (*Milla uniflora, Triteleia uniflora Ipheion uniflorum*) —Spring Star-Flower, native of the Argentine, 6–8″, flowers solitary, white tinted with blue, foliage with onion-like odor when bruised (variety *caerulea* has bluer flowers, those of variety *violacea* are violet); *volubilis* (Snake-Lily), stem twining, 36″, or if supported up to 90″, pink.

**BRUNSDONNA.** Bigeneric hybrids between *Brunsvigia Josephinae* and *Amaryllis Belladonna.*

**Culture:** As for *Amaryllis Belladonna.*

**Propagation:** Offsets at potting time; bulb cuttings, August.

**Kinds:** "Harboard;" "Haythor;" *multiflora rosea; multiflora alba;* "Ovieto;" *Parkeri,* 18″, rose with yellowish white base; *Tubergenii,* 18″, violet-pink.

**BRUNSVIGIA.** South African summer- and fall-flowering bulbs related to *Amaryllis.*

**Culture** and **Propagation:** As for *Amaryllis.*

**Kinds:** *gigantea* (*orientalis*), 12″, red; *Josephinae* (Josephines-Lily), 12–18″, bright red; *natalensis,* 12–18″, pink; *Slateriana,* 9″, red; *undulata,* 12–20″, deep red. The plant sometimes called "*Brunsvigia rosea*" is in this book treated under *Amaryllis Belladonna.*

**BULBOCODIUM** (Spring Meadow-Saffron). A Eurasian corm with crocus-like flowers before the leaves appear in early spring. Suitable for rock gardens.

**Culture:** Soil—gritty, fertile. Location—full sun. Plant in Sept., 3″ deep, 3–4″ apart. Lift and replant in fresh soil every 2–3 years.

**Propagation:** By offsets at planting time; by seeds sown when ripe.

**Kind:** *vernum,* 6″, lavender-pink.

**BUPHANE.** *See Boophone.*

**BUTTERFLY-TULIP.** *See Calochortus.*

# C

**CALADIUM.** Easily grown, tropical American deciduous tuberous plants cultivated for their handsomely colored heart-shaped leaves, beautifully variegated with green, red, pink, and white in a great variety of patterns, blotches, spots, and veinings. They belong in the arum family and produce cream- or other-colored, jack-in-the-pulpit-like, fleeting flowers that have no decorative importance because they are hidden by the foliage. For pot plants, window and porch boxes, and outdoor beds and borders. Most of those grown are named varieties of *bicolor*. Another plant sometimes called *"Caladium"* is the Elephants-Ear, *Colocasia antiquorum.*

**Culture for Outdoor Use:** Soil—rich, moist but not water-logged, rather loose, containing generous amounts of organic matter. Location—semi-shaded, sheltered from wind. In far South plant tubers 2–3″ deep, outdoors, as soon as weather is settled and warm; in North start tubers indoors 8 weeks before setting them outdoors, which should not be done until the weather is quite warm and settled (about June 10th near New York City). Set the tubers in flats of peatmoss and sand, leafmold, or sphagnum moss with their tops covered to a depth of 2″. Keep moist, in temperature 70°–80°, atmosphere humid. When roots are 2″ long transfer tubers individually to 5″ pots and grow in warm, moist atmosphere. Gradually harden before planting outside; alternatively, plants may be potted on into larger containers and plunged to their rims in soil outdoors rather than removed from the pots and planted. Keep foliage sprayed with water frequently after setting out. Water well during dry spells. After frost has damaged foliage, dig, dry, clean off foliage, and store tubers in peatmoss, dry sand, or vermiculite, temperature 60°–65°.

**Culture Indoors:** Soil—as recommended in paragraph above for outdoor culture. Location—greenhouse or window, with shade from strong sun, night temperature 60°–70°

(higher in early stages), fairly humid atmosphere. Start tubers into growth Feb.–May either according to directions given under "Culture for Outdoor Use" or by planting them directly in well-drained pots or pans of soil with the tops of the tubers covered 2–3″. To obtain large specimens plant two or three tubers in an 8″ or 9″ azalea (deep) pan. Water moderately at first, abundantly when in good leaf; reduce water when foliage begins to die naturally in fall, finally withhold entirely and store tubers in soil in which they grew, or in peatmoss or sand over winter. Fertilize regularly from when plants fill their containers with roots until they begin their dormant season.

**Propagation:** By division of tubers that have just started growth, spring; by seeds sown in sandy, humusy soil, spring, temperature 70°–80°.

**Kinds:** *bicolor* in many different varieties, 12–24″; *Humboldtii* (*argyrites*), 9″, small green leaves with white veins. A selection of varieties of *bicolor* (the kinds known as Fancy Leaf Caladiums) follows: Ace of Hearts, red and green; Candidum, white with green veins; Edith Mead, white with green margins, red veins; John Peed, metallic red and moss green; Keystone, green with pink veins and spots; Macahyba, green and red with lilac spots; Marie Moir, white with red blotches; Sorocaba, pink and white with green ribs.

**CALLA-LILY.** *See Zantedeschia.*

**CALLICORE.** *See Amaryllis Belladonna.*

**CALLIPSYCHE.** South African bulbs that require the same general culture as *Hippeastrum.*

**Kind:** *aurantiaca*, 24–36″, yellow, fall. Flowers appear when plants are leafless.

**CALOCHORTUS** (Fairy-Lanterns, Mariposa-Lily, Globe-Tulip, Butterfly-Tulip). Western American bulbs, many of extraordinary beauty, but, unfortunately, not generally long-lived in eastern gardens. For rock gardens, wild gardens, and cut flowers. They are divided into distinct groups, the cultural requirements of each of which vary somewhat.

**Propagation:** May be effected in all by offsets taken when foliage dies down, and by seeds sown in light sandy soil in spring.

FAIRY-LANTERNS OR GLOBE-TULIPS

Flowers globular, nodding, remindful of hanging lanterns.

**Culture:** Soil—freely drained, gritty, rich with humus or leafmold. Location—lightly shaded during heat of day; a west slope with shade from the south is favorable. Plant in fall, cover with twice their depth of soil; after ground has frozen protect with covering of leaves or salt-marsh hay for winter.

**Kinds:** *albus,* 12–24″, white or pink; *amabilis* (Golden Globe-Tulip), 18″, golden yellow; *amoenus,* (Purple Globe-Tulip), 18″, rose purple.

STAR-TULIPS, CATS-EARS, OR OWLS-EARS

Flowers upturned, smaller than those of the Mariposa-Lily group and less brilliant, their interiors hairy after the fashion of a cat's ear. Low growing, suited for rock gardens.

**Culture:** Soil—sharply drained and containing liberal amounts of leafmold or other thoroughly decayed organic matter. Location—a slope with lightest shade from midday sun. Other details as for Fairy-Lantern group.

**Kinds:** *caeruleus,* 6″, blue; *Maweanus,* 6–8″, white or purple-tinged (*grandiflorus, purpurescens,* and *roseus* are varieties of *Maweanus*); *monophyllus* (Yellow Star-Tulip), 6–9″, bright yellow with brown petal bases; *uniflorus,* 8–10″, lilac.

MARIPOSA-LILIES OR BUTTERFLY-TULIPS

Flowers large (3–4″ across), upturned, brilliantly colored; stems tall, with sparse foliage. For borders, wild gardens, cut flowers.

**Culture:** Soil—gritty, perfectly drained. Location—full sun. Plant as for Fairy-Lantern group. Protect well in winter with leaves, salt-marsh hay.

**Kinds:** *clavatus,* 24″, yellow lined with brown; *eurycarpus,* 12–18″, lavender; *Greenei,* 12–18″, lilac and yellow; *Gunnisonii,* 12–18″, white tinted with lavender; *Howellii,* 12–18″, white; *Kennedyi,* 6–12″, vermillion; *Leichtlinii,* 8–12″, white tinted

with purple, yellow with a dark spot at bases of petals; *luteus,* 20–24″, yellow or orange lined with brown (variety *citrinus* is lemon-yellow with dark basal spots bordered with yellow); *macrocarpus,* 24″, lavender with green bands on outsides of petals; *Nuttallii* (Sego-Lily), 18″, white lined with purple and with purple basal spots; *splendens* (*Lilac Mariposa*), 24″, lilac; *Venustus* (*White Mariposa*), 9–12″, very variable, white, yellow, pink, lavender, or vinous, with conspicuous dark center or eyes to the flowers and contrasting markings on the petals. Shortly after flowering the foliage dies completely.

**CALOSTEMMA.** Australian bulbs that are hardy in mild climates such as that of California and require the same culture as the Belladonna-Lily, Amaryllis.

**Kinds:** *album,* 12″, white, spring; *luteum,* 12″, yellow, summer or fall; *purpureum,* 12″, rosy-purple, summer, appearing before the leaves.

**CAMASS.** *See Camassia.*

**CAMASSIA** (Camass). Hardy North American bulbs for borders, wild gardens, and cut flowers. They have tall spires of starry flowers in spring.

**Culture:** Soil—deep, rich, retentive of moisture but not waterlogged. Location—light shade or sun, well suited for waterside planting. Plant in colonies in early fall, 4–5″ deep, 6–9″ apart. Mulch each fall with leafmold or compost. Do not disturb as long as plants thrive and bloom well. Water freely if weather is dry during spring growing season.

**Propagation:** By seeds sown in early fall or early spring in light, porous soil; by offsets removed when foliage dies down.

**Kinds:** *Cusickii,* 30–36″, pale blue; *esculenta,* 20–24″, light blue or white; *Leichtlinii,* 24″, dark blue to nearly white; *Leichtlinii semiplena,* 24″, semidouble, creamy white flowers; *Quamash,* 30–36″, dark blue to nearly white.

**CAMPERNELLE.** *See Narcissus odorus.*

**CANNA.** Easily grown summer-blooming plants with tuberous root stocks. Of South

American and West Indian ancestry. Their foliage and flowers have a distinctly tropical effect. Modern varieties are great improvements over older types. For beds, borders, and cut flowers.

**Culture:** Soil—preferably deep, fertile, fairly moist, but will thrive in any reasonably good garden earth. Location—sunny. Plant divisions of tubers directly outdoors when danger of frost is passed (about the time the first corn is planted); or, in the North, start plants indoors in sandy soil, temperature 60°–70°, 4–10 weeks before planting-out time. Allow the lesser period if they are to be set out from flats, longer if they are to be potted individually and set outdoors from 4″ or 5″ pots. Space 18–24″ apart according to vigor or variety. Plant with tops of tubers 2″ beneath surface. In the far South cannas may be left in the garden all year; elsewhere cut off tops and dig them after first frost, with as much soil attached as will adhere to roots, and store over winter packed in sand or dry soil, temperature 40°–50°.

**Propagation:** By division of tuberous root stocks just before starting into growth in spring; by seeds (to raise new varieties) sown after their hard coats have been nicked through with a file, in a peaty, sandy soil, temperature 70°–80°, spring.

**Kinds:** Aida, old rose and salmon; America, dark red, bronze leaves; Apricot, apricot, bronze leaves; King Humbert, scarlet, bronze leaves; La Bohème, peach-pink; La Traviata, old rose; Mme. Butterfly, yellowish pink; Mrs. Alfred Conard, salmon; The President, scarlet; Rigoletto, yellow; R. Wallace, canary-yellow; Wyoming, yellow-bronze; Yellow King Humbert, yellow.

**CAPE-COWSLIP.** See *Lachenalia*.

**CATS-EAR.** See *Calochortus*.

**CELANDINE,** LESSER. See *Ranunculus Ficaria*.

**CHASMANTHE.** South African summer-flowering cormous plants related to *Gladiolus* that have been grown in gardens under the name "*Antholyza*," a name which properly belongs to other plants. For beds and borders and cut flowers.

**Culture:** As for *Gladiolus*.
**Kinds:** *aethiopica*, 36″, red and yellow; *caffra*, 20″, bright red; *floribunda*, 36″, red and yellow; *vittigera*, 36″, red-yellow with red stripes or clear lemon-yellow.

**CHECKERED-LILY.** See *Fritillaria Meleagris*.

**CHILEAN-CROCUS.** See *Tecophilaea*.

**CHINCHERINCHEE.** See *Ornithogalum thyrsoides*.

**CHINESE YAM.** See *Dioscorea*.

**CHIONODOXA** (Glory-of-the-Snow). Hardy, spring-flowering bulbs native to Asia Minor and Crete that thrive without trouble. For rock gardens, borders, naturalizing at the fringes of shrubberies, etc., and for forcing for winter bloom indoors.

**Outdoor Culture:** Soil—fertile, well drained. Location—sunny. Plant in early fall, 2″ deep, 2–3″ apart, 12–18 bulbs to each square foot. Allow seeds to ripen and self-sow. When they become so crowded that the flower display deteriorates lift and replant immediately after foliage dies.

**Indoor Culture:** As for *Crocus*.
**Kinds:** all 3–6″ tall: *Luciliae*, blue with white eye (variety *alba*, white; *rosea*, pink); *sardensis*, dark blue; *tmolusii* (*Tmolii*), dark blue.

**CHIONOSCILLA.** A natural bigeneric hybrid between *Chionodoxa Luciliae* and *Scilla bifolia*. It blooms in spring.

**Culture:** As for *Chionodoxa*.
**Kind:** *Allenii*, 3–6″, light blue.

**CHLIDANTHUS.** South American summer-blooming bulb, hardy in mild climates. For outdoor beds and borders and pots.

**Outdoor Culture:** Soil—deep, well drained, enriched with compost or leafmold. Location—sunny, sheltered. Plant 3″ deep in April. In cold climates lift after frost and store in sand in a cool, frost-free place over winter.

**Pot Culture:** Soil—rich, gritty. Plant several together (about 1″ between bulbs) in 5″ pots or 6″ pans, April. Water moderately at first, freely when in full growth. Apply dilute fertilizers when well rooted and actively growing. When leaves die in fall gradually withhold water and store dry in temperature 40°–50° until repotting time.

**Propagation:** By offsets, April; by seeds, when ripe or in spring, in pots indoors; by bulb cuttings, August.

**Kind:** *fragrans,* 8–10″, yellow.

**CHLOROGALUM.** Californian natives, one sometimes cultivated. Easy to grow; useful for wild gardens. *Pomeridianum* is a good bee plant.

**Culture:** As for *Camassia.*

**Kind:** *pomeridianum* (Soap-Plant, Amole), 36–60″, white with purple veins, opening in the afternoon.

**CINNAMON-VINE.** *See Dioscorea.*

**CLAYTONIA** (Spring Beauty). Cultivated tuberous kinds are spring-blooming natives suitable for rock gardens and wild gardens. Their foliage dies in early summer.

**Culture:** Soil—dampish, rich, humusy. Location—slopes, rock gardens, and wild gardens in part shade. Plant in early fall or as soon as foliage has died in generous colonies, 2–3″ deep and about the same distance apart. Leave undisturbed as long as possible.

**Propagation:** By seeds sown when ripe; by offsets taken when foliage dies or in fall.

**Kinds:** *caroliniana,* 4–8″, pink; *virginica,* 4–8″, blush-pink.

**CLIVIA** (Kafir-Lily). Somewhat bulbous, fleshy-rooted, evergreen natives of South Africa. Grown in large pots and tubs and valued for their foliage for the summer decoration of patios, terraces, etc., as well as for their handsome flowers borne earlier in the year. These are magnificent greenhouse and house plants and may be grown permanently in the open far South. The finest are hybrids and selected varieties of *miniata.* These are a great improvement over older types.

**Culture:** Soil—fertile loam enriched with well-rotted manure, with enough sand or grit to make it porous. Repot in spring, just as new growth begins, at intervals of several years only (pack soil firm); in other years top-dress in spring. Keep warm and in a moist atmosphere after repotting; spray with water frequently. Location—in frostless or nearly frostless regions shady beds outdoors; elsewhere in greenhouse, sunroom, or light window from first fall frost until weather is really warm and settled (early June in vicinity of New York City); in summer in greenhouse, sunroom, window garden, or outdoors. Shade from strong sun April–Sept. Night temperatures Oct.–March, 45°–55°; March–May 55°–65°. Water copiously and spray foliage with water daily from time new growth begins until Oct.; keep nearly dry at other times. Apply dilute liquid fertilizer regularly to well-rooted specimens March–Sept. Remove faded flowers to prevent seed formation.

**Propagation:** By division at potting time; by seeds in shady, peaty soil, temperature 70°–75°, spring; by leaf cuttings, summer.

**Kinds:** *caulescens,* orange with green tips, spring; *cyrtanthiflora,* orange, winter and spring; *Gardenii,* reddish orange or orange-yellow, winter; *miniata,* typically orange-red with yellow throat, but showing considerable variation in color pattern and intensity (there are pure yellow forms and selected hybrid varieties), spring; *nobilis,* reddish yellow with green petal tips, spring. All are 12–24″ tall.

**COLCHICUM** (Autumn-Crocus). The common name is confusing because there are true crocuses that flower in the autumn which are entirely different from colchicums; to add to the confusion, not all colchicums are autumn-flowering. Colchicums are cormous natives of Europe and Asia most of which bear flowers naked of foliage in late summer and in fall and leaves the following spring which die in early summer. For borders, wild gardens, and rock gardens. Colchicums are sometimes offered as "wonder" bulbs that bloom in the house without soil. It is true that they do bloom even if not planted, but this weakens the bulb; if they are intended for the garden they should be put in soil as soon as received. They may be planted in pots of soil, enjoyed as indoor plants in bloom, and be planted in the garden when they are through blooming.

**Culture:** Soil—deep, sandy loam preferred, enriched with leafmold or compost, fairly moist but not wet. Plant in Aug., 6–9" apart, tops of bulbs 2–3" beneath surface. Location—partial shade or full sun, not windswept. Water freely when in leaf. Do not disturb while flowering well. Transplant, when necessary, as soon as foliage dies.

**Propagation:** By offsets at replanting time; by seeds sown in light soil in cold frame in summer as soon as ripe. Transplant seedlings to nursery bed when two years old. Seedlings do not bloom until 4–5 years old.

**Kinds:** *agrippinum*, 3–4", lilac-purple and white; *autumnale*, 8", typically rose-purple but comes in many variations including white-flowered and double-flowered varieties; *Bornmuelleri*, 8–12", rosy lilac; *latifolium* (*Sibthorpii*), 6–8", tessellated lilac-purple; *luteum*, 3–4", yellow, spring-flowering; *speciosum*, 6", lilac-purple, but comes in many variations including white; *variegatum*, 6", rose and purple. In addition a number of splendid large-flowered hybrids have been distributed in recent years from Holland. These include Autumn Queen, Lilac Wonder, Princess Astrid, Violet Queen, and Waterlily, the last-named having full double pink flowers.

## COLOCASIA (Elephants-Ear).

Magnificent tropical Asiatic tuberous plants grown for their huge, green, heart-shaped leaves. The common *antiquorum* is often misnamed *Caladium esculenta* in catalogs. For beds and borders.

**Culture:** Soil—deep, rich, moist. Location—sheltered, preferably partly shaded. In the far South may be left in ground all year, elsewhere lift annually at first frost and store over winter like cannas. Start tubers into growth in a humid greenhouse, temperature 70°–75°, 8–10 weeks before the plants are to be planted outdoors, which must not be until really warm weather has come to stay. Space 36–72" apart. Water freely during dry weather.

**Propagation:** By division of tubers just before growth starts in spring.

**Kind:** *antiquorum* (Elephants-Ear) 70–100".

## CONVALLARIA (Lily-of-the-Valley).

Not a bulbous plant but often treated as such. A circumboreal deciduous perennial with fragrant flowers in spring. Grown outdoors as a groundcover, indoors in pots; useful as a cut flower.

**Outdoor Culture:** Soil—deep, humusy, fairly moist: Location—cool, shaded, or partly shaded. Plant in spring or early fall, setting single crowns (growth buds with roots attached) 6–8" apart. Mulch with rotted manure or compost in fall, apply complete fertilizer in spring. Water copiously in dry weather. When plants become crowded and number and quality of flowers deteriorate lift and replant in enriched soil.

**Indoor Culture:** Best results are obtained by purchasing crowns (pips) especially grown for forcing. These are held in cold storage by dealers and are available at any season. Take delivery 3–4 weeks before flowers are wanted. Shorten roots slightly and plant 1–2" apart with tips just protruding above surface, in pots or decorative containers in sphagnum moss, peatmoss, vermiculite, sand, or soil. Location—dark, humid, temperature 70°–75°. (If grown in the house a ventilated covered box with an inch or two of moist material in the bottom, placed in a dark closet, will provide the requisite conditions.) At end of ten days bring gradually into light in the same temperature. Strong clumps may be lifted from the garden and potted in well-drained containers of light soil in fall. Bury the pots to their rims in sand or ashes outdoors; then bring indoors Jan.–Feb., and place in light position, night temperature 50°–55°. Flowers expand in 5–7 weeks.

**Kinds:** *majalis*, 6–8", white (variety *albostriata* has yellow-striped leaves, *florepleno* has double flowers, *Fortini*—Fortin's Giant—has larger flowers, *rosea* has pale lavender-pink flowers.

## COOPERANTHES.

Bigeneric hybrids between *Cooperia* and *Zephyranthes*. They have same uses and need same culture as *Zephyranthes* but cannot be propagated by seeds; they are propagated by offset bulbs.

**Kinds:** Alipore Beauty, lilac-rose; Mary, pink.

**COOPERIA** (Rain-Lily, Prairie-Lily). Summer-blooming bulbs, natives of the southwestern United States, Mexico, and Peru. For rock gardens and naturalizing. Flowers open late afternoon or evening. They are hardy about as far north as Virginia; in harsher climates may be lifted in fall and stored over winter packed in sand or peatmoss, temperature 35°–45°.
**Culture:** Soil—sandy, well drained. Location—sunny. Plant in spring about 2″ apart, 1–2″ deep.
**Propagation:** By seeds sown when ripe or in spring.
**Kinds:** *Drummondii*, 6–9″, white tinged with red; *pedunculata*, 4–9″, white tinged with red; *Smallii*, 6–8″, yellow; *Traubii*, 6–9″, white tinged with pink.

**COPPERTIP.** *See Crocosmia.*

**CORAL-DROPS.** *See Bessera.*

**CORN-LILY.** *See Ixia.*

**CORYDALIS** (Fumitory). Hardy spring-flowering tubers, natives of Europe. For rock gardens and woodlands.
**Culture:** Soil—light, humusy, moderately moist, well drained. Location—lightly shaded. Plant in early fall or when foliage dies.
**Propagation:** By offsets, early spring; by seeds, when ripe, in cold frame.
**Kinds:** *angustifolia*, 6–8″, white or pink, very early; *cava* (*bulbosa*), 6″, rosy purple (variety *albiflora* has white flowers); *Halleri* (*solida, densifolia*), 6–8″, rose to rose-purple (variety *australis* blooms earlier, has larger flowers).

**CORYTHOLOMA.** Tropical American summer- and fall-flowering plants for greenhouses. Often called *Gesneria.*
**Culture** and **Propagation:** As for *Achimenes* except that the round tubers cannot be broken into pieces as can the caterpillar-like rhizomes of *Achimenes,* and the stems should not be pinched. Grow singly in 4″ or 5″ pots, 4–5 together in 6″ or 7″ pans.

**Kinds:** *cardinalis,* 8–12″, scarlet, fall and early winter; *Donkelaeriana,* 12–24″, red, summer and fall; *Lindleyi,* 12–24″, rosy pink, yellow speckled with red beneath, summer.

**CRINODONNA** (Amarcrinum). Bigeneric hybrids between *Crinum Moorei* and *Amaryllis Belladonna,* raised simultaneously in Italy and California. Deciduous bulbs bearing handsome, fragrant flowers in late summer and fall. For borders, cut flowers, and pot plants.
**Outdoor Culture:** Soil—deep, fertile, well drained. Location—sunny. Plant in spring with tips of bulbs 2–3″ beneath surface. In the South can be grown permanently outdoors; in the North lift in fall, with as many roots attached as possible, and store over winter in slightly moist sand or sand and peatmoss, temperature 35°–45°.
**Indoor Culture:** Pot in spring with upper third of bulb above surface. Location—sunny greenhouse, night temperature 50°–55°. In summer plunge to rim of pot in bed of sand or cinders outdoors. Water moderately at beginning of growth, freely when well rooted and in foliage. Fertilize regularly through summer. Cease watering when foliage begins to die naturally; keep quite dry while dormant. Repot every several years only. Top-dress each spring. Remove side bulbs not needed for propagation while young.
**Propagation:** By offsets, spring.
**Kinds:** *Corsii,* 24–36″, pink; *Howardii* (*Amarcrinum Howardii*), 24–36″, pink.

**CRINUM.** Large evergreen and deciduous bulbs of the tropics and subtropics with handsome, often fragrant, lily-like flowers. Most common kinds are summer-bloomers, hardy South. *Erubescens* and others with red and white flowers are called milk-and-wine-lilies. *Longifolium, Moorei, Powellii,* and their varieties are generally hardy as far north as Washington, D. C.; by protecting them heavily in winter the author has grown them successfully for many years against a south-facing wall in New York City. In general too large for greenhouses or pot plants although of easy cultivation when so grown.
**Outdoor Culture:** Soil—rich, humusy,

well drained; for *americanum* moist or swampy. Location—sunny for most, light shade for *caribaeum, giganteum,* and *Moorei*. Plant in spring, 18–36″ apart, tops of bulbs 6″ deep. Water freely during dry weather. Fertilize in spring. Will remain for many years without replanting. At northern limits of cultivation apply heavy winter mulch of salt-marsh hay or leaves.

**Indoor Culture:** Soil—rich, coarse. Pot in spring, leaving the necks of the bulbs of those kinds that have long, elongated bulbs well above the surface and only the lower part of the bulb buried in the soil. Repot established plants at intervals of several years only. Top-dress each spring, also remove all small offset bulbs not needed for propagation. Water and fertilize freely when growing, keep nearly dry when dormant; evergreen kinds must be kept moist at all times but drier in winter than in summer. In the North pots or tubs may be set outdoors during summer and stored in a light, cool cellar or similar place in winter.

**Propagation:** By offsets, spring; seed when ripe.

**Kinds:** *abyssinicum,* 12–24″, white, fragrant, summer; *amabile,* 24–36″, red outside, paler within, fragrant, summer, evergreen; *americanum* (Swamp-Lily), 18–24″, white, spring; *asiaticum* (Poison Bulb), 36–60″, white, fragrant, blooms all year, evergreen; *augustum,* 24–36″, crimson-purple outside, pink within, fragrant, fall and winter, evergreen; *erubescens,* 18–24″, white inside, purple-red outside, fragrant, summer; *fimbriatulum,* 24″, white with red stripe on each petal, summer; *giganteum,* 24–36″, white, fragrant, fall and winter, evergreen; *Kirkii,* 12–18″, white, petals red-striped, late summer and fall; *Kunthianum,* 12″, white, fragrant, summer; *longifolium* (*bulbispermum*), 12–18″, white or pink (varieties *album,* white; *roseum,* pink, are recognized), spring–summer; *Macowanii,* 24–36″, white tinged red-purple, fall; *Moorei,* 24–36″, deep pink (white in variety *album*), summer; *pedunculatum,* 24–36″, white, summer, evergreen; *scabrum,* 12–24″, white with crimson stripe on each petal, fragrant, early summer; *yemense,* 12–24″, white, summer; *zeylanicum,* 24–36″, white, fragrant, spring. A number of hybrid kinds

have been named. Noteworthy are *Powellii* (*longifolium* x *Moorei*), pink (variety *album* white), summer; *Powellii* Cecil Houdyshel, deep pink, spring through fall; *Powellii Krelagei,* pink, summer; J. C. Harvey (*Moorei* x *Kirkii*), pink, summer; Virginia Lee, bright pink, pale throat, summer; Ellen Bosanquet, deep rose, summer; White Queen, white, summer.

**CROCOSMIA** (Coppertip, Montbretia). Summer- and autumn-flowering corms for borders and cut flowers, natives of South Africa. Plants known in gardens as montbretias are hybrids of these.

**Culture:** Soil—preferably fertile, well drained, somewhat sandy. With light protection hardy about as far north as Philadelphia and in favorable places to New York City if heavily covered with leaves or similar material after ground has frozen. Location—sunny or slightly shaded. Plant in early spring 3″ deep, 2–3″ apart. Water in dry weather, apply dressing of fertilizer when half grown. Mulch soil with compost, peat-moss, or other suitable material. Dig after first frost, pack closely together in shallow boxes of soil, and store over winter, temperature 40°–50°.

**Propagation:** By offsets; seeds, spring.

**Kinds:** *aurea* (Coppertip), 24–36″, golden yellow to reddish yellow (a double-flowered form and other varieties based on color have been named); *Pottsii,* 36–48″, bright yellow flushed with red outside; *masonorum,* 36″, orange-flame. The name *C. crocosmiiflora* (Montbretia) covers a series of hybrids between *aurea* and *Pottsii.* The montbretias are splendid garden plants and excellent cut flowers. Many fine named garden varieties are available and are listed in catalogs. They vary from yellow through bronzes and coppers to reds and are from 30–36″ or more in height.

**CROCUS.** Hardy corms blooming in spring, fall, and in fairly mild climates in winter, according to kind. For naturalizing in lawns and other grassy places and shrubberies, for rock gardens, and for forcing in pots.

**Outdoor Culture:** Soil—light, rich, well drained. Location—sunny or very light shade. Plant spring-flowering kinds in fall, fall-blooming kinds Aug.–Sept., 2–3″ deep, 3–4″ apart. Under no circumstances cut foliage before it dies naturally. Fertilize established plantings lightly in fall or early spring.

**Propagation:** By offsets removed when foliage has died; seeds in sandy soil in a cold frame, fall. Space seeds 1″ apart, transplant at end of second year; seedlings bloom when 3–4 years old.

**Indoor Culture:** Soil—light, rich. Plant 8–10 corms in early fall in a 5″ pot or rather more in a 6″ pan. Plunge outdoors under sand or ashes or keep in cool cellar. In Jan.–Feb., bring indoors, night temperature 45°–50°. For a few days shade from direct sunshine, but when shoots turn green expose fully. Give plenty of water. Corms of no use for forcing a second time. If kept watered until foliage naturally dies they may be planted in the garden to bloom in future years.

**Kinds:** In addition to the common Dutch crocuses that are available in many charming colors and varieties and are described in the catalogs of bulb dealers there are many charming species. They are 2–4″ tall. Among the best are the following.

(1) To bloom in late winter and spring: *aureus,* yellow; *Balansae,* orange or buff-orange; *biflorus* (Scotch Crocus), lavender to white; *chrysanthus,* yellow or orange-yellow to white with yellow throat, sometimes feathered with purple on outside of petals, some forms fragrant; *etruscus,* lilac with purple markings; *Fleischeri,* white or white striped lilac; *Imperati,* lilac; *Korolkowii,* yellow; *minimus,* light violet; *Sieberi,* lilac and yellow; *stellaris,* orange striped with brown; *susianus* (Cloth-of-Gold Crocus), orange-yellow; *Suterianus,* orange-yellow; *Tomasinianus,* lavender or white; *vernus,* lilac, lavender, and white; *versicolor,* purple to white. (2) To bloom in fall: *asturicus,* lavender or purple; *cancellatus,* white or pale lavender; *laevigatus,* white to lilac; *laevigatus Fontenayi,* soft violet, later-blooming than *laevigatus; longiflorus,* pinkish lilac and purple, fragrant; *medius,* lavender-purple; *nudiflorus,* lilac; *ochroleucus,* cream or white with orange throat; *pulchellus,* lilac, fragrant; *sativus* (Saffron Crocus), lilac or white (*Elwesii, Cartwrightianus* and *Pallassii* are varieties of *sativus*); *speciosus,* lilac, purple, and white; *zonatus,* rosy lilac and yellow. There are named varieties of some of the above-named species which are of particular interest. For other plants called "Autumn-Crocus" *see Colchicum.* For Chilean-Crocus *see Tecophilaea.*

**CROWN IMPERIAL.** *See Fritillaria Imperialis.*

**CUBAN LILY.** *See Scilla peruviana.*

**CUCKOO PINT.** *See Arum maculatum.*

**CURTONUS.** One South African early-summer-flowering corm related to Gladiolus and previously included in the genus *Antholyza.* For beds, borders, and cutting and for pot culture. In mild climates it is hardy outdoors but in the North the corms should be lifted in the fall and stored like gladioluses.

**Outdoor Culture:** As for *Crocosmia* (Montbretia), except that the bulbs may be spaced slightly further (3–5″) apart.

**Greenhouse Culture:** As for gladioluses indoors. Eight corms in an 8″ pot provide a satisfactory display. In a night temperature of 50° corms planted in Sept. or Oct. bloom in Feb.

**Propagation:** By offset corms; by seeds sown in fall or early spring in light, sandy soil in a greenhouse, temperature 50–60°.

**Kind:** *paniculatus.*

**CYANELLA.** Attractive spring- or summer-blooming South African bulbs having the same general uses and requiring the same culture as *Ixia.*

**Kinds:** *capensis,* 12″, purple; *odoratissima* (*lutea*), 12″, rose fading to yellow or clear yellow.

**CYCLAMEN.** Garden and greenhouse tuberous plants, natives of the Mediterranean region and central Europe. The greenhouse kinds are winter-flowering pot plants, the others are for naturalizing beneath shrubs and in rock gardens.

**Culture, Greenhouse Kinds:** Soil—mellow, loamy, well drained. Location—cool greenhouse (or cold frame in summer), temperature 50°–55°; 45°–50° when in bloom. Keep growing steadily from seedling to flowering stage without check to growth. Transfer to flowerpots in Sept. for Christmas bloom, Dec.–Jan. for later flowering. Keep early flower buds picked off plants needed for late bloom. Apply dilute liquid fertilizers regularly to pot-bound specimens. Spray foliage with clear water on all bright days. After blooming it is usual to discard greenhouse cyclamens and to raise a new crop from seed each year; however, they can be retained for many years, although a small proportion invariably fail to survive the dormant period. After flowering is through, gradually reduce water and finally keep dry. Repot July–Aug. Water moderately at first, more freely as growth develops.

**Propagation:** By seeds spaced 1″ apart in light, humusy soil, Aug.–Sept. or Jan.–Feb. It takes 15–18 months for plants to reach blooming size from seeds. Seeds germinate slowly.

**Culture, Outdoor Kinds:** Soil—porous, loamy, with leafmold and a little lime added. Location—shaded. Plant Aug.–Sept. 4–5″ apart, 2″ deep. Keep top of corm level with soil surface. Top-dress annually after leaves die by removing surface soil to tops of tubers and replacing with rotted cow manure and soil or with rich compost. Leave undisturbed as long as thriving.

**Propagation:** By seeds sown in light soil in a cold frame, fall.

**Kinds:** The greenhouse, winter-flowering kinds are selected strains of *indicum* (*persicum*). Outdoor kinds (which can also be grown in pots or pans in a cool greenhouse) are *Atkinsii*, 4″, white to red; *coum*, 4″, red, pink, or white, early spring; *europaeum*, 4″, red, late summer and fall; *neapolitanum*, 4″, red (a white variety of this is called *album*), fall. Other species including *cilicium, cyprium, libanoticum, pseudo-ibericum* and *repandum* are worth growing.

**CYPELLA.** South American plants that bloom in late summer and fall. For rock gardens in mild climates; for pots.

**Culture:** Soil—light, rich, sandy. Location—full sun. Plant in fall, 4″ deep, 2–3″

apart, or 5–6 bulbs in a 5″ pot. Water pot-grown plants moderately at first, freely when in active growth; keep dry during dormant season. Night temperature, 40°–50°. Lift and replant outdoor bulbs and repot indoor ones annually.

**Propagation:** By offsets at planting time; by seeds sown indoors in early spring.

**Kinds:** *Herbertii*, 12″, yellow; *peruviana*, 12″, yellow and brown; *plumbea*, 36″, grayish lilac; *plumbea platensis*, 36″, blue.

**CYRTANTHUS.** South African bulbs, deciduous and evergreen, for outdoor cultivation in California and similar mild climates, as cool greenhouse and window garden pot plants.

**Culture:** Soil—sandy, peaty, fertile. Location—sunny. Plant 2″ deep, 1–2″ apart, in well-drained pots at beginning of growing season (Aug.–Oct.). Water sparingly at first, freely when in full growth, deciduous (leaf-losing) kinds not at all when at rest, evergreen kinds moderately when not growing actively. Night temperature, 50°–55°.

**Propagation:** By offsets at planting time; by seeds, in light soil, spring or early fall.

**Kinds:** *angustifolius*, 12–18″, red, summer; *Mackenii*, 8–12″, creamy white, late fall or winter; *obliquus*, 6–12″, yellow, green, and red, early summer; *parviflorus*, 12″, orange-scarlet, winter; *sanguineus*, 12″, bright red, summer; *Tuckii*, 12–18″, yellow and red (variety *viridiflorus*, pink and green), summer.

# D

**DAFFODIL.** *See Narcissus.*

**DAHLIA.** Summer-blooming, tuberous-rooted plants that grow wild in Mexico and Guatemala. For beds, borders, cut flowers.

**Culture:** Soil—well-drained, fertile loam, deeply spaded and enriched with organic matter, bone meal, and wood ashes or, in place of the last two, a complete fertilizer low in nitrogen and high in phosphate and potash. Location—protected from strong winds, full sun, or part-day shade. Plant tubers outdoors about the time the common lilac passes out of bloom, or young green plants about ten days later when the weather is warm and settled. Drive stakes before planting (dwarf kinds need no stakes). Set young green plants in slight saucer-shaped depressions, tubers in 6" deep holes. Cover tubers with 2–3" of soil. As plants grow fill in soil until level around them. Except with dwarfs allow only 1–2 shoots to develop from each plant; pinch out their tips when 12" tall (except in northern gardens where the 10–14 day delay that results from pinching prevents the production of flowers before frost). If branches obviously crowd prune out ill-placed and weaker ones. When large-flowered varieties produce terminal flower buds remove the smaller lateral buds beside them and also all side growths from the axils of 2–4 pairs of leaves immediately below the terminal bud. Tie to stakes securely, not tightly. Keep free of weeds; cultivate shallowly, frequently. In July–Aug. mulch with compost, rotted manure, peat-moss, or other appropriate material. Fertilize poor soils every month from the time plants are 12" tall; fertilize good soils during mid-Aug. Use fertilizer high in potash and phosphate, low in nitrogen. Water copiously during dry weather. Keep plants growing throughout season without check. After killing frost dig without breaking root clumps, shorten stems to about 1", turn the clumps upside down to drain cut stems for a few hours, and let them dry; then dust cut surfaces with sulphur, pack in peatmoss or dry sand or wrap in newspapers, and store in temperature 35°–45°.

**Propagation:** By division at planting time (each division must include a small piece of the old stem with a growth bud); by cuttings in a greenhouse propagating case, temperature 60°–70°, late winter or early spring; by seeds in light sandy soil sown indoors, night temperature 55°–60°, Feb.–March, or directly outdoors when trees begin to leaf. Plants from outdoor-sown seeds bloom later than those started early indoors. Cuttings and seeds produce "green plants" for planting which are preferred by some to tuber divisions.

**Kinds:** Garden varieties are very numerous and may be had in practically every color except blue. New ones are introduced each year and are described in the catalogs of dealers and specialists. They are classified into "types" by the American Dahlia Society according to habit of growth and form of flower. The types presently recognized are: single, mignon, orchid flowered, anemone, collarette, peony, incurved cactus, straight cactus, semi-cactus, formal decorative, informal decorative, ball, miniature, and pompon.

**DEVILS-TONGUE.** *See Hydrosme.*

**DICENTRA.** Hardy plants for rock gardens, wild gardens, and woodlands. The kinds dealt with here have clusters of small tubers. Natives of North America.

**Culture:** Soil—woodsy, fairly moist. Plant in early fall or as soon as foliage dies in spring, 1–2" deep, 3–4" apart. Location —shaded.

**Propagation:** By separation of tubers at planting time; seed sown in woodsy soil in cold frame when ripe.

**Kinds:** *canadensis* (Squirrel-Corn), 6–12", greenish white tinged with purple, spring; *Cucullaria* (Dutchmans-Breeches), 6–10", cream tipped with yellow, spring.

**DIERAMA** (Wand-Flower). South African corms blooming in late summer and fall. They have long, slender stems terminating in graceful spikes of drooping flowers and are closely related to *Ixia*. For borders and cutting.

**Culture:** Soil—sandy, fertile, well drained. Location—sunny. Where hardy (to Washington, D. C., and perhaps further north) plant outdoors in fall, 3" deep, 3" apart, elsewhere in pots for growing in cool greenhouse in same manner as ixias. Lift and replant outdoor bulbs every third year; repot pot-grown bulbs yearly.

**Propagation:** By offsets at planting time; seeds, indoors, fall.

**Kinds:** *pendula,* 36–48", bluish white to purple-red; *pulcherrima,* 36–48", wine-purple or white.

**DIOSCOREA** (Cinnamon-Vine, Chinese Yams). Tuberous-rooted fast-growing vine from China. Root-hardy to southern Massachusetts and possibly further north. Stems die down in fall. For trellises, arbors, porches, etc.

**Culture:** Soil—sandy, well drained. Location—sun or part shade. Plant in spring. In cold climates protect over winter with a heavy mulch, or lift and store like dahlias.

**Propagation:** By division of clumps of ground tubers; by taking small air tubers that form on the stems in fall, storing them, and planting in spring. These small tubers do not produce full-sized plants the first year.

**Kind:** *Batatas* (Cinnamon-Vine), 10–25′, white, fragrant.

**DIPCADI.** Little-known African, European, and Indian bulbs for planting outdoors in mild climates, elsewhere for pots in cool greenhouse or window garden. The author has grown only *serotinum* which has something of the appearance of a tawny-brown-flowered English bluebell (*Scilla nonscripta*). When grown indoors it thrives under the same conditions as *Lachenalia* and blooms in Feb. Probably hardy at least as far north as Philadelphia with protection. Various South African species are more attractive but less hardy.

**DIPIDAX.** Two rare South African bulbs, spring-flowering and decidedly attractive. For pots in a cool greenhouse or window; outdoors in California and similar climates. The author has grown only *triquetra*, which has somewhat sparaxis-like flowers that last well. It is a splendid decorative plant that thrives under the same conditions that suit *Lachenalia* and blooms in March.

**Kinds:** *ciliata*, 8–12″, white, lilac, or purple; *triquetra*, 12–18″, white flushed with pink, with purple-crimson spots at base of each petal.

**DOGS-TOOTH-VIOLET.** *See Erythronium.*

**DRACUNCULUS.** Early-summer-blooming tuberous plants from the Canary Islands and the Mediterranean region, related to Jack-in-the-Pulpit. Not reliably hardy; in sheltered places *vulgaris* will survive at New York City if heavily protected with leaves or similar material. Grown as a curiosity outdoors in mild climates and as a pot plant. Flowers (inflorescences) malodorous.

**Culture** and **Propagation:** As for *Arum*.

**Kinds:** *canariensis*, 16–24″, pale green with yellow central column; *vulgaris* (*Arum Dracunculus*), 12–30″, brown to purplish white, striped purple in mouth.

**DRAGONROOT.** *See Arisaema dracontium.*

**DUTCHMANS-BREECHES.** *See Dicentra Cucularia.*

# E

**EASTER-BELLS.** *See Erythronium grandiflorum.*

**ELEPHANTS-EAR.** *See Colocasia.*

**ELISENA.** Andean bulbs closely related to *Hymenocallis*. The author has grown *longipetala* outdoors for many years in New York City against a south-facing wall by covering it well with salt-marsh hay during winter.

**Culture:** As for deciduous crinums.

**Kind:** *longipetala;* 24–36″, white, summer. A bigeneric hybrid between *longipetala* and *Hymenocallis calathina* is known as *Hymenocallis festalis.*

**ENDYMION.** The plants treated in this book as *Scilla hispanica* and *Scilla nonscripta* are by some botanists named *Endymion hispanicus* and *Endymion nonscriptus.*

**ENGLISH BLUEBELL.** *See Scilla nonscripta.*

**ERANTHIS** (Winter Aconite). Hardy, very early spring-flowering tubers. For rock gardens and naturalizing. Natives of Europe and Asia.

**Culture:** Soil—rich, loose, woodsy, moderately moist but not wet. Location—light shade. Plant July–Aug. (later planting is very detrimental; tubers must not be held out of the ground long), 3–4″ apart, 3″ deep. Lift and replant only when quantity of bloom begins to deteriorate.

**Propagation:** By division of tubers at

planting time; by seeds in cold frame when ripe.

**Kinds:** *hyemalis*, 2–4″, yellow (variety *cilicica* later flowering and deeper yellow flower); *Tubergenii*, 3–6″, large yellow flowers, the handsomest; does not produce seed. *Tubergenii* is presumably a hybrid between *hyemalis* and *cilicica*.

**EREMURUS** (Foxtail-Lily). Magnificent Asiatic tuberous-rooted plants that have bold, tall, many-flowered spikes in summer. For borders and cut flowers.

**Culture:** Soil—deep, rich, well drained. Location—sunny, sheltered. Plant in early fall with crowns 6–8″ deep. Take care to dig wide holes and spread roots without breaking. In North protect over winter with heavy covering of leaves, salt-marsh hay, or ashes. Protect young shoots (which appear early) from late frosts by covering at night with a box. Mulch with decayed manure or compost. Apply organic fertilizer in spring. Water freely in dry weather. Do not transplant unless absolutely necessary. Avoid deep cultivating near roots.

**Propagation:** By division, fall; by seeds, early fall. Seedlings take 4–7 years to bloom.

**Kinds:** *Bungei*, 24–36″, yellow; *himalaicus*, 80–100″, white; *robustus*, 70–90″, pink; *robustus Elwesii*, 90–100″, pink. Many fine hybrid kinds have been raised including Him-rob, Shelford, Shelford Isabela, Shelford Rosalind, Shelford White Beauty, and *Tubergenii*. Among the hybrids are many enchanting pastel colors.

**ERYTHRONIUM** (Dogs-Tooth-Violet, Adders-Tongue, Trout-Lily). Mostly American spring-blooming bulbs for woodland gardens and rock gardens. Not all the western American kinds are long-lived in eastern gardens although most can be persuaded to prosper if soil and location are carefully chosen; they are certainly easier to make at home in the East than are many other western bulbs.

**Culture:** Soil—deep, loose, humusy, decidedly moist but not waterlogged. Location—shaded from strong sun; the dappled shade of deep-rooting deciduous trees is ideal. Plant in late Aug. or early Sept. The

bulbs deteriorate seriously if kept out of the ground for long periods; plant as early as they can be obtained, covered to a depth of 3″, 2–3″ apart. Leave established plantings undisturbed as long as possible. Mulch soil annually with rotted compost, manure, or leafmold. Water freely in dry weather.

**Propagation:** By offsets (not all kinds form offsets) at planting time; by seeds, early fall.

**Kinds:** *americanum*, 6–10″, yellow, a shy bloomer; *californicum* (Fawn-Lily), 6–12″, cream and yellow (white varieties exist); *citrinum*, 6–8″, cream and yellow; *grandiflorum* (Easter-Bells), 12–20″, bright yellow (white in variety *album*); *Hendersonii* (Pink Trout-Lily), 6–12″, pink-lilac; *montanum* (Avalanche-Lily), 12–18″, white and orange, very difficult; *multiscapoideum* (*Hartwegii*, *Purdyi*), 6″, white or cream and yellow; *revolutum*, 8–12″, white, lavender, pink, or purple; *tuolumnense*, 9–14″, golden yellow.

**EUCHARIS** (Amazon-Lily). Tropical American evergreen bulbs with handsome foliage and splendid fragrant flowers, two or three crops of which are produced each year. For pots and cut flowers.

**Culture:** Soil—rich, loamy, porous, containing old rotted manure and bone meal. Location—shaded, moist greenhouse, night temperatures Oct.–Jan., 60°–65°; Feb.–March, 65°–70°; April–Sept., 70°. Pot May–June, 5 in an 8″ or 9″ pot. Set with bulb tips 1″ beneath surface; make soil firm. Repot only when obviously necessary (at intervals of several years); top-dress in March in intervening years. These plants resent root disturbance. Water sparingly until well rooted, established plants freely April–Oct., moderately Nov.–March. Spray foliage with water on bright days. Apply liquid fertilizer weekly (twice weekly when flower stems are developing).

**Propagation:** By offsets, spring or early summer; seeds, in light soil, temperature 70°–80°, spring.

**Kinds:** *grandiflora* (*amazonica*), 15–24″, white; *subedentata*, 18″, white, winter.

**EUCOMIS** (Pineapple-Flower). Summer-flowering South African bulbs, generally hardy only in the South although the author has grown and flowered them successfully for many years at the foot of a south-facing wall in New York City by covering them each winter with a heavy layer of salt-marsh hay. For borders and pot plants. Flowers in cyclindrical spikes surmounted by tufts of green leaves after the fashion of crown imperials.

**Culture:** Soil—fertile, well drained. Location—sunny. Plant or pot in fall or early spring, outdoors 9″ apart, bulbs covered to a depth of 6″; indoors singly in 5″ or 6″ pots, tips of bulbs barely covered. Leave outdoor bulbs undisturbed as long as thriving. Repot pot specimens every 3–4 years in spring, as new growth begins; top-dress in intervening years. Water freely when growing vigorously, keep dry while leafless and dormant. Apply dilute fertilizers to well-rooted specimens in active growth.

**Propagation:** By offsets, just as new growth begins; by seeds, in light sandy soil, spring. Seedlings bloom in 2–5 years.

**Kinds:** *bicolor,* 12–18″, pale green with lilac margin to petals; *comosa* (*punctata*), 12–18″, greenish white, fragrant; *Pole-Evansii,* 48–72″, cream; *undulata,* 12–15″, green and greenish white. ,

**EUSTEPHIA.** South American spring-flowering bulbs closely related to Phaedranassa, requiring the same culture and responding to the same methods of propagation.

**Kinds:** *coccinea* (*Phaedranassa rubroviridis*), 12–18″, red with pale margins and green keels to petals; *Pamiana,* 12–18″, green and red; *yuyuensis,* 18–24″, orange-scarlet.

**EUSTYLIS.** An early-summer-blooming native of Louisiana, Texas, and Mexico. For wild gardens and rock gardens in the milder parts of the country.

**Culture:** Soil—well drained, sandy. Location—light shade or sun. Plant in fall, 2–4″ deep, 3–4″ apart.

**Propagation:** By seeds sown in sandy soil as soon as ripe; by offsets.

**Kind:** *purpurea* (*Nemastylis purpurea*), 6–15″, lavender and violet, attractively marked with yellow and brown-purple or purple. Flowers are short-lived.

# F

**FAIRY-LANTERNS.** *See Calochortus.*

**FALSE-GARLIC.** *See Nothoscordum.*

**FAWN-LILY.** *See Erythronium californicum.*

**FEATHER-HYACINTH.** *See Muscari comosum monstrosum.*

**FERRARIA.** Mostly South African corms that bloom in spring. Hardy in mild climates only. For rock gardens; as pot plants in window or greenhouse. Flowers very attractive, although somewhat ill-scented and not long-lived.

**Culture:** Soil—sandy, peaty, well drained. Location—full sun. Plant in early fall, 2″ deep and 3″ apart outdoors; in pots or pans, 2″ apart, bulbs just covered. Night temperature 40°–45° from potting time until Jan., then 45°–50°. Water sparingly for some weeks after potting, more freely from Jan. until flowering. Gradually dry off when foliage begins to die naturally after flowering. Keep dry during summer dormant season.

**Propagation:** By offsets at planting time; seeds, Sept., in sandy soil, night temperature 40°–50°.

**Kind:** *undulata,* 6–10″, brown and purple.

**FLORAL FIRE-CRACKER.** *See Brevoortia.*

**FLY-POISON.** *See Amianthium.*

**FOXTAIL-LILY.** *See Eremurus.*

**FREESIA.** South African corms that produce fragrant flowers in winter and spring. By making several plantings a succession of blooms may be had for several months. For pots and cut flowers. In frostless and nearly frostless climates they may be grown outdoors, but essentially they are cool greenhouse bulbs; even in sunrooms they are rarely entirely satisfactory. They need coolness and plenty of sun. Given a suitable environment they are easy to grow.

**Culture:** Soil—light, loamy, fertile, porous. Location—sunny, airy, greenhouse atmosphere moderately moist. Plant 2″ apart, ½–1″ deep in adequately drained 5″ or 6″ pots or deep pans, at end of Aug. to bloom late Dec. and Jan.; in Oct. to bloom Jan.; Nov. for March flowering; Dec. for April flowering. Night temperature 40°–50°. Use bulbs ¾″ or more in diameter for early planting; for later plantings those ⅝″ are satisfactory and even ½″ size will do. After planting, water; put Aug.-planted pots in a cold frame, cover surface of soil with moss, and shade from sun until young shoots appear; put later-planted bulbs directly in greenhouse; no period of darkness is necessary. Water moderately until well rooted, then generously; excessive dryness results in yellow leaf tips and blind flower buds. However, unless the pots are very well drained, equally disastrous results may occur from overwetness. Apply weak, liquid fertilizers regularly from the time flower stems show until flowers begin to open. Stake and tie neatly. After flowering keep watered and fertilized as long as foliage remains green; when yellowing begins dry gradually and finally withhold water altogether. Store dry until planting time in pots of soil in which plants grew, or remove and store in dry, airy place out of sun. Bulbs are inexpensive and most growers discard them after blooming and purchase new ones each year; this is by far the best plan if the flowers are cut with foliage but is unnecessary otherwise.

**Propagation:** By offsets at planting time; to obtain new varieties and to raise natural species, by seeds in pots of light, sandy soil, Sept.

**Kinds:** Practically all grown today are named varieties that are great improvements over the wild species. They may be had in white and a wide range of colors (almost every color except red); *refracta*, 12–18″, greenish yellow (white in variety *alba*), is very fragrant.

**FRITILLARIA** (Fritillary). A large group of spring-blooming bulbs, natives of the North Temperate Zone; a considerable number from the American West. Many are difficult to grow or are tantalizingly capricious, often gradually petering out and finally disappearing after two or three years; all are worth trying. For rock gardens, wild gardens, and *imperialis* for borders. Among those that have proved fairly reliable in eastern gardens are: *camschatcensis, lanceolata, meleagris* and its varieties, *pudica, pyrenaica,* and, in some places, *imperialis*.

**Culture:** Soil—deep, rich, sandy, fairly moist but not wet, with limestone or lime added for *imperialis* and other alien kinds. Location—sun or light shade. Plant as early in fall as bulbs can be obtained; they are harmed by being out of the ground longer than necessary. Set most 4–8″ apart, 3–4″ deep; *imperialis*, 6–8″ apart, 5–6″ deep. Mulch in fall with leafmold, very old rotted manure, or compost. Water copiously in dry weather. Do not transplant or disturb oftener than absolutely necessary.

**Propagation:** By offsets at planting time; by seeds in cold frame when ripe. Do not transplant seedlings until second year; they bloom when 4–6 years old.

**Kinds:** *camschatcensis*, 12–18″, black-purple; *glauca*, 8″, purple and greenish yellow; *imperialis* (Crown Imperial) 36–48″, purplish, orange- or yellow-red; *lanceolata*, 18–24″, purple mottled with greenish yellow; *liliacea*, 12″, dull white, fragrant; *Meleagris* (Snakes-Head, Checkered-Lily, Guinea-Hen-Flower), 12–18″, checkered with maroon (variety *alba* is creamy white; variety *purpurea*, deep purplish); *pluriflora* (Pink Adobe-Lily), 12″, pink-purple; *pudica*, 9″, yellow or orange tinged with purple; *pyrenaica*, 12″, purple spotted with green.

**FRITILLARY.** *See Fritillaria.*

# G

**GAGEA.** Small, spring-flowering bulbs, natives of Europe, Asia, and north Africa. Suitable for rock gardens.

**Culture:** Soil—porous, fertile. Location—sunny. Plant in fall, 3″ deep, 3″ apart. Lift and replant not oftener than necessary.

**Propagation:** By offsets at lifting time; by

seeds sown in sandy soil in a cold frame, summer or fall.

**Kinds:** *arvensis,* 6″; *pratensis,* 4″; *silvatica (lutea),* 6″. All are yellow with greenish outsides to the petals.

**GALANTHUS** (Snowdrop). Hardy bulbs with nodding flowers, those ordinarily grown flowering in late winter and earliest spring. Easy to grow and increasing naturally when comfortably located. For rock gardens, light woodlands, borders, and cut flowers.

**Outdoor Culture:** Soil—deep, mellow, not too dry (for *nivalis* distinctly moist but not wet). Location—lightly shaded, beneath deciduous trees or shrubs but not evergreens. Plant Aug.–Sept., 2–4″ apart, 2–3″ deep. Mulch lightly in fall with humus or leafmold. Fertilize in early spring. Do not transplant unless signs of deterioration are apparent, then lift and transplant as soon as foliage dies.

**Propagation:** By offsets at transplanting time; by seeds in cold frame as soon as ripe. Seedlings flower when 3 years old.

**Indoor Culture:** As for *Crocus.*

**Kinds:** *byzantinus,* 6–9″, white with green spots, Dec.–Feb.; *cilicicus,* 5–6″, white, Dec.–Feb.; *Elwesii,* 9–12″, white and green, Dec.–Feb.; *latifolius,* 6–8″, white and green, Feb.–March; *nivalis* (common Snowdrop), 6–8″, white with green spots, Jan.–March (varieties of *nivalis* include *flore-pleno* with double flowers, *Imperati* with earlier and larger flowers, and *Scharlokii* and *Viridi-apice* with much greener flowers); *plicatus,* 6–12″, green and white, Jan.–March.

**GALTONIA** (Summer-Hyacinth). Summer-blooming South African bulb hardy at Philadelphia with winter covering. For borders, groups, and cut flowers.

**Culture:** Soil—rich, fairly moist. Location—sunny. Plant in spring 5–6″ deep, 18–24″ apart. Leave undisturbed several years. Mulch with leaves, salt-marsh hay, etc., over winter; or in cold climates lift in fall and store like gladioluses.

**Propagation:** By seeds, spring or fall, in cold frame or greenhouse; offsets, spring. Seedlings bloom when 4–5 years old.

**Kind:** *candicans (Hyacinthus candicans),* 24–48″, white, summer.

**GAYLAXIA.** Spring- or summer-blooming South African corms having the same general uses and requiring the same culture as *Ixia.*

**Kinds:** *graminea,* light yellow; *ovata,* dark yellow (variety *grandiflora* has larger flowers).

**GEISSORHIZA.** Spring-blooming South African corms having the same general uses and requiring the same culture as *Ixia.*

**Kinds:** *hirta,* 12″, bright red; *inaequalis,* 12″, gray-blue to lavender; *secunda,* 12″, white.

**GESNERIA.** True gesnerias appear not to be in cultivation. For plants grown as such *see Corytholoma,* and *Smithiantha.*

**GETHYLLIS.** Fragrant, crocus-like, South African bulbs that bloom in spring or summer. The fruits, which are fragrant and pleasant to the taste, are eaten in its native country. They may be grown in pots in a cool greenhouse in the same manner as *Oxalis* and should be suited for outdoor cultivation in southern California and similar mild climates.

**Kinds:** *afra,* 3–4″, white or flushed pink; *ciaris,* 6″, white; *spiralis,* 9″, white.

**GLADIOLUS.** Cormous natives of Africa and the Mediterranean region now including many hybrids and garden varieties. Popular for garden decoration, for early bloom in greenhouses, as cut flowers. By making successional plantings a continuity of flowers may be had in the garden for many weeks.

**Culture for Summer Bloom Outdoors:** Soil—fertile, well drained, enriched with compost, leafmold, or some such organic matter but not containing fresh manure. Location—preferably full sun but will stand a little part-day shade. In cut-flower garden plant in single or double rows, 24–30″ apart; in group plantings in borders space 6–9″ apart. Set 4–6″ deep, the lesser depth if corms are small or soil is heavy, the greater if reverse conditions exist. Make first planting about the time trees leaf out, successive plantings every 2–3 weeks until the latest date a planting can be made with expectation of bloom before frost. For the late plantings use early-maturing varieties (dealers indicate the average number of days it takes each variety to bloom from planting; this varies from 60 to 90 days or more). Extra-early blooms may be had by planting in a cold frame 3–4 weeks before it is safe to plant outdoors, or by potting bulbs singly in 4″ pots a month ahead of planting time and transplanting them to the outdoor garden when all danger of frost is passed. Clean cultivation is important; cultivate surface soil frequently but shallowly. If supports seem necessary stake and tie before plants keel over or are broken. In borders other nearby plants may afford adequate support; deep-planted bulbs are less likely to need support than others. Three or four inches of soil hilled up to the bases of plants grown in rows may give support enough. When second leaves have fully developed give a light application of fertilizer and repeat twice monthly until flowers show color. Water copiously at weekly intervals in dry weather. After blooming continue to encourage growth as long as leaves remain green. After they have turned brown, or with the coming of frost, if that occurs before the leaves have died, dig corms, cut off foliage, and spread corms to dry in a shaded frostproof place. After about ten days clean them off, dust with DDT powder, and store in a dry, dark, or shaded place, temperature 40°–50°.

**Culture for Winter and Spring Bloom:** In the far South gladioluses of the "baby" (*nanus*) and other spring-blooming types may be planted in fall for early bloom and in mild climates may be left without disturbance for 2–3 years. In the North these, as well as corms of the ordinary summer-flowering kinds (specially prepared for early forcing), are grown in greenhouses. Plant *tristis, nanus,* and other spring-flowering gladioluses in Sept.–Oct., in benches or 5″ or 6″ pots, the bulbs 2″ apart and 2″ deep; plant prepared bulbs of the large-flowering varieties (summer-blooming types) in late Dec.–March, in benches or 8″ or 9″ pots,

bulbs 3″ deep and 3–4″ apart. Cultural requirements same as for freesias.

**Propagation:** By offset corms; by cormels (tiny corms found clustered around corms at digging time) stored over winter in barely moist sand or peatmoss, temperature 40°–45°, and in spring sown outdoors 2″ apart in 2″ deep drills after first being soaked for 2–4 days in tepid water (cormels produce good corms the first year, flowers the second); by seeds to raise new varieties and to increase natural species.

**Kinds:** Modern gladioluses of hybrid origin are available in a vast number of varieties described in the catalogs of dealers and specialists. They fall into a few distinct groups including the *nanus* (*Colvillei*) group which blooms in late winter and spring and includes such well-established varieties as The Bride and Peach Blossom; the *Tubergenii* group which is similar but of taller growth; and the Herald group, also winter- and spring-flowering, but with stouter spikes and larger flowers. Certain species, notably *tristis,* are also winter- and spring-bloomers. Summer-flowering varieties, once grouped as *primulinus* hybrids, large flowered, orchid flowered, etc., are classified as formal or informal—the former having flowers regularly arranged, close together, and approximately in opposite pairs on the spike; the latter with flowers less regular, in somewhat looser spikes, and spaced alternately in two rows, and within that informal classification are further divided into groups based on diameter of individual flowers (giant, 5½″ or more; large, 4½–5½″; medium, 3¼–4½″; small, 2½–3¼″; and miniature, under 2½″), and still further into groups according to their color. Species sometimes grown include *segetum,* 24″, bright purple, early summer; *tristis,* 24–36″, yellowish white with purplish markings, fragrant, late winter (its variety *concolor* is similar but with creamy white flowers).

**GLOBE-TULIP.** *See Calochortus.*

**GLORIOSA** (Glory-Lily). Tuberous-rooted vines with annual stems. They bear handsome flowers in summer and fall. Natives of tropical Africa and Asia. In far South may be grown permanently outdoors, elsewhere in greenhouses, window gardens, and outdoors in summer. For cut flowers, garden decoration, and as pot plants.

**Indoor Culture:** Soil—light, well drained, fertile. Location—sunny, with light shade in summer. Plant Feb.–April, 2″ deep, singly in a 6″ or 3 in an 8″ pot. Water moderately until growth is well advanced, then freely. Spray with water on bright days. Night temperature 65°–70°. Provide supports around which leaf tendrils can twine. Apply weak liquid fertilizers regularly from when half grown until dormant season is at hand. After flowering, when foliage begins to fade, reduce watering, finally withhold and keep quite dry until planting time.

**Outdoor Culture:** Where too cold to leave tubers in ground permanently set out started plants from pots in sheltered locations when weather is really warm and settled. Water freely in dry weather. Dig before frost, taking great care not to break or damage tubers; store over winter in peatmoss or sand, temperature 55°–65°.

**Propagation:** By offset tubers, complete with bud at upper end, removed at planting time; seeds in light soil, temperature 70°–75°, Jan.–Feb.

**Kinds:** *Carsoni*, 36–48″, red and yellow; *lutea*, 60–80″, buff-yellow; *Rothschildiana*, 70–120″, red and yellow (variety *citrina* is citron-yellow and claret); *superba*, 70–120″, yellow-orange changing to red; *Verschuuri*, 60″, red and yellow; *virescens* (*simplex*), 60–80″, orange and yellow (variety *grandiflora* is larger with yellow flowers, variety *Plantii* has reddish yellow flowers).

**GLORY-LILY.** *See Gloriosa.*

**GLORY-OF-THE-SNOW.** *See Chionodoxa.*

**GLORY-OF-THE-SUN.** *See Leucocoryne ixioides.*

**GLOXINIA.** Common name of *Sinningia*, which see.

**GOLDEN-STARS.** *See Bloomeria crocea.*

**GRAPE-HYACINTH.** *See Muscari.*

**GRASS-NUT.** *See Brodiaea laxa.*

**GUERNSEY-LILY.** *See Nerine sarniensis.*

**GUINEA-HEN-FLOWER.** *See Fritillaria Meleagris.*

# H

**HABRANTHUS.** Chiefly South American (one species in Texas) summer-flowering bulbs some of which have been known as *Zephyranthes*, others as *Hippeastrum*. Hardy in the South, elsewhere for cultivation in pots, or planted in the garden in spring and lifted and stored over winter. For rock gardens, borders, and window gardens.

**Cultivation:** As for *Zephyranthes*.

**Kinds:** *Andersonii*, 6″, yellow with red stripings; *brachyandrus*, 12″, lavender-pink shading to brownish purple; *robustus*, 9″, rose-red; *texanus*, 9″, yellow with reddish markings.

**HAEMANTHUS** (Blood-Lily). South African spring-, summer- and fall-flowering bulbs with spherical or hemispherical heads of star-shaped flowers. For window gardens, greenhouses, and the larger ones as summer plants on terraces and porches.

**Culture:** Soil—rich, loamy, well drained. Location—sunny, with a little light shade during hottest summer months. Pot at beginning of growing season, e.g. *albiflos* and *coccineus* in Aug., *Katherinae* and *multiflorus* March–April. Leave top half of bulb protruding above soil. Do not repot more frequently than is necessary; in intermediate seasons top-dress. Water freely when in growth; keep deciduous kinds quite dry while dormant, water evergreen kinds rather sparingly during their seasons of rest. Apply weak liquid fertilizers when actively growing. Night temperature 55°–65°.

**Propagation:** By offsets removed at potting time; by bulb cuttings, Aug.; by seeds in sandy soil, temperature 60°–65°, spring.

**Kinds:** *albiflos*, 9–12″, white, red berries, evergreen, fall; *coccineus*, 12–24″, bright red, deciduous, fall; *Katherinae*, 12–24″, salmon-red, evergreen or nearly so, summer;

*multiflorus*, 12–30″, coral-red, deciduous, summer; *puniceus*, 12″, red, pink, or nearly white, deciduous, summer. Some excellent summer-blooming hybrids of *Katherinae* exist including Andromeda (*Katherinae* x *magnificus*), salmon-crimson; and King Albert (*Katherinae* x *puniceus*), red, low growing.

**HELICODICEROS** (Twist-Arum). A Jack-in-the-Pulpit relative from Corsica and the Balearic Islands. For growing as a curiosity in the South and in greenhouses.

**Culture** and **Propagation:** As for *Arum*.

**Kind:** *muscivorus* (*Arum crinitum*), 12–18″, brown-purple, flowers (inflorescences) possessing an offensive odor, early spring.

**HESPERANTHERA.** Mostly spring-blooming South African corms resembling *Ixia* but less decorative. Their delightfully fragrant flowers open in the afternoon or evening according to kind.

**Culture:** As for *Ixia*.

**Kinds:** *Bauri*, 8–10″, white, pink outside, anthers golden yellow; *Stanfordiae*, 12″, bright yellow.

**HEXAGLOTTIS.** South African spring-blooming corms with yellow flowers of short duration.

**Culture:** As for *Ixia*.

**Kinds:** *longifolia*, 18″; *virgata*, 18″.

**HIPPEASTRUM.** South American bulbs, popularly known as amaryllises, quite distinct from the botanical genus *Amaryllis*. Handsome flowering plants for window gardens, greenhouses, and, in the far South, permanent planting outdoors. Popular hybrid kinds bloom chiefly in winter and spring, occasionally in summer; natural species bloom at various seasons according to kind.

**Culture:** Soil—rich, loamy, well drained. Location—full sun Sept.–April (except when dormant), light shade at other times; night temperature when growing 65°–70°, when dormant 55°. Pot new bulbs (which when bought have had their roots trimmed off) Nov.–Dec., with upper third of bulb protruding above surface; place in dark or shaded place, temperature 55°–60°, and

water very sparingly (but do not allow soil to become really dry) until new roots are established (by Jan.–Feb.), then bring into light and treat as for repotted established specimens. Repot or top-dress established plants at first signs of new growth (Jan.–Feb. for hybrid kinds); repot every few years only. Water well when first repotted, moderately until new growth is well advanced, then freely. Apply liquid fertilizers throughout active growing season. During summer plants may be plunged almost to the rims of their pots in a bed of sand or ashes outdoors. Some growers remove the plants from their pots and plant in rich soil in the garden for the summer, lifting and repotting them before frost; this is a less desirable method but offers advantages if for any reason one cannot give them regular care during the summer. At end of growing season (fall for hybrid kinds) gradually reduce water and store dry until new growth begins. Most indicate the approach of the resting season by ceasing growth and by their leaves beginning to yellow, but some hybrids tend to remain green as long as moisture is supplied; these should be forced to rest by withholding water from Oct. to Jan. or Feb.

**Propagation:** By offsets at potting time; by bulb cuttings, Aug.; by seeds, spring, in light, sandy soil, temperature 70°–75°. If seedlings are kept growing without rest until first bloom many will bloom in 1½ to 2 years; if allowed to go dormant each year, they take longer.

**Kinds:** Many magnificent named hybrid varieties are available as well as unnamed seedlings of hybrid origin. These hybrids come in a magnificent color range from pure white to deepest crimson and include all shades between but not yellows or blues. They include miniature-flowered kinds as well as those with immense blooms. It is worth-while to go to some effort to obtain the finest-flowering types of these hybrids. In addition a number of natural species are grown including: *advenum*, 9–18″, old rose or red, Sept.; *aulicum*, 24″, red and green, winter, stands cooler conditions than most species; *candidum* (*immaculatum*), 30″, white, fragrant; *Harrisonii*, 20″, white and red, fragrant, spring; *miniatum*, 12–18″, **red,**

fall; *pratense,* 12–24″, bright red, spring, hardier than most; *procerum* (Blue Amaryllis), 20–36″, lavender-blue, winter (notoriously difficult to flower); *psittacinum,* 24″, red and green, spring; *puniceum* (*equestre*), salmon-red, spring or early summer; *reticulatum,* 12″, red, spring (variety *striatifolium* has prominent white stripe down center of leaf); *rutilum,* 12″, red and pale green (variety *crocatum,* salmon and pale green), winter and spring; *solandriflorum,* 24–30″, cream or greenish, fragrant; *vittatum,* 12–24″, red and white, fragrant, spring. A bulb grown in the lower South as St. Joseph's Lily is apparently the old hybrid *H. Johnsonii* or a variant of it. It blooms in spring, its flowers deep red with a white center band to each petal.

**HOMERIA.** Pretty South African corms that have the same uses and require the same culture as *Ixia;* their flowers close on dull days.

Kinds: *collina,* 18″, red with yellowish base (variations in color exist and some have been given varietal names such as *aurantiaca,* orange-red and yellow, and *ochroleuca,* pale yellow); *elegans,* 18″, yellow with green or brownish blotch; *lilacina,* 12″, lilac with purple veins and yellow-speckled purple blotch.

**HOMOGLOSSUM.** African corms that were once included in the genus *Antholyza.* They require the same culture and are propagated in the same manner as *Freesia.*

Kind: *Priori* variety *Salteri,* bright red, winter.

**HYACINTH.** *See Hyacinthus.*

**HYACINTHUS** (Hyacinth). Mostly hardy, mostly spring-flowering bulbs, natives chiefly of the Mediterranean region. Best known are the common hyacinth and the Roman hyacinth which are valuable for beds, borders, and early forcing indoors. The smaller species are suitable for rock gardens and require the same culture as *Chionodoxa.* They may be forced indoors like crocuses.

**Outdoor Culture (Common Hyacinth and Roman Hyacinth):** Soil—deep, fertile, well drained, preferably sandy. Location—sunny. Plant Sept.–mid-Oct., 6–8″ apart, bulb tops 5–6″ deep. If fall is dry keep well watered. Mulch over winter with marsh hay, leaves, or evergreen branches. Apply light dressing of complete fertilizer early spring. After foliage dies, lift and store in dry, cool, shaded place until fall, or leave undisturbed in ground. In many American gardens hyacinths tend to deteriorate with the passing years, although when favorably located they persist and bloom for years.

**Indoor Culture:** Soil—fertile, well drained. Plant Aug.–Oct., large bulbs singly in 5″ pots, or several together, nearly touching, in pans; Romans and Dutch Romans 3–4 together in 5″ pots. Water well, then plunge outdoors under 8″ of sand or ashes or place in cool bulb cellar. When well rooted and before young shoots are 3″ high, transfer to light position indoors. Keep in dark until leaves and flower stems are 6–8″ tall, then gradually expose to light, full sun after leaves turn green. Night temperature 50°–55° is suitable; somewhat higher may be given if flowers are wanted quickly, somewhat lower if they are to be held back for later bloom. Water freely. After blooming, bulbs are of no further use. May also be forced in bulb fiber, pebbles, and water, or in plain water in special hyacinth glasses. When grown in these media it is not practical to plunge the containers outdoors; keep them in a dark place, temperature 40°–45° during rooting period. Romans bloom Nov.–Jan. indoors.

**Propagation:** Small rock garden kinds freely by seeds sown in cold frame in early fall; by offsets at planting time. Common hyacinths and Roman hyacinths are rarely propagated in this country except by natural offsets. In Holland propagation is effected by scooping or slashing the bases of the bulbs; new varieties are raised from seed.

Kinds: Common hyacinths or Dutch hyacinths (varieties of *orientalis*) are 12–18″ tall, have dense cylindrical spikes of fragrant blooms—white, pale yellow, pink, red, blue, or purple—and may be obtained in a number of named varieties that are described in dealers' catalogs. The miniature, Dutch Roman, or Cynthella hyacinths are younger and smaller bulbs of the common or Dutch varieties that are specially preferred for early forcing. They bear less massive spikes and are offered in the same color range. Roman hyacinths (*orientalis albulus*), sometimes called "French Roman," are white flowered, have daintier spikes than the common hyacinth, bloom much earlier, and are less hardy; they are particularly valuable for very early forcing indoors. The following species are suitable for rock gardens and naturalizing: *amethystinus*, 6", light blue, spring (variety *albus* has white flowers); *ciliatus* (*azureus*) 9–12", blue, spring; *dalmaticus*, 3–4", pale blue, spring; *romanus*, 9–15", greenish white shaded blue, spring. They need the same culture as *Muscari*.

**HYDROSME** (Devils-Tongue, Snake-Palm). Allied to *Amorphophallus* and sometimes grown under that name. A curious Calla-Lily relative, native of Cochin-China and bearing in late winter or spring tall calla-like blooms of somber color and offensive odor. The bloom, which lasts but a few days, is followed by a single, large, much-divided umbrella-shaped decorative leaf that remains all summer. For subtropical effect in the summer border; as a porch or terrace plant.

**Culture:** Generally as for *Amorphophallus;* may be planted in garden after weather is warm and settled and be lifted before fall frost and stored over winter in cellar, temperature 50°–55°.

**Propagation:** This species produces offset tubers freely and these afford a ready means of propagation.

**Kind:** *Rivieri*, leaf 36–60" tall, flower (inflorescence) 36–48" tall, dull reddish purple.

**HYMENOCALLIS** (Spider-Lily). Mostly summer-flowering bulbs, natives of the Americas including the U. S. For outdoor beds and borders in mild climates, and *calathina* (Ismene, Basket-Flower, Peruvian Daffodil) for summer culture outdoors North; for pots and cut flowers.

**Outdoor Culture:** Soil—rich, deep, plentifully supplied with organic matter. Where

hardy plant in spring, 6–12" apart, 4–6" deep. Mulch with compost or leafmold; lift and replant only when blooming deteriorates. Plant *calathina* after weather is warm and settled, the tips of bulbs at a distance beneath the surface equal to three times the depth of the bulb, 8–12" apart. Water freely in dry weather. After frost dig without damaging roots more than necessary, pack soil around roots, and store over winter dry, temperature 60°.

**Indoor Culture:** Soil—rich, coarse, well drained. Location—moist greenhouse shaded lightly from strong summer sun. Pot in spring or summer, when new growth is about to begin, with tips of bulbs just buried. Water freely during active growth; water evergreen kinds moderately during resting season, but keep deciduous kinds dry while dormant. Apply dilute liquid fertilizers regularly when growing actively. Repot every few years only; top-dress in spring, intermediate years. Night temperature for tropical kinds 65°–70°, for temperate kinds 50°–55°.

**Propagation:** By offsets, spring; by bulb cuttings, Aug.; seeds, spring, temperature 70°–74°.

**Tropical Kinds:** *caribaea*, 8–12", white; *Horsmannii*, white; *littoralis*, 12–24", white; *Macrostephana*, 24", white, winter (probably a hybrid); *speciosa*, 18–24", white; *tenuiflora*, 12–18", white.

**Temperate Kinds:** *Amancaes*, 18–24", yellow and green; *calathina*, 24", white (variety Advance, white, more vigorous growth; Olympia, cream to light yellow, larger); *galvestonensis*, 24", white; *Harrisiana*, 12", white; *Macleana*, 12–18", yellowish and green; *occidentalis*, 18"; *rotata*, 18", white, spring. Hybrids and varieties: *festalis* (*Elisena longipetala* x *H. calathina*), Sulphur Queen (*calathina* x *Amancaes*).

**HYPOXIS** (Star-Grass). A grassy-leaved cormous plant that is scarcely ever without blooms from late spring to frost. For rock gardens and wild gardens.

**Culture:** Soil—well drained, preferably sandy. Location—sunny. Plant in spring or early fall, 5–6" apart, 2" deep.

**Propagation:** By division at planting time; by seeds in early fall or spring.

Kind: *hirsuta (erecta)*, 6–12", bright yellow.

# I

INDIAN-TURNIP. *See Arisaema triphyllum.*

IPHEION. The plant treated in this book as *Brodiaea uniflora* is by some botanists named *Ipheion uniflorum.*

IRIS. Irises that have true bulbs require quite different treatment from the better-known kinds that grow from rhizomes. Bulbous kinds only are discussed here. They bloom naturally in spring (early or late, according to kind) and are useful, the low-growing species for rock gardens and for early forcing indoors, the Spanish, Dutch, and English kinds for borders, beds, cut flowers, and for forcing for early bloom. *Iris tingitana* is similar in its uses to the Spanish irises but is best suited for mild climates.

**Culture of Rock Garden Kinds Outdoors:** Soil—gritty, fertile, well drained. Location—full sun. Plant 3" deep, 3" apart, early fall, preferably among low groundcover plants such as thyme. Lift and replant every 3–4 years.

**Culture of Rock Garden Kinds Indoors:** Soil—gritty, fertile. Plant in 4" pots or 6" pans, early fall, 2–3" apart, 1" deep. Treat same as Spanish and Dutch kinds. When well rooted bring into greenhouse or sunroom, night temperature 40°–50°. Keep well watered. After flowering continue to water, gradually harden, and after danger from frost is passed plant in rock garden.

**Culture of Spanish, English, and Dutch Irises Outdoors:** Soil—deep, well drained, porous, fertile, distinctly more moist for the English than for the Spanish and Dutch, and, for the English, decidedly rich with organic matter. Location—sunny, sheltered. Plant in early fall, 3–4" deep, 5–6" apart. In the North protect with generous layer of leaves, marsh hay, etc., after the ground has frozen; remove this in spring. Lift and replant every third year.

**Culture of Spanish and Dutch Irises and**

**Iris tingitana in Greenhouses:** Soil—light, fertile. Location—sunny. Pot in Oct., about 7 bulbs in a 6" pot or plant in deep flats 4" apart. Plant with tops of bulbs 1" deep. Bury outdoors under 8" of sand or ashes or place in a frost-free cellar or cold frame, temperature 35°–45°, until well rooted; then bring into greenhouse, night temperature 45°–50°. Keep well watered. Apply dilute liquid fertilizer once or twice a week. After blooming, forced bulbs are of no further value for indoor growing but may be kept watered until foliage dies, then be dried off and planted in an outdoor garden in fall.

**Propagation:** By offsets at planting time; by seeds in light sandy soil in cold frame early fall or spring.

**Kinds:** Dutch irises (hybrids of *Xiphium praecox, tingitana,* and perhaps other species) resemble Spanish irises, but bloom earlier, have larger flowers, and are of sturdier appearance. They are magnificent for garden decoration and cutting. There are a great many named varieties (described in dealers' catalogs), in a wide range of colors including white, white and yellow, yellow, orange-yellow, lilac, light blue, and deep blue. They grow 18–24" tall and flower outdoors the latter part of May at New York City. Spanish irises (varieties of *Xiphium*) bloom in early June at New York City, are 12–24" tall, and have lovely white, yellow, bronze, blue, violet, or intermediate-toned fragrant flowers atop wiry stems. They are splendid in the garden or as cut flowers. Dealers' catalogs describe many varieties. English irises (varieties of *xiphioides*) are rather more difficult to grow than the Spanish and Dutch kinds. They bloom in late June at New York City. They are of stouter growth and are of less fragile appearance than others. Their color range includes blue, mauve, purple, plain and with various featherings and flakings, rose tone, clarets, and white; there are no yellows. Varieties are described in dealers' catalogs. Rock garden kinds that are hardy in the North where they bloom in late winter and spring include *Bakeriana*, 6–12", white, violet, and blue; *Danfordiae*, 2–4", yellow with brownish green markings; *histrioides*, 12", blue-purple, white, and yellow; *reticulata*,

4–10″, deep violet with orange and white, fragrant on warm days (varieties of this include *Cantab, coerulea, cyanea,* Harmony, Hercules, J. S. Dijt, Joyce, *Krelagei, major, purpurea,* Royal Blue, *sophenensis,* and Wentworth). Rock garden kinds not reliably hardy north of Washington, D. C., are: *juncea,* 12″, yellow; *palestina,* yellow, greenish, or blue, and *Vartanii,* 9–18″, slaty lilac to white. Bulbous irises of the Juno group are little known in cultivation in North America. They include *bucharica, caucasica, orchioides, persica, Rosenbachiana, sindjarensis,* and the Sindpur hybrids between *sindjarensis* and *persica.* They are early-bloomers, interesting to the collector of the unusual, but generally less attractive than other bulbous kinds recommended. They are best suited for milder sections of the country. In the North they should be protected by a heavy winter covering of leaves, evergreen branches, etc. They need light soil and a sunny exposure.

**ISMENE.** *See Hymenocallis calathina.*

**ISOLOMA.** A name often applied to plants correctly named *Kohleria. See Kohleria.*

**IXIA** (Corn-Lily). South African spring-blooming corms with grassy foliage and slender racemes of attractive, brilliantly colored flowers. For outdoor cultivation in the South and for cultivation in greenhouses. The author has grown them successfully outdoors in New York City in a sheltered place at the base of a south-facing wall by covering heavily with leaves over winter.

**Outdoor Culture:** Soil—light, fertile, well drained. Location—sunny. Plant outdoors Oct.–Nov., 3″ deep, 3–4″ apart, and protect with a winter covering of leaves, salt-marsh hay, or similar material. Lift after foliage has died, dry, and store in a cool, dry, shaded place until planting time. Where dry summers prevail, as in southern California, they may remain permanently in the ground.

**Indoor Culture:** As for *Freesia.*

**Propagation:** By offsets; by seeds, Sept., in light, sandy soil, night temperature 50°–55°.

**Kinds:** *azurea,* 18″, blue with purple-black centers; *campanulata* (*crateroides*), 12″, pink or red, early; *maculata,* 24″, typically yellow with dark purple blotches at bases of petals, but occurring in other colors including cream, purplish, and pinkish; *paniculata,* 24–36″, creamy white with dark basal blotches, sometimes pink tinged (variety *tenuiflora* has no basal blotches); *patens* 12″, crimson to pale red, fragrant; *polystachya,* 24″, pink; *viridiflora,* 24″, pale green with black throat. In addition to the species a number of fine named varieties are offered in catalogs.

**IXIOLIRION.** Asiatic bulbs that bloom in spring. For rock gardens and borders.

**Culture:** Soil—sandy, well drained. Location—sunny. Plant 3″ deep, 4″ apart, fall. In North protect over winter with leaves, salt-marsh hay, or similar covering. May be grown in greenhouses in the same manner as *Freesia.*

**Propagation:** By offsets; by seeds sown in fall or early spring in sandy soil, temperature 45°–55°.

**Kind:** *montanum* (*Ledebouri*), 12″, lilac-blue.

# J

**JACK-IN-THE-PULPIT.** *See Arisaema triphyllum.*

**JACOBEAN-LILY.** *See Sprekelia.*

**JONQUIL.** *See Narcissus.*

**JOSEPHINES-LILY.** *See Brunsvigia Josephinae.*

# K

**KAFIR-LILY.** *See Clivia.*

**KOHLERIA.** Tuberous-rooted summer-blooming plants related to *Achimenes.* Frequently grown in gardens under the name *Isoloma.* Natives of tropical South America. For greenhouses and window gardens.

**Culture** and **Propagation:** As for *Achi-*

*menes,* except that plants should be grown singly in 5″ pots or 4–5 in 6″ pots and shoots should not be pinched.

Kinds: *amabilis,* 24″, dark pink dotted with purple; *bogotensis,* 24″, red, below is yellow spotted with red; *digitaliflora,* 24″, green with pink and white tube to flower; *eriantha* (often misnamed *hirsutum*), 24–36″, orange-red, spotted; *Lindenianum,* white and violet with yellow and purple markings; *pictum,* 18–36″, scarlet, yellow beneath, fall or early winter; several hybrids are in cultivation.

# L

LACHENALIA (Cape-Cowslip). Attractive winter- and spring-blooming plants from South Africa with spikes of drooping tubular flowers in a range of interesting colors. For cool greenhouses and sun porches; in frostless and nearly frostless climates for cultivation outdoors.

Culture: As for *Freesia,* except that bulbs may be set somewhat closer together, 10–15 in a 6″ pan, according to size of bulbs.

Kinds: *contaminata,* 9–12″, white or tinged pink; *glaucina,* 12″, white, red, or yellow; *mediana,* 12–15″, greenish white or bluish; *orchioides,* 12–18″, bluish white or creamy yellow with green tips (in variety *mutabilis* the buds are clear blue); *pallida,* 10–12″, pale yellow; *pendula,* 12–15″, red or rose-pink, purple tipped (variety *superba* is an improved form); *purpureo-caerulea,* 12″, blue and purple, fragrant; *pustulata,* 12″, white and tinted red; *reflexa,* 6–8″, yellowish; *Roodeae,* 12–15″, blue and purple; *tricolor,* 9–12″, yellow and red (varieties include *aurea,* golden yellow; *luteola,* citron-yellow tipped with green; *Nelsonii,* butter-yellow tipped with green; *Pearsonii,* 20″, orange and red, a hybrid; *quadricolor,* red and yellow tipped with green); *unifolia,* 12″, white tinged with red or blue.

LAPEIROUSIA. South African corms. For garden beds and pot plants. They bloom for a comparatively long season in summer outdoors and in spring in greenhouses. Hardy as far north as Washington, D. C., and further north with adequate winter protection.

Culture and Propagation: Outdoors, as for *Crocosmia;* indoors as for *Freesia.*

Kinds: *cruenta* (*Anomatheca cruenta*), 12″, red; *juncea,* 18–24″, pale red.

LESSER CELANDINE. See Ranunculus Ficaria.

LEUCOCORYNE (Glory-of-the-Sun). Spring-blooming Chilean bulbs, hardy in mild climates, and in places favored with such suitable for borders and rock gardens, elsewhere as pot plants and cut flowers. Ixioides and its variety *odorata* are delightfully fragrant and last long when cut.

Culture and Propagation: As for *Freesia;* 9–12 bulbs in a 5″ pot are satisfactory.

Kind: *ixioides* (*odorata*), 18″, fairly deep lavender-blue with white centers to, occasionally, pure white.

LEUCOCRINUM (Sand-Lily, Star-Lily). Native of western North America, spring-blooming. For rock gardens.

Culture: Soil—sandy, well drained. Location—full sun. Plant in early fall, 3–4″ apart, 4″ deep.

Propagation: By seeds, early fall, in sandy soil in cold frame.

Kind: *montanum,* 3–4″, white, fragrant.

LEUCOJUM (Snowflake). European and North African bulbs some of which bear a general resemblance to snowdrops, although the spring and summer snowflakes are more robust in appearance and the autumn snowflake is frailer in appearance than snowdrops. Both spring and summer snowflakes are hardy in the North and the author has grown the autumn snowflake (which is more tender) outdoors in a sheltered location in a rock garden in New York City for many years; the autumn snowflake also succeeds well when grown in a pan in a cold frame or cool greenhouse. In American catalogs the summer snowflake (*aestivum*) is often offered under the name of the spring snowflake (*vernum*). The latter has one (occasionally two) flowers on a stem, whereas the summer snowflake has 3–6 (occasionally two); the spring snowflake blooms earlier—before late snowdrops go—and is shorter. Spring and autumn snowflakes are best suited for rock gardens; the summer snowflake for borders, naturalizing, and for cut flowers.

**Culture:** Soil—rich with organic matter, well drained but fairly moist; decidedly gritty for *autumnalis.* Location—sun or light shade for *aestivum,* sunny for *autumnalis,* lightly shaded for *vernum.* Plant in summer or early fall, covering the bulbs to their own depth. Set *vernum* and *aestivum* 3–4″, *autumnale* 1–2″ apart. Do not dig up or disturb oftener than necessary. Never keep bulbs out of the ground longer than necessary. When transplanting is necessary do it as soon as leaves die down.

**Propagation:** By offsets at transplanting time; by seeds sown in cold frame, fall.

**Kinds:** *aestivum* (Summer Snowflake), 12–18″, white tipped with green; *autumnale* (Autumn Snowflake) 6–9″, white flushed with pink, Sept.; *vernum* (Spring Snowflake), 6–9″, white tipped with green (variety *carpathicum* has flowers tipped with yellow; variety *Vagneri* is sturdier and has two, occasionally three, flowers on each stem).

**LILIUM** (Lily). All true lilies belong here; many plants of which "lily" forms part of the common name, such as lily-of-the-valley and glory-lily, belong in other genera, and are treated in this book under their approved botanical names with cross references given under their common names. Lilies are bulbs native to the Northern Hemisphere and include a great many species, some of which are extremely difficult to grow, others comparatively easy. In recent years many splendid hybrid lilies have been raised, a very considerable number by American breeders. It seems certain that as yet only the first possibilities of lily breeding have been explored; we may confidently expect that breeders will continue for some time to provide new and often better kinds. Here we consider only lilies that are reasonably easy to grow; connoisseurs interested in more difficult kinds may consult specialized works. Easily grown lilies are useful for borders and beds, naturalizing, cut flowers, and a few low ones for rock gardens and for pot plants.

**Culture Outdoors:** Soil—deep, fertile, abundantly supplied with organic matter, well drained. Location—sun or part shade, not windswept. Ideal conditions for most—roots and lower stem shaded by other plants, heads in the sun. Even those that prefer some shade grow well in full sun if they do not suffer from dryness, and if the soil surface is mulched to keep it cool; the flowers of a few, such as *Henryi,* tend to bleach in strong sun, but the plants grow well. Plant in fall preferably (*candidum,* Aug.). Purchased bulbs have usually had most of their roots removed and are not available as early as one would wish, sometimes not until after the ground is frozen; for these prepare sites in advance and cover with a thick layer of leaves, straw, or other mulch so that the bulbs may be planted immediately upon arrival. Before planting, pick off damaged scales, cut back withered roots, dust with Fermate, Arasan, or other fungicide. Lilies, particularly stem-rooting kinds, can be successfully planted in spring provided they have been properly stored through the winter, but fall planting is preferable. Bulbs that cannot be planted in fall may be potted and carried through the winter buried beneath a few inches of sand or peatmoss in a cold frame outdoors, or they may be wintered in a cellar, temperature 35°–45°. Established bulbs need digging and transplanting only when they become obviously crowded. Move such bulbs Sept.–Oct. (those of *candidum,* Aug.); take care not to damage roots more than can be helped; do not let them dry. All lilies form permanent roots from the bases of the bulbs, some develop annual roots from the stems above the bulbs as well. Lilies in the latter group need to be planted deeper than the others. Most stem-rooters will be planted at a suitable depth if the tops of the bulbs are covered with 8–10″ of soil; for *concolor, dauricum,* and *rubellum* 5–6″ is sufficient. In all cases plant small bulbs somewhat less deeply. For non-stem-rooters, cover tops of bulbs with 4″ of soil, except *candidum* and *testaceum* which should be set with their tops 1–2″ beneath the surface. Suitable spacing for smaller kinds is 5–6″, for larger kinds 9–15″. Keep soil covered with a loose organic mulch such as peatmoss, compost, leafmold, buckwheat hulls, or pine needles.

Water freely in dry weather. Fertilize in spring, when shoots are a few inches tall, and immediately after flowering with fertilizer rather low in nitrogen, high in phosphorus and potash. Steamed bone meal and unleached wood ashes with some cottonseed meal or other source of organic nitrogen added provides a suitable fertilizer. Remove all faded blooms unless seed is desired. Cut stems near ground only after all leaves on them have withered.

**Indoor Cultivation:** Soil—light, mellow loam enriched with leafmold or peatmoss, and some bone meal. Pot Sept.–March, one bulb in a 5″, 6″, or 7″ pot (according to size of bulb) or three in a 7″, 8″, or 9″ pot. Provide good drainage. Set bulbs (except those of *candidum* and others which do not form stem roots) low in pots and cover so that tips are 1″ beneath surface; later, when stem is well up and pot is filled with roots, add additional rich soil. Plant non-stem-rooters in pots filled to normal level with soil, tips of bulbs 1″ beneath surface. After potting put in cool place to root, temperature 40°–50° for most, 55° for Easter lilies, then bring into greenhouse where growing temperature is maintained. The most favorable temperature varies somewhat according to kind and to the time of year; it is always better to grow lilies rather slowly than to push them with too much heat. Give full sun. Water moderately at first, freely when in full growth and pots are well filled with roots; at the latter stage too apply weekly dilute liquid fertilizer. A night temperature of 50° is ample when forcing *candidum* and many other hardy kinds, but the lilies that are more usually used for forcing such as *longiflorum* varieties and the *speciosum* varieties require 60°–65° after they are well rooted. For these a steady night temperature of 60° is generally best; at this temperature they take about 12–13 weeks from the time the leaves begin to open on the shoots until flowering.

**Propagation:** By offsets at transplanting time; bulbils and stem bulblets in late summer or fall; scales immediately after blooming; seeds, as soon as ripe, in light, peaty, sandy soil in cold frame, covered with soil to depth of ⅛″. Seedlings bloom in 1–7 years according to kind. Among those that

bloom quickly from seed are; *formosanum, Henryi, longiflorum, pumilum, regale, superbum*. Some lilies show no growth above ground the first year when raised from seeds but do make tiny bulbs under the surface; top growth appears after the first winter. Among these are *auratum, canadense*, and *speciosum*.

**Kinds for Outdoor Cultivation:** (\* indicates stem-rooting kinds) \**amabile*, 36″, orange-red, dark spots, June; \**auratum*, (Goldband Lily) 36–60″, white with red spots and yellow band (many varieties, based chiefly on variations of the flower markings, exist), Aug.–Sept.; \**Brownii*, 48″, white, rosy purple outside, July; \**bulbiferum*, 48″, orange-red, spotted dark purple (variety *croceum*, the Orange Lily, is crimson spotted), June; *canadense* (Meadow Lily), 36–60″, orange-yellow to red, spotted purplish brown, July; *candidum* (Madonna Lily), 36–48″, white, June; \**cernuum*, 24″, pink, July; *chalcedonicum* (Scarlet Turks-Cap Lily), 48″, scarlet, July; \**concolor*, 48″, vermillion, June–July; \**dauricum* 18–36″, red, brown-purple spots dark purple (several named color varieties exist), June; \**formosanum*, 60–80″, white, usually tinged with green or reddish purple outside, Sept.; *Grayi*, 36–48″, red and orange spotted with brown, July; \**Hansonii*, 60″, orange-yellow, brown spotted, June–July; \**Henryi*, 70–100″, yellow-orange, spotted brown, Aug.–Sept.; \**Hollandicum* (*umbellatum* of gardens), 18–42″, red, orange, yellow, often marked with darker spots, June–July (a group of hybrids that includes several named varieties); \**longiflorum* (Easter Lily), 36–60″, white (many varieties are grown), June–July; \**maculatum* (*elegans*), yellow to red, usually spotted (many varieties, varying from each other chiefly in color, exist), 18–24″, June–July; *Martagon* (Turks-Cap Lily), 48–72″, rose or dark purple, spotted black-purple (variety *album*, white), June–July; *pardalinum* (Leopard Lily), 70–90″, orange-red and yellow, spotted purple, July (several color forms have varietal names); *philadelphicum*, 36″, orange-red, spotted purple, June; \**pumilum* (*tenuifolium*—Coral Lily), 18–36″, bright red to yellow (in variety Golden Gleam), June; \**regale* (Regal Lily), 60″, white, purplish outside, July; *rubellum*, 24″, pink, June; *Sargentiae*, 70″, cream, brownish purple outside, Aug.; *speciosum*, 40–50″, white, pink, and crimson, usually spotted with red, Aug.–Sept. (several named varieties exist); *superbum* (American Turks-Cap Lily), 70–100″, orange-scarlet, spotted purplish brown, July–Aug.; *Szovitzianum*, 70″, lemon-yellow, spotted purple, June–July; *testaceum* (Nankeen Lily), 60–80″, apricot, July; *tigrinum* (Tiger Lily), 50–60″, orange-red, spotted black (several varieties exist), Aug. In addition to the above-mentioned lilies there are now available many very fine hybrids that will be found described in dealers' catalogs. Among the best of these are Aurelian hybrids, Bellingham hybrids, Fiesta hybrids, Golden Chalice hybrids, Green Mountain hybrids, Mid-Century hybrids, Rainbow hybrids, and Backhouse hybrids; many of these, as well as some other hybrid lilies such as T. A. Havemeyer, have been given individual varietal names.

**Kinds for Indoor Cultivation:** Almost all lilies can be grown in pots indoors provided they are not forced in high temperatures, but in practice only a few ordinarily are. Of these *longiflorum* (which stands considerable forcing) is most popular, *speciosum* and its varieties being of next importance.

**LILY.** *See Lilium.*

**LILY-OF-THE-NILE.** *See Agapanthus.*

**LILY-OF-THE-VALLEY.** *See Convallaria.*

**LITTONIA.** Spring- or early-summer-blooming natives of South Africa; a climbing, tuberous plant related to *Gloriosa* and requiring identical treatment.

**Kind:** *modesta*, 36–48″, orange-yellow (the variety *Keitii* is more free flowering and more vigorous).

**LLOYDIA.** Hardy bulbs of North America, Europe, and Asia. For rock gardens.

**Culture:** Soil—sandy, dryish. Location—sunny. Plant in fall, 3–4″ deep, 3–4″ apart. Lift and replant only when plants begin to deteriorate.

**Propagation:** By offsets, fall; seeds, fall or spring.

**Kind:** *serotina*, 6″, white, yellowish purple at base.

**LORDS AND LADIES.** *See Arum maculatum.*

**LYCORIS.** Chinese and Japanese bulbs blooming in late summer and fall. *Squamigera* (Hardy Amaryllis) is hardy in the North, the others are suitable for growing outdoors in the South; elsewhere they may be grown indoors. For borders and naturalizing where hardy; for cut flowers.

**Culture Outdoors:** Soil—deep, fertile, sandy loam, containing an abundance of organic matter. Location—light shade or sunny. Plant in Aug., *squamigera* 6″ deep, 6–9″ apart; the others 4″ deep, 4–6″ apart. Do not disturb more often than necessary; the bulbs often fail to bloom for a year or two following transplanting.

**Culture Indoors:** Soil—light, fertile, enriched with leafmold or humus. Location—sunny greenhouse or window. Night temperature 55°–60°. Pot in Aug. with upper third of bulb showing above soil surface. Water moderately at first, freely when leaves are well developed. Fertilize established plants regularly during growing season with dilute fertilizers. At end of growing season, when foliage begins to fade, gradually reduce water; keep quite dry during resting season. Repot every 3–4 years; in intermediate seasons top-dress at beginning of growing season.

**Propagation:** By offsets at planting time; by bulb cuttings in Aug.; by seeds in spring, temperature 55°–60°.

**Kinds:** *aurea*, 12–18″, yellow; *incarnata*, 12–20″, flesh-pink; *radiata*, 12–18″, bright red (white in variety *alba*); *sanguinea*, 12–18″, red; *sprengeri*, 18–24″, pink or purplish; *squamigera* (*Amaryllis Hallii*—Hardy Amaryllis), 24″, lavender-pink, fragrant.

# M

**MADEIRA-VINE.** *See Boussingaultia.*

**MARIPOSA-LILY.** *See Calochortus.*

**MERENDERA.** Spring-flowering bulbs closely related to *Colchicum* and natives of the Mediterranean region and an area extending east to Afghanistan. They require the same culture and are propagated in the same manner as *Colchicum*.

Kinds: *sobolifera*, 3–5″, bluish white; *trigyna* (*caucasica*), pale pink or white.

**MEXICAN SHELL-FLOWER.** See *Tigridia*.

**MEXICAN-STAR.** See *Milla*.

**MIGNONETTE-VINE.** See *Boussingaultia*.

**MILK-AND-WINE-LILY.** See *Crinum*.

**MILLA** (Mexican-Star). A native of the southwestern United States and Mexico that blooms in late winter and spring. Hardy in mild climates only; may be grown indoors in pots. *Biflora* is the only species; the plant sometimes called "*Milla uniflora*" is *Brodiaea uniflora*. For naturalizing and rock gardens where hardy.

Culture: Soil—sandy, well drained. Location—sunny. Plant in fall, or pot several bulbs together in 5″ pot or 6″ pan. Grow through winter in greenhouse, sun porch, or window garden, night temperature 45°–50°. Keep dry when dormant, water established plants freely when in growth. Apply dilute fertilizers when well rooted.

Propagation: by offsets and seeds.

Kind: *biflora*, 12–18″, white, fragrant.

**MONARCH-OF-THE-EAST.** See *Sauromatum*.

**MONTBRETIA.** See *Crocosmia crocosmiiflora*.

**MORAEA.** Mostly cormous plants; the few non-cormous ones are not considered here. Individual flowers are short-lived but a succession appear. Natives of Africa and Australia. Hardy outdoors in mild climates; suitable for pots in greenhouses and sunrooms.

Culture: Soil—rich, sandy. Location—full sun. Plant or pot in fall, setting bulbs outdoors 4″ deep, 2–3″ apart; in pots, 5–6 bulbs in a 5″ container, 2″ deep.

General Care and Propagation: As for *Ixia*.

Kinds: *pavonia* (Peacock-Iris), 12–24″, orange-red with blue basal blotches (in some varieties, yellow, purple, or white), June–July; *polystachya*, 24–36″, bright lilac, summer, poisonous to stock; *ramosa*, 24–36″, bright yellow with brown basal blotches, May–June; *spathacea*, 40–50″, bright yellow, late winter or spring; *tricuspis*, 12–24″, white, tinted lilac, May–June; *tristis*, 12–18″, lilac or pink, May; *undulata*, 12–24″, lilac, May.

**MUSCARI** (Grape-Hyacinth). Hardy spring-blooming bulbs, natives of the Mediterranean region. For rock gardens, borders, naturalizing at fringes of shrubbery, and as pot plants. Foliage often appears in fall; is not injured by winter weather.

Culture and Propagation: As for *Chionodoxa*.

Kinds: *armeniacum* (Heavenly Blue), 6–12″, bright blue, fragrant (variety Fairway Seedling is a plumose form like *comosum monstrosum*); *botryoides*, 6–9″, blue (variety *album* white, *carneum* an indifferent pink, *pallidum* pale blue); *comosum*, 12″, lower flowers bluish olive, upper flowers blue (variety *monstrosum*, Feather-Hyacinth, has a feathery spike of bluish violet, petals shredded into fine filaments); *conicum*, 6″, violet-blue; *Heldreichii*, 4–8″, blue; *latifolium*, 12″, blue; *moschatum* (Musk-Hyacinth), 6–9″, greenish yellow tinged with violet (varieties *flavum* and *luteum* are more yellow), not showy but deliciously fragrant; *neglectum*, 9″, blackish blue, fragrant; *paradoxum*, 5–6″, blue-black; *Pinardii*, 6–9″, gray-blue with light blue tips; *polyanthum*, 9–12″, deep blue (variety *album* white); *tubergenianum*, 8″, upper flowers light blue, lower flowers dark blue.

**MUSK-HYACINTH.** See *Muscari moschatum*.

# N

**NAEGELIA.** *See Smithiantha.*

**NARCISSUS** (Daffodil, Jonquil). Mostly hardy (the Tazettas are not hardy in the North), and mostly spring-flowering bulbs (a few bloom in autumn). For beds, borders, naturalizing in meadows, open woodlands, under scattered trees, at the fringes of shrubberies, and in orchards, the smaller kinds for rock gardens; for forcing. The name "daffodil" is sometimes used to include all narcissuses but is more often restricted to those that have large trumpets. The name "jonquil" originally referred only to *Narcissus jonquilla* and its hybrids but now, in some parts of the country, is freely applied to other kinds of narcissuses, particularly the large-trumpet kinds. Yellow, varying to orange, is the commonest color among narcissuses; a few exhibit delightful pinkish hues, many are white or predominantly so.

**Outdoor Culture:** Soil—deep, fertile, well drained but not dry; for *Bulbocodium* sandy, for *cyclamineus* peaty. Location—sun or light shade with shelter from sweeping winds. Plant as early as bulbs can be obtained in fall, robust kinds that have large bulbs 5–6″ deep to round part of bulb (disregarding the slender neck), less vigorous kinds with smaller bulbs 3–4″, tiny species 3″ (increase these depths somewhat if soil is sandy). Space vigorous growers 6–9″, moderately vigorous growers, 4–5″, small species 2–4″ apart. In naturalized planting these distances are varied considerably; they are for rough guidance only. If soil is dry water thoroughly after planting. Where winters are severe protect bulbs not planted in grass with covering of salt-marsh hay, leaves, or other suitable material. Fertilize established plantings in early fall and early spring using a quickly available complete fertilizer in spring, a slower-acting organic fertilizer in fall. Water copiously during dry spells when foliage is above ground. Never remove foliage until it has died naturally. When plantings become crowded so that bloom deteriorates in quantity and quality,

lift, separate, and replant as soon as foliage has died.

**Indoor Cultivation in Soil:** Soil—light, loamy, well drained. Plant with just clearing distance between bulbs and with their tips just showing above surface in 5–8″ pots or deep pans, or 4″ deep flats, early fall (early planting is important, particularly for forcing). Location—when first planted, in bulb cellar (temperature 40°–45°) or buried outdoors under 8″ of sand or cinders except for Paper White, Grand Soleil d'Or, Chinese Sacred Lily, and others of the *Tazetta* division which may be placed outdoors in temperature 45°–50° without burying; when well rooted remove to greenhouse, sunroom, or window, shading until shoots turn green, then in full sun (temperature 50°–55° at first, then 55°–60°). Apply dilute fertilizers weekly until flowers begin to open. Water freely; dryness causes buds to blast. After flowering continue to water, harden gradually, and plant outdoors after danger of frost is passed; or keep watered as long as foliage is green, then dry and store bulbs in cool dry place, and plant outdoors in early fall.

**Indoor Cultivation Without Soil:** Plant in bulb fiber or in pebbles and water as described in Chapter 10. Paper White, Grand Soleil d'Or, and the Chinese Sacred Lily particularly lend themselves to these modes of culture, and an extended succession of bloom is easily maintained from late November well into winter by planting every ten days or two weeks from early Oct. until the new year or even into Feb. provided the bulbs remain plump and in good condition.

**Propagation:** By offsets at lifting time; by bulb cuttings, July–Aug.; by seeds (species, and to raise new varieties) in fall in a shaded cold frame. Seedlings bloom in 3–7 years.

**Kinds:** Narcissuses are classified into eleven divisions and several subdivisions based on flower form and ancestral parentage. Chief divisions are: I. Trumpet—trumpet (corona) as long as or longer than petals, one flower to stem; II. Large-Cupped—cup (corona) more than one third as long but not as long as the petals, one flower to

stem; III. Small-Cupped—cup (corona) no
more than one third as long as petals, one
flower to stem; IV. Double—with double
flowers; V. *Triandrus*—hybrids or varieties
of *Narcissus triandrus* with parental character clearly evident; VI. *Cyclamineus*—hybrids or varieties of *cyclamineus* with parental character clearly evident; VII. *Jonquilla*
—hybrids or varieties that have characters
of the *Narcissus Jonquilla* group clearly
evident. VIII. *Tazetta*—hybrids or varieties
of *Tazetta* with parental character clearly
evident; IX. *Poeticus*—with characteristics
of *Narcissus poeticus* without admixture of
other species; X. Species and Wild Forms—
all species and wild, or supposedly wild,
forms and hybrids; XI. Miscellaneous—narcissuses not belonging in any of the afore-
mentioned divisions. Within each division
and subdivision are numerous named varieties which are described in dealers' catalogs.
Species and wild forms include: *Bulbocodium* (Hoop Petticoat Daffodil), 6", yellow
(variety *citrinus*, sulphur-yellow; *con-
spicuus*, yellow; *Graellsii*, primrose-yellow;
*monophyllus* white, winter-blooming, not
reliably hardy in the North); *calcicola*, 4–
6", bright yellow; *cyclamineus*, 6", yellow
flowers solitary, drooping, petals strongly reflexed, corona narrow, as long as petals;
*Jonquilla*, 12", bright yellow, leaves cylindrical, rushlike, corona less than half as long
as petals, 2–6 flowers on each stem;
*juncifolius*, 6–8", bright yellow; *minimus* (a
tiny form of *Pseudo-Narcissus*), 3–6", yellow; *minor*, 5–6", yellow; *nanus*, 6–8", yellow; *odorus* (Campernelle), 12–18", bright
yellow; *poeticus*, 12", white, fragrant, one
flower to stem, corona shallow, red edged;
*rupicola*, 4", yellow; *scaberulus*, 6–9",
orange-yellow; *serotinus*, 6–10", white, fall;
*Tazetta*, 12–18", white or white with cream
corona, corona much shorter than petals, 4–
8 flowers on each stem; *tenuior*, 8–9", cream
and sulphur; *triandrus* (Angels-Tears), 12",
white or yellow, corona half as long as petals, 1–6 flowers on each stem, leaves cylindrical, rushlike; *viridiflorus*, 12–18", green,
fall; *watieri*, 4", white.

**NEMASTYLIS.** Natives of the southern
U. S. Not hardy in the North, suitable for

wild gardens in milder parts of the country.
Flowers last a few hours only.

**Culture** and **Propagation:** As for *Eustylis*.

**Kinds:** *acuta* (*geminiflora*), 24", blue,
spring; *floridana*, 18–48", violet, fall. For
other plants previously called *"Nemastylis"*
see *Eustylis* and *Salpingostylis*.

**NERINE.** South African fall- and early-
winter-blooming bulbs, hardy in the mild
climates and excellent as cool greenhouse
pot plants.

**Culture:** Soil—fertile, well drained. Plant
at beginning of growing season (Aug.–
Oct.), outdoors 3–4" deep, in pots with
upper half of bulb exposed. Space 3–4"
apart outdoors; indoors, one bulb in 4" pot
or three in 5" or 6" pot. Top-dress bulbs in
garden in Aug., with rich compost and complete fertilizer; lift and replant every 3–5
years. Location—full sun. Night temperature indoors, 40°–45°. When grown in pots
top-dress annually at beginning of growing
season but do not repot oftener than necessary; they flower better when pot-bound.
Water freely from time when growth begins
(late summer or fall) until foliage naturally
dies (spring or early summer); keep quite
dry while resting. Feed pot plants regularly
with dilute liquid fertilizers through growing
season. Unless needed for propagation remove all surplus side bulbs that appear
while they are quite small.

**Propagation:** By offsets at potting time;
by bulb cuttings in Aug.; by seeds sown in
sandy soil, early fall.

**Kinds:** *Bowdenii*, 15–18", pink; *curvi-
folia*, 18", scarlet (variety Fothergillii is more
robust); *filifolia*, 12", clear, soft pink (not
red as often stated); *flexuosa*, 18–36", pink;
*humilis*, 6–18", light pink or lavender-pink;
*sarniensis* (Guernsey-Lily), 24", salmon-
pink (variety *corusca*, scarlet; *Plantii*, dull
crimson; *rosea*, rose-red; *venusta*, scarlet);
*undulata*, 12–18", pale pink. There are also
numerous garden varieties and hybrids,
some of the best of which are Aurora, Empire Day, His Majesty, Peter Barr, and
Princess Mary.

**NOMOCHARIS.** Hardy lily-like bulbs that
are natives of high mountain regions of the

Himalaya, Tibet, Upper Burma, and western China. Except in the most favored climates they are impossible or difficult to grow. They are essentially plants for cool, moist regions and may be expected to succeed best in the Pacific Northwest.

**Culture:** Soil—fertile, porous loam to which generous amounts of peatmoss and sand have been added. Location—with their roots and lower stems shaded from strong sunshine. Plant in spring, when plants are 1–3 years old. Leave undisturbed after planting. Bulbs normally flower when 4–6 years old.

**Propagation:** By seeds sown in a greenhouse where a temperature of 55°–60° is maintained, in Jan. or Feb. The seedlings are transplanted (take great care not to break their roots) to 4″ deep flats of light, porous, peaty soil and are kept growing in a cold frame until early the following spring, when they are transplanted to other flats. They may be set in their permanent position the next spring or may be grown in frames for another year or two.

**Kinds:** *aperata*, 18–36″, rose or rose-purple with crimson spots and blotches; *Farreri*, 30–36″, pale pink with red spots near bases of petals; *Mairei*, 18–48″, white or white suffused with purple on outsides of flowers; *pardanthina*, 12–30″, rose spotted with crimson; *saluenensis*, 18–36″, white or pale yellow flushed with purplish rose and lightly spotted.

**NOTHOSCORDUM** (False Garlic). A small group of tropical and temperate region bulbs related to *Allium*, two native species of which are sometimes cultivated and are hardy at least as far north as New York City. *Fragrans* self-sows and becomes something of a weed. For wild gardens; *bivalve* for rock gardens.

**Culture:** Soil—well drained, preferably sandy. Location—sunny. Plant in fall or early spring, 2–3″ deep, 3–4″ apart.

**Propagation:** By offsets at planting time; by seeds in spring or fall.

**Kinds:** *bivalve*, 6–12″, pale yellow, spring and sometimes again in late summer; *fragrans*, 12–24″, white with lavender streak, fragrant, early summer.

# O

**ORNITHOGALUM.** Hardy and tender bulbs, natives of Europe, Asia, and Africa. For wild gardens, rock gardens, cut flowers, and pot plants. *Umbellatum* (Star-of-Bethlehem) spreads freely, should be kept out of choice rock garden areas, is excellent for naturalizing beneath shrubs or in grass; *nutans* is lovely for light woodland and for cutting; *arabicum*, not reliably hardy in the North unless planted in a protected cold frame, is magnificent for cutting and pot culture. *Thyrsoides* lasts so well when cut that its flowers are sent from South Africa to American markets and remain in good condition in water for several weeks after arrival.

**Outdoor Culture:** Soil—rich, porous. Location—full sun; or light shade for *nutans*. Plant in fall, small bulbs 3″, large bulbs 4–6″ deep, 2–3″ apart. Fertilize in spring. Lift and replant when crowded.

**Indoor Culture:** Soil—rich, well drained. Location—sunny. Night temperature 40°–50°; for *thyrsoides aureum* 55°. Pot at beginning of growing season (fall for most, Feb.–March for *caudatum*). Repot most each year in 5–6″ pots or pans, several bulbs in each; *caudatum* every few years only, singly in pots. Leave greater portion of bulb of *caudatum* exposed above soil surface, cover bulbs of others 1″ deep. Water moderately when growth first begins, freely when growing actively; when foliage begins to die naturally after flowering gradually reduce water, finally withhold, and keep dry through dormant season. Fertilize with dilute liquid stimulants when in full growth.

**Propagation:** By offsets at planting time; seeds in early fall or spring.

**Hardy Kinds:** *narbonense*, 18″, white and green, early summer; *nutans*, 12–18″, gray-green and white, spring; *pyramidale*, 24″, white and green, summer; *umbellatum*, 6–10″, white and green, spring.

**Tender Kinds:** *arabicum*, 18–30″, creamy white and black, fragrant, spring (variety *corymbosum* is robust and free flowering); *caudatum*, 36″, green and white, spring and summer; *lacteum*, 24″, white, spring; *Saundersiae,* 24–36″, white, spring; *thyrsoides* (*Chincherinchee*), 12–24″, white (variety *aureum,* yellow; *flavescens,* pale yellow).

## OWLS-EAR. *See Calochortus.*

## OXALIS.

Hardy and tender plants of wide natural distribution. Bulbous kinds only are considered here. The tender kinds can be grown outdoors in mild climates. For rock gardens, wild gardens, borders, and pot plants.

**Outdoor Culture:** Soil—sandy loam. Location—sunny, except *violacea* which needs light shade. Plant in spring or fall, 2–3″ deep, 2–4″ apart. Summer-flowering kinds may be lifted in cold climates and stored over winter indoors, temperature 40°–50°.

**Indoor Culture:** Pot at beginning of growing season (fall for spring-bloomers, spring for summer-flowerers, July–Aug. for fall-bloomers). *Bowieana* may be planted in fall or spring according to when flowers are wanted. Soil—light, nourishing, well drained. Location—full sun, night temperature 45°–50°. Set bulbs 6–9″ deep in a 6″ pan, slightly fewer in a 5″ pot, 1–2″ deep. Water sparingly at first, freely when in full growth; dry when foliage naturally dies after blooming, keep dry when dormant. Repot in fresh soil each year.

**Propagation:** By offsets at planting time; by seeds in sandy soil at beginning of growing season.

**Hardy Kind:** *violacea,* 3–6″, rose-purple, summer.

**Tender Kinds:** *Bowieana,* 6–10″, pink, spring or summer; *brasiliensis,* 3–6″, reddish purple, spring; *cernua* (Bermuda Buttercup), 9–12″, yellow (variety *flore-pleno* is double flowered), spring; *Deppei,* 6–10″, red or purplish, spring; *hirta,* 12″, pink, fall or early winter; *incarnata,* 6–10″, purplish or lavender and yellow, spring; *lasiandra,* 12″, purple-crimson, summer; *lobata,* 3–4″, yellow, fall; *purpurata,* 6–12″, purple or purplish red, spring; *variabilis* (here belong the varieties cataloged as "Grand Dutchess"), 9–12″, pink, lavender-pink, and red, late fall and early winter.

# P

**PAMIANTHE.** Tropical American bulb related to *Hymenocallis.* For outdoors in mild climates; for pots.

**Culture** and **Propagation:** As for tropical *Hymenocallis.*

**Kind:** *peruviana,* 12–18″, white with yellowish green stripe on petals, fragrant, spring.

**PANCRATIUM.** Natives of Europe, Asia, and Africa. *Maritimum* and *illyricum* may be grown outdoors in the South in the same way as *Crinum;* others are for pots and need the same culture as indicated for *Hymenocallis.* Hymenocallis are often miscalled pancratiums.

**Propagation:** As for *Hymenocallis.*

**Kinds:** *canariense,* 24″, white, fall; *illyricum,* 18″, white, fragrant, summer; *maritimum,* 24″, white, summer; *zeylanicum,* white, June.

**PEACOCK-IRIS.** *See Moraea pavonia.*

**PERUVIAN DAFFODIL.** *See Hymenocallis calathina.*

**PHAEDRANASSA.** South and Central American spring-flowering bulbs for outdoor cultivation in mild climates only, elsewhere as pot plants.

**Culture:** Soil—fertile, loamy, well drained. Location—sunny. Indoor night temperature Sept.–March, 40°–45°, after that 55°–60°. Plant or pot in spring, tips of bulbs just beneath surface. Repot annually, placing bulbs in small pots at first and transferring to larger ones as growth demands. Water moderately until well rooted, then freely. In October gradually dry off; keep quite dry when dormant. Apply dilute liquid fertilizer to well-rooted specimens in active growth.

**Propagation:** By offsets at potting time; bulb cuttings in Aug.; seeds in fall or spring, temperature 60°–65°.

**Kinds:** *Carmiolii,* 24″, red and green; *chloracea,* 18″, scarlet and green.

**PINEAPPLE-FLOWER.** *See Eucomis.*

**POISON-BULB.** *See Crinum asiaticum.*

**POLIANTHES** (Tuberose). Tender summer-blooming bulbs for planting outdoors during warm season and storing indoors over winter. Second-year bulbs often fail to bloom satisfactorily; this is especially likely if they are stored in too low a temperature. For borders and, unless their very strong scent is considered objectionable, for cutting. Natives of Mexico.

**Outdoor Culture:** Soil—rich, well drained but not excessively dry. Location—sheltered, sunny. Plant after weather is settled and danger of frost has passed, 3″ deep, 6″ apart; or start indoors in pots 6–8 weeks before they are wanted for planting outside and set in garden when weather is warm. Dig before frost and store in a dry place, temperature 60°.

**Indoor Culture:** Soil—rich, well drained. Location—humid greenhouse. Pot singly in a 5″ pot or 3 bulbs in a 6″ pot, leaving top half of bulbs out of soil, Jan.–Feb. for bloom April–June; bulbs that have been retarded by keeping in a cool, dry place, late Aug. for Nov. flowers. Water sparingly at first, freely after well rooted. Spray with water on clear days. Apply liquid fertilizers regularly from time roots fill pots until flowers open. Temperature 65°–70°.

**Propagation:** By offsets at planting time.

**Kinds:** *tuberosa* (Tuberose) 30–48″, white, fragrant. Both double-flowered and single-flowered forms are available.

**PRAIRIE-LILY.** *See Cooperia.*

**PRETTY FACE.** *See Brodiaea ixioides.*

**PUSCHKINIA** (Striped-Squill). Hardy bulbs from Asia Minor resembling scillas. For rock gardens, naturalizing, and pot culture.

**Culture** and **Propagation:** As for *Chionodoxa.*

**Kind:** *scilloides* (*libanotica*), 6–10″, milky blue with a deeper blue line down each petal (variety *alba* is creamy white), spring.

# R

**RAIN-LILY.** *See Cooperia.*

**RANUNCULUS.** A few members of this large genus are tuberous. Most noteworthy is *asiaticus* and its varieties which have large flowers, single or double, in a wide variety of colors. These are not hardy in the North. They are useful for beds, borders, cut flowers, and greenhouses. They require the same culture and propagation as poppy anemones; see *Anemone*. *Ficaria* (Lesser Celandine) blooms early, then its foliage dies down until following year. For rock gardens, wild gardens, and bog gardens.

**Culture:** Soil—rich, woodsy, moist or wet. Location—part shade or sun. Plant in fall 1″ deep, 3–4″ apart.

**Propagation:** By division of clumps of tubers in fall; the single type by seed as soon as ripe.

**Kinds:** *asiaticus* (Turban Ranunculus and Persian Ranunculus), 12–18″, wild type yellow, garden varieties white, yellow, orange, pink, scarlet, and crimson, late winter and spring; *Ficaria* (Lesser Celandine), 3–5″, glossy yellow (variety *albus*, white; *cuprea*, coppery, very early flowering; *florepleno*, double flowered; *grandiflorus*, larger in all parts).

**RHODOHYPOXIS.** South African summer-flowering bulbs related to *Hypoxis*, not reliably hardy in the North (the author has grown them successfully in New York City in a protected cold frame). Best suited for climates like that of the Pacific Northwest.

**Culture:** Soil—light, well drained, moderately moist. For rock gardens and naturalizing. Location—sunny. Plant in spring, 1–2″ deep, 2–3″ apart.

**Propagation:** By offsets at planting time; by seeds in fall.

**Kinds:** *Baueri*, 4″, deep pink (variety *platypetala*, white).

**RICHARDIA.** A name sometimes applied to *Zantedeschia*, which see.

**RIGIDELLA.** Mexican bulbs related closely to *Tigridia* and requiring the same general culture.

**Kinds:** *flammea,* 36–60″, bright scarlet, striped deep purple in throat; *immaculata,* 36–60″, red.

**ROMULEA.** Mediterranean basin and African corms related to *Crocus.* Not considered hardy North, although *Bulbocodium* and *Columnae* would probably prove so in New York City in a sheltered location if well protected. For rock gardens, naturalizing, and pots.

**Culture** and **Propagation:** As for *Ixia.*

**Kinds:** *Bulbocodium,* 6″, greenish yellow, summer; *Clusiana,* 6–9″, white, yellow, and violet, spring; *Columnae,* 6″, blue, violet, or white with yellow base, spring; *ramiflora,* 6–8″, lilac and yellow, spring; *rosea,* 6″, pink and yellow, summer.

**RUE-ANEMONE.** *See Anemonella.*

# S

**ST. JAMES-LILY.** *See Sprekelia.*

**ST. JOSEPH'S LILY.** A name applied to a form of *Hippeastrum Johnsonii* that is common in Louisiana and some other southern states.

**SALPINGOSTYLIS.** A native of the southeastern U. S. Summer-blooming, the flowers opening from sunrise until about 8 A.M. For wild gardens and rock gardens. Not hardy in the North.

**Culture** and **Propagation:** As for *Eustylis.*

**Kind:** *coelestina,* 12–20″, violet with white eye.

**SANDERSONIA.** South African tuberous climbing plant, related to *Gloriosa* but with bell-shaped, nodding flowers. Hardier than *Gloriosa* and may perhaps live outdoors as far north as Washington, D. C. The author has cultivated it successfully in New York City in a greenhouse exactly as *Gloriosa* but in a night temperature of 50°–55°.

**Propagation:** Division of tubers at potting time; seeds in spring in sandy soil. Seedlings bloom when 3 years old.

**Kind:** *aurantiaca,* 12–24″, bright orange-yellow; seed pods open to reveal red pea-like seed.

**SAND-LILY.** *See Leucocrinum.*

**SANGUINARIA** (Bloodroot). Not really a bulb but sometimes considered such. Native of eastern North America. For naturalizing in woodlands and other shady places including rock gardens. Spring-blooming.

**Culture:** Soil—preferably sandy, rich with organic matter, fairly moist but not wet. Location—light shade. Plant when foliage dies or in early fall, 2″ deep, 4–6″ apart. Mulch in fall with leafmold or other organic material. Leave undisturbed as long as doing well.

**Propagation:** By seeds sown in sandy soil in a cold frame when ripe; by division in August.

**Kinds:** *canadensis,* 4–8″, white or tinged pink (variety *multiplex* has double flowers).

**SAUROMATUM** (Monarch-of-the-East). Curious Asiatic and African plants related to Jack-in-the-Pulpit (*Arisaema*). Flowers in late winter or spring before leaves. Nearly hardy North, in New York City surviving outdoors in sheltered locations if well protected over winter. For borders, naturalizing, and pot plants.

**Culture:** Soil—woodsy, rich, moderately moist but well drained. Pot or plant in early spring. May be lifted before frost and stored over winter, temperature 40°–50°. Water freely when in full growth; keep pot specimens dry when dormant.

**Propagation:** As for *Arum.*

**Kinds:** *guttatum,* 18–24″, yellow, purple, and green (varieties *pedatum, punctatum,* and *venosum* differ in their color markings).

**SCARBOROUGH-LILY.** *See Vallota.*

**SCHIZOBASOPSIS.** Curious, leafless, South African bulb that produces branched, twining green stem of graceful, ferny appearance. Flowers insignificant. For greenhouses and window gardens, night temperature 45°–55°; outdoors in climates such as that of southern California.

**Culture:** Soil—porous, well drained, moderately rich. Location—full sun. Pot in fall, with only lower third of bulb beneath surface. Repot only at intervals of several years. Water moderately when in leaf; keep dry when dormant.

**Propagation:** By offsets at potting time; bulb cuttings, Aug.; seeds in early fall.

**Kind:** *volubilis* (*Bowiea volubilis*), 36″, green.

**SCILLA** (Squill). Hardy and tender bulbs from Europe, Asia, and Africa, mostly spring-flowering. Hardy kinds for rock gardens, naturalizing, pots, and cut flowers; tender kinds for pots and outdoors in mild climates. All are easy.

**Culture of Hardy Kinds:** As for *Chionodoxa;* except *nonscripta* (English Bluebell) and *hispanica* (Spanish Bluebell), which need deep, fertile, moderately moist, woodsy soil and preferably dappled shade or part-day shade. Plant these in fall, 4–5″ deep, 3–5″ apart. Mulch annually in fall with compost, peatmoss, or leafmold. Lift and replant only when obviously too crowded.

**Culture of Tender Kinds:** Soil—rich, fertile, well drained. Pot at beginning of growing season with tip of bulb just beneath surface. Repot every 3–4 years, in intermediate years top-dress; one or more bulbs to each container according to size. Water freely and fertilize regularly when in active growth; reduce water and finally withhold when leaves die naturally after blooming.

**Propagation:** By offsets; by seeds in fall or spring; bulb cuttings, Aug.

**Hardy kinds:** *amoena* (Star-Hyacinth), 6″, blue-purple, spring; *autumnalis,* 6″, rosy lilac, late summer or fall; *bifolia,* 6″, blue (variety *alba,* creamy white; *praecox,* more robust; *rosea,* pink; *taurica,* purple-blue with deeper mid-stripe on each petal, more robust), spring; *chinensis,* 6–12″, lilac-pink, Aug.–Sept.; *hispanica* (*campanulata*— Spanish Bluebell), 12–24″, blue (variety *alba,* white; *rosea,* lilac-pink; many named varieties are offered by specialists), spring; *nonscripta* (*nutans*—English Bluebell), 12–18″, blue (variety *alba,* white; *rosea,* pink), fragrant, spring; *pratensis,* 6–8″, blue-purple, fragrant, late spring; *sibirica* (Siberian Squill), 6″, deep blue (variety *alba,* white; *atrocoerulea* or Spring Beauty, deeper blue,

more robust; *azurea,* bright blue; *taurica,* light blue, early), spring; *Tubergeniana,* 4″, light blue with deeper veining.

**Tender Kinds:** *latifolia,* 12″, lilac, winter or early spring; *peruviana* (Cuban Lily), 8–12″, lilac (variety *alba,* white), late winter or spring; *prasina,* 4–6″, green, tinged purple, spring.

**SEA-ONION.** *See Urginea.*

**SEGO-LILY.** *See Calochortus Nuttallii.*

**SINNINGIA.** Commonly known as gloxinias; *Gloxinia* of the botanist is a non-tuberous relative. Tender, tuberous, summer-blooming pot plants, natives of Brazil.

**Culture:** Soil—rich, humusy, coarse (except for small seedlings). Location—humid greenhouse, shaded from strong sun; window gardens when in bloom. Start tubers into growth Jan.–April by setting them 3–4″ apart, just covered, in shallow boxes of leafmold or peatmoss and sand. Keep moist but not sodden, night temperature 60°–70°. When masses of roots 1–2″ long have formed, pot individually in 4″ pots in coarse, rich, humusy soil, made only moderately firm. When nicely rooted transfer to 5″ or 6″ pots according to vigor of plants; set with tops of tubers 1″ below surface. Keep soil always moist but not saturated; avoid wetting foliage. Apply weak liquid fertilizer weekly from time flower buds show. After flowering gradually withhold water when foliage begins to die naturally, then store dry until potting time.

**Propagation:** By seeds sown without soil covering in sandy, peaty soil, temperature 65°–75°, Jan.–March; by leaf cuttings in spring or early summer.

**Kinds:** *speciosa* (prototype of modern gloxinias), 6–12″, violet, late summer and fall. Many fine garden hybrids with flowers ranging from pure white to deepest purple and deepest crimson with all intermediate hues and many beautifully variegated are available. Buell hybrids are particularly noteworthy.

**SMITHIANTHA.** Tropical American plants allied to *Achimenes* and often grown under the name *Naegelia.*

**Culture** and **Propagation:** As for *Achimenes* except that shoots should not be pinched, and plants should be grown singly in 5″ pots or 3 in a 6″ pot.

**Kinds:** *cinnabarina*, 24″, cinnabar red spotted with white; *exoniensis*, 12″, orange-scarlet, summer, of uncertain hybrid origin; *refulgens*, 12–18″, deep red, summer, hybrid of *exoniensis* relationship; *zebrina*, 36″, red, yellow spotted with red beneath. Several hybrids and hybrids between *Smithiantha* and *Achimenes* have been raised.

**SPANISH BLUEBELL.** *See Scilla hispanica.*

**SNAKE-LILY.** *See Brodiaea volubilis.*

**SNAKE-PALM.** *See Hydrosme.*

**SNOWDROP.** *See Galanthus.*

**SNOWFLAKE.** *See Leucojum.*

**SOAP-PLANT.** *See Chlorogalum.*

**SPARAXIS** (Wand-Flower). South African corms closely related to *Ixia* but generally with larger flowers and lower growth. They occur in a range of brilliant colors.

**Uses, Propagation,** and **Culture:** As for *Ixia.*

**Kinds:** *bulbifera*, 12″, yellow; *grandiflora*, 12″, violet-purple, white, or variegated (several color forms have been given varietal names; *Liliago*, white; *purpurea*, deep purple; *stellaris*, deep purple, paler outside); *tricolor*, 12″, each flower orange, yellow, and black (variety *blanda*, white flushed with pink; *Griffinii*, yellow and violet-purple with dark blotch; *versicolor*, yellow and purple with dark blotch, paler margins).

**SPIDER-LILY.** *See Hymenocallis.*

**SPREKELIA** (Jacobean-Lily, St. James-Lily). Mexican bulb hardy only in the South. For borders, rock gardens, and pots.

**Outdoor Culture:** Soil—light, fertile, well drained. Location—sunny. Plant in spring, 3–4″ deep, 4–6″ apart.

**Indoor Culture:** As for *Hippeastrum,* but temperatures 5–10° lower, and in smaller pots (4″ for single bulbs).

**Kind:** *formosissima*, 12″, bright crimson, spring and summer.

**SPRING BEAUTY.** *See Claytonia.*

**SPRING MEADOW-SAFFRON.** *See Bulbocodium vernum.*

**SPRING SNOWFLAKE.** *See Leucojum vernum.*

**SPRING STAR-FLOWER.** *See Brodiaea uniflora.*

**SQUILL.** *See Scilla.* For **Striped-Squill** see *Puschkinia.*

**SQUIRREL-CORN.** *See Dicentra canadensis.*

**STAR-GRASS.** *See Hypoxis.*

**STAR-HYACINTH.** *See Scilla amoena.*

**STAR-LILY.** *See Leucocrinum.*

**STAR-OF-BETHLEHEM.** *See Ornithogalum umbellatum.*

**STAR-TULIP.** *See Calochortus.*

**STENONOMESSON.** South American bulbs that require the same culture as *Hippeastrum.* Adapted for greenhouses and window gardens; in the far South they may be cultivated outdoors. They bloom in winter and spring.

**Kinds:** *coccineum*, 12″, red; *flavum*, 12″, yellow; *incarnatum*, 18–24″, red or tawny.

**STERNBERGIA.** Hardy bulbs with flowers resembling substantial crocuses. For rock gardens and borders.

**Culture:** Soil—light, rich, well drained, not wet. Location—sheltered, full sun. Plant as early in fall as bulbs can be obtained, 4″ deep, 3–4″ apart. Leave undisturbed as long as doing well. Transplant, when necessary, in Aug.

**Propagation:** By offsets, bulb cuttings and seeds.

**Kind:** *lutea,* yellow (varieties *angustifolia, graeca,* and *sicula* differ in minor details), fall.

**STREPTANTHERA.** Tender South African spring-blooming bulbs related to *Ixia* and having similar uses.

**Culture** and **Propagation:** As for *Ixia.*

**Kinds:** *cuprea,* 8–9″, yellowish copper, purple base (variety *coccinea* is bright orange with nearly black base); *elegans,* 8–9″, white or blush with purple center and a zone of black with yellow spots.

**STRIPED-SQUILL.** See *Puschkinia.*

**STROXINIA.** Name given to reputed hybrids between *Streptocarpus* and *Sinningia* (**Gloxinia**).

**SUMMER-HYACINTH.** See *Galtonia.*

**SUMMER-SNOWFLAKE.** See *Leucojum-aestivum.*

**SWAMP-LILY.** See *Crinum americanum.*

**SYNNOTIA.** South African cormous plants requiring the same culture as *Ixia.*

**Kinds:** *bicolor,* 18″, yellow, tinged violet; *metelerkampiae,* 6–10″, violet; *variegata,* 18″, yellow and violet.

# T

**TECOPHILAEA** (Chilean-Crocus). Tender South American spring-flowering corms. Rare in cultivation. Probably adapted for outdoor cultivation in Southwest only where winters are not too severe and where soil can be kept dry through the summer after blooming. Elsewhere suitable for cool greenhouse.

**Culture:** Soil—rich, sandy, well drained. Pot or plant in fall, 2–3″ deep, 2–3″ apart. Water carefully at first, freely when in growth; keep quite dry while resting, night temperature 40°–50°.

**Propagation:** By offsets at planting time; by seeds when ripe.

**Kind:** *cyanocrocus,* 6″, blue with white throat (variety *Leichtlinii* has paler flowers;

a variety with violet-blue flowers is offered as violacea).

**TIGER-FLOWER.** See *Tigridia.*

**TIGRIDIA** (Tiger-Flower, Mexican Shell-Flower). Summer-blooming bulbs native from Mexico to Chile. Flowers brilliantly colored, lasting but one day but following each other in succession. For beds, borders, cut flowers.

**Outdoor Culture:** Soil—fertile, well drained. Location—full sun. Plant in spring, 3″ deep, 5–6″ apart. Mulch when 3–4″ tall. Dig before frost and store like gladioluses over winter.

**Indoor Culture:** Soil—rich, well drained. Location—sunny. Plant 5–6 bulbs in an 8″ pan in Feb. for May–June bloom. Start in night temperature 50°, when well rooted 55°. Water sparingly at first, freely when well rooted. Apply dilute fertilizers weekly when containers are filled with roots.

**Propagation:** By offsets; by seeds in sandy soil, spring.

**Kinds:** *Pavonia,* 12–24″, comes in a wide range of brilliant colors including red, yellow, white, and combinations, often spotted with purple or lavender. Many of the color forms have been given varietal names.

**TRILLIUM.** Not strictly bulbs but often considered such. Natives of North America and Asia. For rock gardens, shady borders, and naturalizing in woodlands. Spring-blooming.

**Culture:** Soil—rich with organic matter, fairly moist but for most not wet. Location—part shade. Plant after flowering or in early fall at depth equal to 4 times diameter of rhizome, 3–6″ apart. Mulch in fall with leafmold or other organic fertilizer. Leave undisturbed as long as doing well.

**Propagation:** By seeds when fruits are ripe; by division at planting time; also by cutting a V-notch longitudinally in the upper side of the rhizome and replanting.

**Kinds:** *Catesbaei,* 9–18″, pink; *cernuum,* 9–18″, white; *erectum,* 9–15″, maroon (variety *album,* white; *flavum,* yellowish green); *grandiflorum,* 9–18″, large flowered, white changing to pale pink; *nivale,* 3–7″, white; *pusillum,* 3–10″, pale pink; *recurva-*

*tum,* 9–18″, brown-purple; *sessile,* 6–12″, red-purple or green (variety *chloropetalum,* white; *luteum,* yellow); *undulatum,* 12–18″, white veined with rose-purple, difficult to grow, needs acid wet soil. Several other native species are sometimes grown.

**TRIPLET-LILY.** *See Brodiaea laxa.*

**TRITELEIA.** *See Brodidea uniflora.*

**TRITONIA.** Tender South African corms related to *Sparaxis* and useful for same purposes. The montbretias of gardens are sometimes included, but in this book are dealt with under *Crocosmia.*

  **Culture** and **Propagation:** As for *Ixia.*

  **Kinds:** *crocata,* 24″, tawny yellow or red-orange (several color variations have been given varietal names); *deusta,* 12″, orange with chocolate blotches; *hyalina,* 12″, orange; *rosea,* 12–18″, bright pink.

**TROUT-LILY.** *See Erythronium.*

**TUBEROSE.** *See Polianthes.*

**TULBAGHIA.** South African summer- and fall-flowering cormous plants. For borders and rock gardens in mild climates; for pots. The author has grown these successfully for many years in New York City against a south-facing wall by covering them heavily in winter with salt-marsh hay or leaves. Water freely when in growth, keep dry while resting. Fertilize well-rooted specimens with dilute liquid fertilizer regularly. Location—sunny; indoor night temperature 45°–50°.

  **Propagation:** By offsets at planting; by seeds in light sandy soil, temperature 50°–55°, spring.

  **Kinds:** *fragrans,* 12–18″, rosy lavender, sweetly fragrant, no onion odor when bruised; *violacea* 12–24″, deep rosy violet, rather unpleasantly scented, foliage when bruised smells of onion.

**TULIP.** *See Tulipa.*

**TULIPA.** Hardy spring-blooming bulbs. Natives of Europe, Asia, and North Africa. Garden varieties, developed as a result of centuries of selection and breeding, are popular for beds, borders, early forcing, and cut flowers; many species or "botanical" tulips (wild forms unimproved by the horticulturist) are useful for rock gardens, some of the more robust for beds, borders, and cutting. As a group tulips are less long-lived in most American gardens than narcissuses, and although vigorous varieties and species sometimes persist for ten, twenty, or more years it is more usual for them to gradually deteriorate and disappear after a much shorter time. Some of the more difficult species rarely last more than 2–3 years despite careful selection of site, and good care, while others—for example, *persica*—may remain productive for two decades or more. A tulip bulb that produces but one leaf will not flower and only a compelling reason makes it worth-while to keep such bulbs and attempt to grow them back to flowering size. In the far South it is possible to grow tulips by purchasing them as soon as available in fall and storing them at 40° temperature until Nov.–Dec., then planting them. New bulbs must be obtained each year.

  **Outdoor Culture:** Soil—light to medium fertile loam, well drained. Location—sunny or with a little light shade during hottest part of day. Plant in fall, 5–10″ deep (the greater depth if the bulbs are to be left in ground rather than dug and stored over summer, and provided several inches of good soil, into which they may root, is beneath them). Space species 4–5″ apart, garden varieties 6″, or 9–12″ if bedding plants are to be set among them. Tulips may be planted later than most bulbs; many growers favor November but provided they are set deeply enough no harm results from planting earlier. The author has planted tulips in New York City in mid-January that flowered well but had shorter stems and somewhat smaller blooms than normal. After soil surface is frozen cover with salt-marsh hay, leaves, evergreen branches, or other suitable protection. Remove this gradually when shoots appear in spring and apply complete fertilizer. Water copiously if weather is dry while foliage is green. Remove faded flowers promptly. If beds are needed for summer plants tulips may be lifted and heeled in, in light shade, to complete their growth, but it is better to leave them undisturbed until the foliage has died naturally; then they may remain in the ground undisturbed or may be lifted, cleaned, dusted with sulphur, and stored in a dry, airy, shaded place until fall planting time. Avoid injuring bulbs when digging; do not expose them to strong sun for extended periods.

**Indoor Culture:** As for *Narcissus,* but forced bulbs are scarcely worth keeping for outdoor planting later.

**Propagation:** By offsets at planting time; species by seeds.

**Kinds:** Tulips are classified in two main groups, Early Flowering and May Flowering, and in 16 divisions. Classification is based on flower form and growth habits. Divisions I–V form the early-flowering group, Divisions VI–XVI the May flowering. May-flowering tulips are from about 24–32″ in height according to variety. Divisions are: I. Duc Van Tol—6″, very early; II. Single Early—9–16″, April; III. Double Early—9–16″, April; IV. Mendel—16–26″, resembling Darwins, but blooming two weeks earlier, some double flowered; V. Triumph—16–26″, resembling Darwins, slightly earlier than Mendels and somewhat stouter, some double flowered; VI. Cottage —all tulips that do not fall into other classes; VII. Dutch Breeders—flowers oval or cupped, brown, purple, red, or bronze, base white or yellow generally stained blue or green; VIII. English Breeders—flowers forming one third to one half of a hollow ball when fully expanded, base white or yellow without other color; IX. Darwin— lower part of flower usually rectangular in outline, flowers of good substance, tall strong stems; X. Broken Dutch Breeders— same as VII but with color feathered or striped, usually on white or yellow ground; XI. Broken English Breeders—same as VIII but with color striped or feathered usually on white or yellow ground; XII. Rembrandt —broken Darwin tulips; XIII. Broken Cottage tulips; XIV. Parrot—varieties with slashes and fringed petals; XV. Late Doubles; XVI. Species and first crosses between species. Broken tulips are self-colored varieties that because of infection with a virus develop their colors in a streaked or feathered pattern on a paler background. If the background is pink or cerise they are termed "Roses"; if the markings are violet or purple on a white ground, "Bybloemens"; if brown, red, or purple on a yellow ground, "Bizarres." Dealers' catalogs list numerous named varieties in each division. Among the best species (botanical) tulips are: *acuminata,* 12–18″, yellow and red, early May; *australis,* 18″, yellow and reddish brown, fragrant, April; *Batalinii,* 5–6″, pale yellow, May; *biflora,* 3–4″, white tinged with pink, March–April; *Billietiana,* 24″, yellow, May; *chrysantha,* 6–8″, yellow and cherry-red, early May; *Clusiana* (Lady Tulip, Peppermint-Candy Tulip), 12–18″, white and red outside, white with red-purple blotch inside, early May; *Didieri,* 8–12″, crimson and purple-black, May; *Eichleri,* 9–12″, scarlet and blue-black, April; *Fosteriana,* 12–18″, scarlet, yellow, and black, April; *Greigii,* 6–9″, scarlet, yellow, and black, April; *Hageri,* 4–6″, copper-red and purple blotch, early May; *ingens,* 10–12″, vermillion and purple-black inside, buff outside; *Kaufmanniana* (Water-Lily Tulip), 6″, cream, yellow, and red, early April; *Kolpakowskyana,* 5–6″, yellow and reddish, April; linifolia, 3–5″, red, April; *Marjolettii,* 18–24″, yellowish, purplish outside, May; *Oculis-solis,* 18″, red, yellow, and black, April; *Orphanidea,* 8–10″, orange, bronze-green outside, April; *persica,* 6–9″, orange-yellow tinted with green and red, May; *polychroma,* 4–8″, white, yellow, and mauve, early April; *praecox,* 15–18″, scarlet and black, April; *praestans,* 10–12″, light scarlet, April; *primulina,* 6″, white and green tinted with red, fragrant, April; *pulchella,* 4–6″, rosy violet and yellow, early April; *saxatilis,* 9–12″, lilac and yellow, May; *Sprengeri,* 10–12″, orange-red and buff, June; *stellata,* 8–12″, white and cherry-red, April–May; *sylvestris,* 12–18″, yellow, greenish outside, fragrant, May; *tarda* (frequently misnamed *dasystemon*), 3–6″, white and yellow or flushed pink, April; *violacea,* 6″, mauve-red with olive blotch, fragrant, May.

**TWIST-ARUM.** *See Helicodiceros.*

**TYDAEA.** *See Kohleria.*

# U

**URCEOLINA.** South American bulbs that bloom in summer. Suitable for outdoor planting in mild, dry climates such as that of southern California, also as pot plants.

Culture and Propagation: As for *Albuca*.

Kinds: *peruviana* (*miniata*), 9–15″, red; *urceolata* (*pendula*), yellow and green, white margins.

**URGINEA.** Tender bulbs flowering in late spring and early summer. *Maritima* (Sea-Onion) is sometimes grown as *Scilla maritima*. For outdoors in mild, dry climates such as that of southern California; as pot plants.

Culture and Propagation: As for *Albuca*.

Kind: *maritima*, 30–48″, whitish.

# V

**VALLOTA** (Scarborough-Lily). Fall-blooming tender evergreen bulb, native of South Africa. For borders and rock gardens in mild climates, elsewhere as pot plant for greenhouse and window garden.

Culture: Soil—rich, loamy, well drained. Location—sunny with light shade from strongest sun. Pot or plant June–July, 6″ deep outdoors, with tips just covered in pots. Never transplant or repot unless quite necessary. Established specimens need repotting only every few years; in intermediate years top-dress at beginning of growing season. Water moderately Sept.–March, freely at other times. Apply dilute liquid fertilizer regularly when growing actively. Indoor temperatures, Sept.–March 40°–50°, other times 55°–65°.

Propagation: By offsets at potting time; seeds in spring; bulb cuttings July–Aug.

Kind: *speciosa* (*purpurea*), 12–24″, orange-scarlet (named varieties vary from white to cherry-red).

**VELTHEIMIA.** Tender South African bulbs for outdoors in mild climates and pot culture in greenhouses and window gardens. Flower spikes, borne in late winter and spring, are like a large lachenalia, or a small aloe or kniphofia.

Culture: As for *Hippeastrum*, but plant or repot when necessary Aug.–Sept., and grow in temperatures 10° lower than for *Hippeastrum*.

Kinds: *glauca*, 12–15″, white or yellowish spotted with red or purple; *viridifolia* (*capensis*), 12–18″, deep flesh-pink.

# W

**WAND-FLOWER.** *See Dierama and Sparaxis.*

**WATSONIA.** Handsome South African deciduous and evergreen tender bulbs for permanent outdoor cultivation in mild climates and as pot plants.

Indoor Culture: Soil—light, fertile loam, well drained. Location—sunny greenhouse, night temperature 45°–50°. Plant in spring, early-summer-flowering kinds in fall, late-summer-flowering kinds in winter or spring, 5 in a 6″ pot, 6–7 in a 7″ pot, 1″ beneath surface. Water sparingly at first, generously when in full growth. Apply weak liquid fertilizers regularly from time flower spikes show until flowers open. After flowering reduce water gradually and finally withhold entirely from deciduous kinds; give just enough to evergreen kinds to retain their foliage, keeping them dry during dormant season. Repot in fresh soil annually.

Outdoor Culture: Soil—deep, fertile, light loam, moderately moist. In mild climates plant in fall, in colder climates plant summer-bloomers in spring and lift and store over winter, temperature 40°–50°. Set 6″ apart, 4″ deep. Protect over winter with evergreen branches, salt-marsh hay, or similar material. Water freely in dry weather. Stake when half grown.

Propagation: By offsets; seeds, in light sandy soil, temperature 55°–60°, fall or early spring.

Kinds: *aletroides*, 18–24″, deep pink to scarlet, spring or early summer; *Ardernei* (*O'Brienii*) 36–50″, white, early summer; *Beatricis*, 36″, bright apricot red, summer; *brevifolia*, orange-red, late spring; *densiflora*, rose-red or white, June; *fulgens* (*angusta*), 36″, scarlet, summer; *Meriana*, 24–36″, rose-red to pink, spring. Several named garden varieties such as Burbank's Lavender, Mrs. Bullard's White, and Mc-Coy's Florist's White, creamy white, are offered.

**WIND FLOWER.** *See Anemone.*

**WILD-HYACINTH.** *See Brodiaea lactea.*

**WINTER ACONITE.** *See Eranthis.*

**WORSLEYA.** A name sometimes applied to *Hippeastrum procerum,* which see.

# Z

**ZANTEDESCHIA** (Calla-Lily). Tender tuberous plants, natives of South Africa. For permanent outdoor cultivation in climates that are nearly or quite frostless; for indoor cultivation in pots and greenhouse benches; valuable for cut flowers.

**Outdoor Culture:** Soil—rich, humusy, moist. Location—light shade from strong sun. Plant in spring or fall, *aethiopica* 24–36″, others 6–12″ apart. Give ample supplies of moisture when growing. Fertilize beginning of growing season. Mulch with manure, compost, or peatmoss.

**Indoor Culture:** Soil—rich, coarse, loamy, with a liberal admixture of organic matter. Location—sunny greenhouse, 45°–55° for *aethiopica* and its varieties, 55°–65° for others. Pot *aethiopica* in Aug. singly in 6″ or 7″ pots or three in an 8″ or 9″ pot or 10″ pan, with their tops barely covered with soil but with space left for 2″ of additional soil to be applied later. Pot other kinds same way, singly in 5″ pots for most (4″ pots for *Rehmannii*), Sept.–Jan. Water moderately after potting, freely when well rooted. Top-dress with rich soil and manure when roots show plentifully at surface. When top-dressing is pervaded by roots apply dilute liquid fertilizers 2–3 times a week. At end of flowering season give less water, finally withhold completely, turn pots on sides in shaded cool place, and keep dry until potting time. Plants kept growing without a dry, dormant period do not bloom well. Repot in new soil every year.

**Propagation:** By offsets at planting time;

by seeds in sandy, peaty soil, temperature 55°–65°, fall or early spring.

**Kinds:** *aethiopica* (Common Calla-Lily), 24–36″, white (varieties are Baby Calla-Lily, 12–18″, small flowers; *Godfreyana,* slightly smaller and freer flowering; and *minor*); *albo-maculata* (Spotted Calla-Lily), 18–24″, creamy white with purplish throat; *angustiloba* (*Pentlandii*), 24″, rich yellow with purple basal blotch; *Elliottiana* (Golden Calla-Lily), 24–36″, yellow; *melanoleuca* (Black-Throated Calla-Lily), pale yellow with black-purple base; *Rehmannii* (Red or Pink Calla-Lily), 9–12″, pink or purplish rose.

**ZEPHYRANTHES** (Zephyr-Lily). Natives of North and South America including the U. S. *Atamasco, candida,* and *grandiflora* hardy at New York City, at foot of a south-facing wall and well covered in winter with leaves, salt-marsh hay or similar material, but generally are not reliably hardy north of Washington, D. C. For borders, naturalizing, and rock gardens in South; as pot plants. Mostly spring- and summer-blooming, but the hardiest, *candida,* flowers in Sept.

**Outdoor Culture:** Soil—light loam, well drained. Location—sunny. In mild climates plant in early fall 3–4 times depth of bulb, 2–3″ apart; where winters are cold plant in spring, 2″ deep, 2–3″ apart. Lift after first frost and store over winter in dry soil, temperature 40°–50°.

**Indoor Culture:** Soil—fertile, sandy, well drained. Plant in fall in 4–6″ pots or pans, 2–3″ apart. Location—sunny, temperature 40°–50°. Water sparingly at first, moderately when in leaf, withhold water when foliage dies naturally after blooming; keep dry until beginning of growing season. Repot only every 3–4 years; in intermediate years top-dress.

**Propagation:** By offsets, early fall; bulb cuttings, Aug.; seeds, late winter or spring, temperature 60°.

**Kinds:** *Atamasco* (Atamasco-Lily), 6–10″, white or flushed pink; *candida,* 2–3″, white, evergreen foliage; *citrina,* 5–10″, bright yellow; *grandiflora* (*carinata*), 4–8″, pink; *longifolia,* 6″, bright yellow, coppery outside; *macrosiphon,* 5–8″, pink; *rosea,* 3–6″, pink; *tubispatha,* 4–8″, white.

**ZEPHYR-LILY.**  *See Zephyranthes.*

**ZIGADENUS.**    American    and    Asiatic
plants resembling camassias; some are bulbous. For wild gardens and bog gardens.
    **Culture:** Soil—rich, moist. Location—
sunny or part-day shade. Plant in fall, 4–8″
apart, 3–4″ deep. Lift and replant every
3–4 years.
    **Propagation:** Offsets at planting time;
seeds, early fall.
    **Kinds:**  *elegans,*  24–36″, yellowish  or
greenish white; *Fremontii,* 24–36″, creamy
white tinted with green.

# GROUPS ESPECIALLY INTERESTED IN BULBS

There are in North America a number of societies that devote all, or a considerable proportion, of their interests and efforts to bulbs and their culture. The following are noteworthy:

American Begonia Society
Mrs. Dorris Motschman, Sec'y.
9601 Haas Avenue
Los Angeles 47, California

American Dahlia Society
Dr. Frederick J. Knocke, Sec'y.
2616 Arlington Avenue
New York 63, New York

American Gesneria Society
Mrs. Lois Williams, Sec'y.
P. O. Box 464
San Leandro, California

American Gloxinia Society
Mrs. Sam Payne, Sec'y.
311 N. 10th
Enid, Oklahoma

American Iris Society
Geddes Douglas, Sec'y.
Franklin Road
Brentwood, Tennessee

American Plant Life Society
Miss Pauline Buck, Sec'y.
26 East Camino Real
Arcadia, California

American Rock Garden Society
Mrs. Dorothy E. Hansell, Corr. Sec'y.

66 Pittsford Way
New Providence, New Jersey

National Gladiolus Society
Mrs. Charles A. Wade, Sec'y.
Route 1
Vienna, Virginia

National Tulip Society
Felix R. Tyroler, Sec'y.
37 West 43rd Street
New York 36, New York

New England Gladiolus Society
Marion Ayer, Sec'y.
12 Newbury Circle
Needham, Mass.

North American Gladiolus Council
J. Elton Carter, Sec'y.
2420 East 25th Street
Des Moines 17, Iowa

North American Lily Society
Forrest E. Kendall, Sec'y.
240–06 53rd Avenue
Douglaston, New York

Western International Gladiolus Society
G. Hilton, Sec'y.
Box 205
Zillah, Washington

Canadian Gladiolus Society
Mrs. J. A. Carleton, Sec'y.
Box 103
Guelph, Ontario
Canada

Canadian Iris Society
L. Laking, Sec'y.
Royal Botanical Gardens
Hamilton, Ontario
Canada

# ABOUT BULB SIZES

The vast majority of bulb producers and dealers are keenly anxious to market none but fine quality bulbs which, if planted under reasonable conditions, will surely give satisfaction. Most of them succeed. Unfortunately a few less conscientious, often fly-by-night, advertisers offer for sale each season substandard bulbs, frequently at prices lower than those at which reliable bulbs can be produced and sold.

Size is a good indication of bulb quality, though there are other indications too, of course, such as firmness, weightiness, freedom from shrivelling, freedom from bruises, etc. Below certain minimum sizes (which differ considerably for different kinds of bulbs and sometimes for different varieties of the same kind) bulbs cannot be expected to bloom the first season after planting nor, unless they are planted and cared for under favorable conditions, will they ever flower. In the vast majority of cases the amateur who purchases bulbs needs and expects to receive those that will bloom the first season after planting. Recognizing this fact, the National Better Business Bureau recommends that "offers of bulbs which will not bloom in the first season after planting should be made to the public."

The Netherlands Government accepts the same principle and actually forbids the export from Holland for resale to consumers bulbs that do not meet certain designated minimum size specifications (in certain cases smaller sizes may be exported to bulb growers for propagation purposes). As a guide to purchasers the minimum sizes of bulbs that may be exported from Holland for sales to consumers are here given. The Dutch list, except in a few cases, specifies *circumference* and gives measurements in *centimeters;* for the convenience of those unfamiliar with the metric measure a list of equivalents giving *diameter* in *inches* is here presented. Remember these are the *smallest* sized bulbs you should purchase. It is of interest to note that a bulb's measurement increases one eighth of an inch in *diameter* with each one centimeter increase in its *circumference.*

| | CIRCUMFERENCE IN CENTIMETERS.* | DIAMETER IN INCHES. | | CIRCUMFERENCE IN CENTIMETERS.* | DIAMETER IN INCHES. |
|---|---|---|---|---|---|
| **Acidanthera** | 4 | ½ | **Chionodoxa** | 4 | ½ |
| **Anemone** (only wings and buttons; no split pieces) | 4 | ½ | **Colchicum** byzantinum | 16 | 2 |
| | | | other types and varieties | 13 | 1⅝ |
| **Begonia** tuberhybrida (Diameter) | 3 | 1⅛ | **Corydalis** | 4 | ½ |
| **Begonia** tuberhybrida multiflora (Diameter) | 2½ | 1 | **Crocosmia** crocosmiiflora (Montbretia) | 6 | ¾ |
| **Brodiaea** | 5 | ⅝ | **Crocus** (except those named below) | 7 | ⅞ |
| **Cammassià** esculenta | 6 | ¾ | candidus, chrysanthus, Sie- | | |

* (except where diameter is specifically stated)

219

| | Circumference in centimeters.* | Diameter in inches. |
|---|---|---|
| **Crocus** (*Continued*) | | |
| beri, speciosus, and susianus | 5 | ⅝ |
| sativus | 8 | 1 |
| Tomasinianus | 4 | ½ |
| **Ferraria** | 5 | ⅝ |
| **Freesia** | 4 | ½ |
| **Fritillaria** | | |
| imperialis | 18 | 2¼ |
| meleagris | 5 | ⅝ |
| **Galanthus** | | |
| nivalis | 4 | ½ |
| **Galtonia** | | |
| candicans | 12 | 1½ |
| **Gladiolus** | | |
| Large Flowered, Primulinus and Herald | 8 | 1 |
| nanus (Colvillei), byzantinus, and communis | 6 | ¾ |
| **Hippeastrum** | 18 | 2⅜ |
| **Hyacinthus** | | |
| orientalis (Common or Dutch Hyacinth) | 14 | 1¾ |
| orientalis "Rosalie" | 13 | 1⅝ |
| **Iris** | | |
| Dutch (except varieties mentioned below) | 6 | ¾ |
| "Professor Blauw" and "Wedgewood" | 8 | 1 |
| "Yellow Queen," "Huchtenburg," "Bronze Beauty," "Golden Bronze," "Ankara," "Bronze Queen" and "Le Mogol" | 5 | ⅝ |
| English | 8 | 1 |
| Spanish | 4 | ½ |
| **Ixia** | 4 | ½ |
| **Lachenalia** | 5 | ⅝ |
| **Lilium** | | |
| bulbiferum croceum | 14 | 1¾ |
| candidum | 17 | 2⅛ |
| Henryi | 16 | 2 |
| hollandicum (umbellatum) | 14 | 1¾ |
| "Maxwill" | 10 | 1¼ |
| philippinense formosanum | 8 | 1 |
| pumilum (tenuifolium) | 7 | ⅞ |
| speciosum (lancifolium album and lancifolium rubrum) | 16 | 2 |

| | Circumference in centimeters.* | Diameter in inches. |
|---|---|---|
| speciosum, double-nosed bulbs | 18 | 2⅜ |
| tigrinum | 10 | 1¼ |
| Willmottiae | 8 | 1 |
| **Muscari** | 5 | ⅝ |
| **Narcissus** Round I and DN III. (Round I refers to single-nosed and DN III to double-nosed bulbs. The classification is highly complex, and is based on how many bulbs fit into baskets of different sizes.) | | |
| **Oxalis** | 3 | ⅜ |
| **Ranunculus:** good meaty claws with at least five prongs. | | |
| **Scilla** | | |
| hispanica (campanulata), round bulbs | 7 | ⅞ |
| nonscripta (nutans), round bulbs | 6 | ¾ |
| sibirica | 6 | ¾ |
| **Sauromatum** | | |
| guttatum (Arum cornutum) | 18 | 2¼ |
| **Sinningia** (Gloxinia) (Diameter) | 3 | 1⅛ |
| **Tritonia** | 4 | ½ |
| **Tulips** | | |
| Early—including T. Fosteriana and its varieties | 10 | 1¼ |
| Late and Parrots (except those named below) | 11 | 1⅜ |
| Parrot "Sunshine" | 10 | 1¼ |
| Parrots "Café Brun," "Café Pourpre," "Amiral de Constantinople," "Crimson Beauty (sometimes misnamed Cramoisi Brillant) "Lutea Major," "Markgraaf" ("Markgraaf van Baden") and "Perfecta." | 9 | 1⅛ |
| Broken Tulips (Rembrandts, Bizarres and miscellaneous) | 10 | 1¼ |
| Species (Botanical Tulips) | | |
| T. Kaufmanniana, T. Eichleri, T. praestans, and their varieties | 8 | 1 |
| T. patens (persica) | 6 | ¾ |
| T. Clusiana and T. sylvestris (florentina) | 5 | ⅝ |

\* (except where diameter is specifically stated)

# INDEX

## A

Achimenes, 136, 167, 244
Acidanthera, 55, 167
Adders-Tongue, *see* Erythronium, 186
Adobe-Lily, *see* Fritillaria, 188
African-Lily, *see* Agapanthus, 167
Agapanthus, 167
Albuca, 167
Allium, 44–46, 62, 85, 138, 168, 244
Alstroemeria, 168
Amacrinum, *see* Crinodonna, 180
Amaryllis, 133–134, 169, 241, 243; *see also* Hippeastrum, 192
Amazon-Lily, *see* Eucharis, 186
Amianthium, 169
Ammocharis, 169
Amole, *see* Chlorogalum, 178
Amorphophallus, 169
Anapalina, 169
Anemone, 78, 170
Anemonella, 170
Angels-Tears, *see* Narcissus triandrus, 203
Anomatheca, *see* Lapeirousia cruenta, 197
Antholyza, *see* Anapalina (169), Chasmanthe (177), Curtonus (182), *and* Homoglossum (193)
Aphids, 157
Apios, 170
Arisaema, 171
Arrangements, 92 *ff.*
Arum, 171
Atamasco-Lily, *see* Zephyranthes, 214
Autumn-Crocus, *see* Colchicum, 178
Autumn-Snowflake, *see* Leucojum, 197
Avalanche-Lily, *see* Erythronium montanum, 186
Azalea, 59

## B

Babiana, 137, 171
Baboon Flower, *see* Babiana, 171
Basal cuttage, 142
Basket-Flower, *see* Hymenocallis calathina, 194
Beds
  formal, 21–24
  planting and culture, 35–38
  spring bulbs, 19 *ff.*
  summer bulbs, 39 *ff.*
Begonia, tuberous, 171–173
  beds, 42–43

Begonia (*Continued*)
  borders, 55
  boxes, 101
  climate, 42
  culture, 172, 173
  diseases, 161
  house plants, 135
  indoors, 135
  kinds, 43, 50, 172, 173
  propagation, 172, 173, 243
Belladonna-Lily, *see* Amaryllis, 169
Bermuda Buttercup, *see* Oxalis cernua, 205
Bessera, 173
Birds, 160
Blights, 161
Blood-Lily, *see* Haemanthus, 191
Bloodroot, *see* Sanguinaria, 207
Bloomeria, 173
Bluebell, 62, 77–78; *see also* Scilla, 208
Blue-Dicks, *see* Brodiaea capitata, 174
Bongardia, 173
Boophane, 173
Boophone, 173
Borders
  informal, 25–35
  spring bulbs, 19 *ff.*
  summer bulbs, 39 *ff.*, 50–55
Botrytis diseases, 161
Boussingaultia, 173
Bowiea, *see* Schizobasopsis, 207
Boxes, 100 *ff.*
Brevoortia, 173–174
Brodiaea, 174
Brunsdonna, 174
Brunsvigia, 174
Bulb fiber, 113–115
Bulb flies, 158
Bulbils, 142
Bulblets, 141–142, 242, 244
Bulbocodium, 174
Bulbs
  arrangements, 92 *ff.*
  attractions of, 4
  autumn bloom, 39 *ff.*
  beds, 19 *ff.*, 39 *ff.*
  borders, 19 *ff.*, 39 *ff.*
  boxes, 100 *ff.*
  buying, 16–18
  culture, 10 *ff.*, 35–38, 63–65, 88, 105–107, 109, 112–116, 156 *ff.*, 239; *see also* entry for individual bulb in *Encyclopedia* section
  cut flowers, 14, 81 *ff.*, 238
  cuttings, 144–146, 243
  definition, xi–xii

# C

# HOW-TO-DO-IT

# PICTURES

## Replanting bulbs in pots

**1.** At the end of the dormant season, tender bulbs that have only annual roots are repotted. Here the old soil ball in which the bulbs have been stored dry is being broken so that the bulbs can be picked from it.

**2.** The bulbs, in this case babianas, are planted in new soil in a clean, dry, well-drained pot. They are covered with soil to a depth of an inch or two, which is then pressed firm with the tips of the fingers.

**3.** The containers are placed in a cool greenhouse, frame, or other frostproof place and are well watered with a fine spray. After watering, a two- or three-inch layer of moss is placed over the surface to prevent excessive drying and thus reduce the necessity for watering until the new growths show above ground.

**Replanting bulbs in pots**

## How to top-dress

**1.** The roots of perennial-rooted bulbs, such as this haemanthus, are examined at the end of the dormant season. Unless repotting is obviously needed—and this is normally done at intervals of several years only—the bulb is top-dressed.

**2.** First the soil is soaked with water and allowed to drain. After making sure that the drainage is not stopped up, a pointed stick is used to pick out some of the old soil from the top of the root ball and perhaps

**3.** a little from the sides, taking care not to damage the roots. The center of the soil ball is left intact.

**4.** The plant is then returned to its pot and some fresh rich soil is put around it. This soil is packed firmly and then soaked with water applied in the form of a fine spray.

**How to top dress**

**1.** Assemble the topsoil, humus or peatmoss, sand, and other ingredients. Include bone meal at the rate of about a pint to the bushel. Mix them together thoroughly while they are just barely moist—not wet enough to be sticky, not dry enough to be dusty.

**2.** To test if the mixture is in the right physical condition squeeze a handful, open the hand and tap the ball of earth lightly with the finger. If it falls apart it is satisfactory.

**3.** If it remains in a hard clod it is too heavy and needs the addition of more organic matter (humus, leafmold, or peatmoss) and sand.

**4.** Crock a clean dry pot by placing over the hole in the bottom a piece of broken pot (hollow side down) or a large cinder or clinker. On top of this place an inch or so of smaller crocks or cinders (not fine ashes), and then

**5.** a layer of coarse leaves, straw, hay, moss, or partly rotted manure to prevent the soil from washing down and clogging the drainage.

**6.** Now add some soil, enough to bring the root ball of the plant to be potted to the desired level.

**7.** Remove the plant from its pot without disturbing its roots (except that the old crocks from the bottom of the old ball are carefully removed).

**8.** Center it in the new pot, fill soil around and firm it with the fingers or with a stick. Water thoroughly.

**9.** This old clivia is in need of repotting and the decision has been made to divide it at potting time.

**10.** With a fork the plant is pried apart so that each shoot or growth is separated and retains a substantial amount of roots.

**11.** The divisions are potted separately in properly drained pots of sizes just large enough to hold the roots without undue crowding. Soil is filled in and is worked well among the roots with the fingers; no large air spaces must be left.

**12.** Then with a potting stick the soil is packed firmly and made level (with sufficient space left for watering). Next, the newly potted divisions are watered thoroughly with a fine spray and are kept out of strong sunshine until they recover from the shock of transplanting.

9

10

11

12

**1.** Drain the pots by placing a large piece of broken pot hollow side down over the hole in the bottom. A large clinker may be substituted for the piece of pot. On top of this place an inch or so of smaller crocks or coarse cinders

**2.** and then a layer of straw, hay, dead leaves, or moss to keep the soil from washing through.

**3.** Then add some porous, fertile (but not over-rich) soil, pressed down but not packed firmly.

**4.** Set the bulbs almost touching each other and in most cases so that their tips will just show at the finished surface as has been done with these tulips. Small bulbs such as crocuses and scillas are buried an inch or two beneath the surface.

**5.** Then soil is added and is pressed very firmly with the tips of the fingers.

**6.** Hyacinths, like tulips and most other forcing bulbs, may be planted several together in a container, the bulbs almost touching each other . . . or they may be planted singly in pots that measure four or five inches in diameter. If planted singly the pots must be drained and the soil filled in

and pressed firm above them in the same way as when several are planted together.

**7.** After potting, water the plants thoroughly. Then bury them outdoors under eight inches of ashes, sand, or peatmoss.

**8.** Alternatively stand the pots in a cool, frostproof cellar, garage, or similar place and cover with a few inches of sand, peatmoss, or cinders to prevent drying.

**9.** Yet another possibility is to put them in a deep box and pack peatmoss around and over them to prevent freezing.

**10.** Finally there is always the possibility of placing a few pots in a cool, dark, frost-free attic, cellar, or closet. If you do this it is a good plan to encase each pot in polyethelene film (the kind used for food in food lockers) to prevent the rooting medium (soil or fiber) from drying too rapidly.

**11.** Under cool moist conditions in the dark roots soon start to grow and develop rapidly. It is important that root growth develop before top growth, as this cut-away pot of hyacinth shows.

**12.** When sturdy roots have filled the containers and the shoots are an inch or two high the pots may be moved into the house.

233

Forcing
hardy bulbs
in soil

## Growing bulbs without soil in fiber

**1.** The ingredients used in preparing bulb fiber are peatmoss, chopped charcoal, and oyster shell or limestone chips.

**2.** The charcoal bits are added to the peatmoss which is just barely moist.

**3.** Limestone or oyster shell chips are added and the whole is mixed very thoroughly.

**4.** No holes are necessary in the containers; simply fill them with the bulb fiber and firm it well. Then with the fingers scoop holes in the surface and plant each bulb individually. These are crocuses.

**5.** Crocuses, scillas, grape-hyacinths, and other small bulbs are just covered with fiber. Taller bulbs, such as narcissuses, are left with their necks protruding.

**6.** Here are crocuses that were grown in fiber in a metal container and were set inside a decorative basket at blooming time.

## Setting out plants

**1.** The Easter lily that has been forced may be planted in the outdoor garden after danger from frost has passed. In late summer it will produce a second crop of short-stemmed blooms. If protected from excessive winter cold, the following year it will bear flowers of normal stem length outside.

**2.** Narcissuses and some other bulbs that have been forced may be taken from their pots after their foliage has died.

**3.** They are separated and planted in the outdoor garden immediately or stored for fall planting. These are the bulbs taken from the pot shown in the previous picture.

1

**Setting
out
plants**

1

5

2         3         4

**4.** When planting green dahlia plants do not break the root ball. Make sure that their roots are moist at planting time. Make the soil firm about the roots, leaving a slight hollow to hold water. Water well. It is better to set the stake in position before planting instead of doing as is done here.

**5.** Cannas, like green plants of dahlias, are set out after the weather is warm and settled. The root ball is not broken, good soil is packed around it, and the newly set plant is well soaked with water.

### Bulbs for forcing without soil

**1.** Vermiculite is a suitable material in which to grow bulbs in undrained containers. It is left loose rather than being packed firm as are other rooting media. Here Paper White narcissuses are beginning to grow.

**2.** Here are the same narcissuses coming into bloom a few weeks later. The vermiculite is kept moist but not flooded.

**3.** Special hyacinth glasses are cupped at the top to fit the bulb. If filled barely to the base of the bulb with water to which a few pieces of charcoal are added, they form interesting receptacles.

**4.** After spending a few weeks in a cool dark place, the hyacinth glass is brought into light and a higher temperature.

**5.** Pebbles or gravel form a suitable anchorage for the roots of bulbs grown in containers filled with water. Water is poured in until the bases of the bulbs are covered.

2         3         4         5

**1.** The soil must be·well prepared to a good depth for outdoor bulbs. Here a bed for tulips has been excavated to a depth of eight inches, compost has been spread over the bottom, and bone meal is being applied.

**2.** The bottom is then forked over and the compost and bone meal mixed in thoroughly. The loosened bottom is compacted moderately by treading it while it is fairly dry, not so wet that it sticks to the shoes.

**3.** If mice or other rodents are apt to be troublesome they may be circumvented by surrounding the bed with fine wire mesh set vertically around the edge of the bed, extending into the ground for eight or nine inches and protruding above it for about two inches.

**4.** A layer of good soil is then spread over the bottom and the bottom is made level and raked smooth.

**5.** The bulbs are then spaced out at appropriate distances and good soil enriched with humus or peatmoss and bone meal is carefully filled in, care being taken not to disturb the bulbs.

**6.** Then the surface is trodden until it is moderately firm and it is raked smooth and level.

**7.** If the undersoil is reasonably good it is not necessary to excavate (remove the topsoil) in preparing for bulb planting. Instead simply spread organic matter and bone meal over the surface

**8.** and fork it in, mixing it very thoroughly with the upper ten or twelve inches of earth. Then tread the bed lightly to firm it somewhat and rake it level and smooth.

**9.** Now space the bulbs—fairly closely together if they are to be used alone . . . more widely apart if other spring blooming plants are to be set among them.

**10.** Plant each bulb individually with a trowel, taking particular care to set it at the correct depth and, so far as is possible, all bulbs of the same kind at the same depth. This makes for even flowering.

**11.** Groups of gladioluses add color to the summer border. After the ground has been thoroughly spaded and fertilized, space the bulbs on the surface.

**12.** Plant each bulb with a trowel, taking care that it is set deeply enough and that it rests on the bottom of the hole.

**13.** When planting dormant dahlia tubers drive the stake in position first and set the tuber horizontally with the "eye" end near to the stake. Then cover the tubers with two or three inches of soil and add more soil as the shoots grow.

**14.** With few exceptions lily bulbs must be set deeply. In heavy soils it is considered a good plan to place a cushion of sand under each bulb and to pour sand around the bulb before the soil is filled in.

**15.** When planting groups of bulbs among foundation plantings and under shrubs, space them irregularly—not in straight lines or set patterns.

**16.** These grape-hyacinths being planted near a sheltering evergreen that is part of a foundation planting are covered with soil to about three times their own depth.

9    10    11

13    14    15

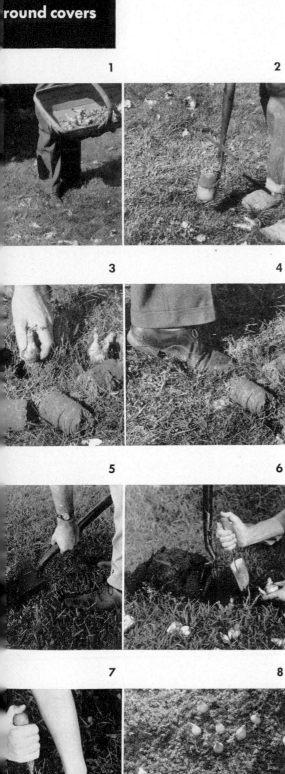

1      2

3      4

5      6

7      8

## Planting bulbs in grass and among groundcovers

**1.** When narcissuses are naturalized the best effects are obtained by strewing them in handfuls and planting them where they fall.

**2.** Special bulb-planting tools such as this may be used for planting in grass. The bulb planter is pressed into the soil and lifts out a plug of sod as it is pulled out. As the next hole is made the plug is pushed out of the planter.

**3.** The bulbs are inserted well to the bottom of the holes.

**4.** Then the turf plugs are replaced and stepped on to firm them. This method is suitable for reasonably deep and fertile soils only.

**5.** Another method is to lift pieces of sod with a sharp spade, then.

**6.** to improve the soil beneath by mixing fertilizer and humus with it. Plant the bulbs with a trowel before flipping the sod back into place and firming it.

**7.** Crocuses and other small bulbs that are to be planted in grass can easily be installed with a trowel.

**8.** In early October grape-hyacinths are being planted among a low groundcover while sternbergias are in full bloom. A narrow trowel such as this, sometimes called a fern trowel, is especially useful for planting bulbs among low groundcovers.

### Some varied tasks with bulbs

**1.** Remove as little foliage as possible when cutting flowers if you want the bulbs to build up strength to flower well in succeeding years. Unless seeds are wanted for increasing stock cut off faded flowers or developing seed pods as soon as the petals have fallen.

**2.** Some kinds of bulbs, such as these grape-hyacinths, increase freely from self-sown seeds. In such cases allow the seeds to mature; do this too if you wish to collect the seeds for sowing elsewhere.

**Some varied tasks with bulbs**

**3.** Always allow the foliage of bulbs to die down naturally before cutting it off. The stems and leaves of these tulips, which are to be left in the ground instead of being lifted and stored for the summer, are being cleared away.

**4.** Narcissus foliage is apt to be untidy in borders during its period of ripening after the flowers are passed. Tying it in small bundles gives a neater appearance to the border.

**5.** When staking bulbs take great care not to push the stake through the bulb. Keep it far enough away to prevent this.

**6.** When tying around the stems of plants such as this dahlia use soft string and tie loosely enough for expansion of the stem as it grows.

**7.** A simple way of supporting gladioluses in the cut-flower garden is to insert stakes at intervals on both sides of the row and connect them with strings.

**8.** Frequent shallow surface cultivation (or, alternatively, mulching) conserves moisture and keeps down weeds.

**9.** The anthers are picked off the stamens of lilies before they are mature enough to shed their yellow pollen and so discolor the flowers.

**10.** Surplus side shoots are removed from dahlias while they are quite small. This is done to limit the number of stems and improve the quality of the blooms of many kinds.

**11.** Surplus flower buds are removed from around the central terminal bud of a dahlia in "disbudding." This results in larger flowers.

# Lifting tulips and narcissuses

1

2

3

4

5

6

7

**1.** If tulips are to be lifted and stored for the summer it is best to wait until the foliage has died. If that cannot be done dig the bulbs carefully.

**2.** Without losing more soil from the roots than can be helped plant them in shallow trenches in an out-of-the-way place. Cover them with soil and keep them well watered and lightly shaded until the foliage has died completely.

**3.** Then clean the bulbs off and store them in a dry, cool, shady place in trays with bottoms of wire mesh

**4.** or, if you wish, by placing them inside old nylon stockings and suspending them in a suitable cellar or shed.

**5.** When narcissuses become so crowded that their flowering deteriorates dig them up as soon as the foliage has died. Separate them and grade them according to size.

**6.** Then either store them in a cool, dry place until fall or replant them immediately in soil that has been enriched with fertilizer and humus.

**7.** Set the bulbs at the required depth and cover them with soil and, if they are in grassland, with a plug of sod. The small bulblets may be planted in a nursery bed for a year or two until they reach flowering size.

241

**1.** Calla-lilies may be rested during the summer by turning the pots in which they are grown on their sides outdoors in a shaded place and keeping them quite dry.

**2.** Amaryllises (*Hippeastrum*) are turned on their sides under a greenhouse bench for dry storage during their fall and winter rest period.

**3.** Gloxinias at the beginning of their winter period of dormancy may be removed from their pots and be packed together in flats for storage in a moderately warm cellar.

**4.** Caladiums, at the approach of winter, are gradually dried off and are stored in their pots in a moderately warm cellar.

**5.** Here is a bulb of crinodonna that is resting. It is kept in its pot and given no water during its period of dormancy.

**6.** Dahlias are carefully dug up after the first touch of frost. The tops are then cut away and the roots are stored in a cool frostproof place until spring.

**7.** Gladioluses are dug after their foliage has browned or has been killed by frost and are then dried off in an airy frostproof place. When they are quite dry the tops are cleaned off, the bulbs freed of loose husks and dusted with DDT powder, and are stored in paper bags or trays in a cool dry cellar.

## Propagating by bulblets, scales and division

**1.** Many lilies form bulblets on the lower parts of their stems. To obtain these place your foot near a stem and, with a sharp twist and jerk, pull up the stem.

**2.** The stem parts from the bulb at its top, bringing with it the stem roots and the bulblets attached to the stem.

**3.** The bulblets are picked off and

**4.** planted an inch or two deep in flats, cold frames, or in prepared beds outdoors.

**5.** Lily bulbs are composed of loose scales that lap each other like the shingles of a roof. The outer scales, picked off individually, can be used to generate new bulbs.

**6.** The scales are planted in a mixture of peatmoss and sand and are kept moderately dry until the young bulbs form.

**7.** Dahlias form clumps of tuberous roots. These are stored over winter and are divided in spring before planting.

**8.** It is important that each division have a small piece of stem attached at its upper end; it is from this that the new shoots arise. Unlike potatoes, buds (eyes) are not formed on the tuberous portion itself.

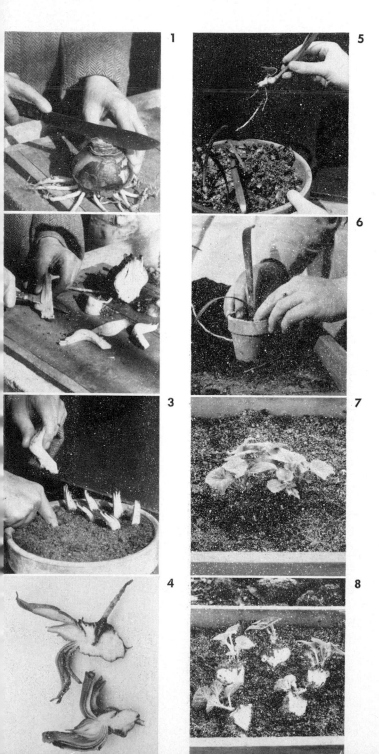

**1.** Bulb cuttings afford a ready means of increasing some bulbs. Here an amaryllis (*Hippeastrum*) bulb is being prepared. First cut it into wedge-shaped segments as a pie is cut.

**2.** Then cut down between the scales that form the wedges to form bulb cuttings; each must have a small piece of the basal plate of the bulb attached.

**3.** The cuttings are then planted in peatmoss and sand and kept warm and moderately moist.

**4.** Small new bulbs form between the scales of the bulb cutting, and roots develop from the piece of basal plate.

**5.** The young bulbs formed by the bulb cuttings will develop more roots and leaves.

**6.** They may then be potted individually or planted in flats or several together to make further growth.

**7.** Old tubers of begonias can be propagated by division. The bulbs are first started into growth in peatmoss and sand and when the new shoots are an inch or two tall

**8.** the bulbs are cut with a sharp knife so that each division has one shoot, a piece of tuber, and some roots. The cut surfaces are dusted with sulphur and the divisions are planted in light loose soil and are kept warm in a humid atmosphere.

# Some methods of propagation

1. Gloxinias are easily propagated by slicing mature leaves to form leaf cuttings.

2. The cuttings are planted in peatmoss and sand and are kept in a shaded moist place. Small bulbs form the first year, leaves and flowers the second.

3. The small white cormlets that cluster around the base of the new gladiolus bulb (the old bulb, shriveled and dark, can be seen beneath the new bulb) offer a rapid means of increase.

4. Lilies multiply by forming offset bulblets from the base of the bulb as well as by tiny bulblets on the bottom of the stem.

5. Offset bulblets have been formed by this amaryllis (*Hippeastrum*). They are ready for removal at the beginning of the next growing season.

6. The caterpillar-like bulbs of *Achimenes* afford a ready means of propagation. At the end of the dormant season they are removed from the old plant,

7. broken into small pieces, and planted in peatmoss and sand, covered to an inch deep. When the new shoots are an inch or two high the plants are transferred to regular soil.

8. Most bulbs are easily raised from seeds. These seedling lilies, not much over a year old, are flowering in the flats to which they were transplanted from the seed pot.

9. Seedling alliums are removed from their pot for transplanting. They are a little too far advanced; it would have been better to transplant them before their roots became quite so matted.

10. With a dibber the young plants are carefully set in fresh soil in other containers and are spaced about two inches apart. Then they are well watered.

11. Immersing the pot in water nearly to its rim so moisture seeps up from below is a safe way of watering seedlings . . . or a very fine spray may be used.